AF608294

ENTERTAINING THE IDEA: SHAKESPEARE, PHILOSOPHY, AND PERFORMANCE

THE UCLA CLARK MEMORIAL LIBRARY SERIES

ENTERTAINING THE IDEA

SHAKESPEARE, PHILOSOPHY, AND PERFORMANCE

Edited by Lowell Gallagher, James Kearney, and Julia Reinhard Lupton

Published by the University of Toronto Press in association with the UCLA Center for Seventeenth- and Eighteenth-Century Studies and the William Andrews Clark Memorial Library utorontopress.com

ISBN 978-1-4875-0743-5 (cloth)
ISBN 978-1-4875-3624-4 (EPUB)
ISBN 978-1-4875-3623-7 (PDF)

Library and Archives Canada Cataloguing in Publication

Title: Entertaining the idea: Shakespeare, philosophy, and performance / edited by Lowell Gallagher, James Kearney, and Julia Reinhard Lupton.
Names: Gallagher, Lowell, 1953– editor. | Kearney, James (James Joseph), editor. | Lupton, Julia Reinhard, 1963– editor.
Series: UCLA Clark Memorial Library series ; 29.
Description: Series statement: UCLA/Clark Memorial Library series ; no. 29 | Includes bibliographical references and index.
Identifiers: Canadiana (print) 20200255657 | Canadiana (ebook) 2020025572X | ISBN 9781487507435 (hardcover) | ISBN 9781487536244 (EPUB) | ISBN 9781487536237 (PDF)
Subjects: LCSH: Shakespeare, William, 1564–1616 – Criticism and interpretation. | LCSH: Shakespeare, William, 1564–1616 – Philosophy. | LCSH: Philosophy in literature. | LCSH: Thought and thinking in literature.
Classification: LCC PR2986.E58 2021 | DDC 822.3/3–dc23

This book has been published with the help of a grant from the UCLA Center for Seventeenth- and Eighteenth-Century Studies.

University of Toronto Press acknowledges the financial assistance to its publishing program of the Canada Council for the Arts and the Ontario Arts Council, an agency of the Government of Ontario.

Canada Council for the Arts   Conseil des Arts du Canada

Funded by the Government of Canada   Financé par le gouvernement du Canada   Canada

Contents

Illustrations

Acknowledgments

This collection grew out of a year-long sequence of symposia on the topic "Entertaining the Idea: Shakespeare, Performance, and Philosophy," held at the UCLA Center for Seventeenth- and Eighteenth-Century Studies and the William Andrews Clark Memorial Library in 2016–17. We would like to thank UCLA and the Clark Library for their generous support of this year of research exchange. As Clark Professors for the year, we had the opportunity to mentor two extraordinary post-doctoral fellows, Sheiba Kian Kaufman and Ariane Helou. Our collaboration originated in an intercampus research group, "w/Shakespeare," funded by the University of California Humanities Research Institute, 2012–14. The UC Irvine New Swan Shakespeare Center provided additional funds to hire Danilo Caputo and Olivia Rall for research assistance for this volume. We would like to thank the center's patron, Dr. Marilyn Sutton, for her generous support of our research endeavours.

Lowell Gallagher,
The University of California, Los Angeles

James Kearney,
The University of California, Santa Barbara

Julia Reinhard Lupton,
The University of California, Irvine

ENTERTAINING THE IDEA: SHAKESPEARE, PHILOSOPHY, AND PERFORMANCE

Introduction

LOWELL GALLAGHER, JAMES KEARNEY, AND JULIA REINHARD LUPTON

To entertain is to delight and amuse (Hamlet wants no "lenten entertainment"), but also to receive guests and hence to court risk, from the real dangers of rape, murder, or jealousy (*Lucrece, Macbeth, The Winter's Tale*) to the more intangible exhilaration of self-disclosure and captivation in response to another (*Romeo and Juliet, As You Like It, Twelfth Night*). To *entertain an idea* is to welcome a compelling thought or beckoning fiction into the disinhibited zone of speculative play. "I'll entertain the offer'd fallacy," says Antipholus of Syracuse as he abandons himself to the comedy of errors (2.2.183).[1] Like Antipholus, readers of fictions and viewers of plays entertain "themes" and "dreams" (2.2.178–9) on their way to recognition and new knowledge, as a mode of testing the significance and reach of the suppositions they encounter in a world co-created by their imaginative participation. To entertain an idea is to take it in, accommodate and pay attention to it, give it breathing room, dwell with it for a time. The conceit of entertaining an idea suggests a temporary visitation or trial period, a flirtation that might turn into more, but for now is a fling, a temporary affair. This welcoming gesture recognizes the multiple sensory channels through which an idea may take shape – not only through vision or abstract cogitation (the Platonic ground of the idea as a species of form or discernible shape) but also in vision's concert or tension with haptic and auditory impressions. The idea so entertained is necessarily a stranger, and to invite a stranger into one's parlour, closet, or confidence is to accept risk by exposing oneself and one's household, including the household of the soul, to unknown incursions or visitations. The practice of entertaining ideas suggests a ruminative and meditative approach to thought, inviting us to think of philosophy as a form of hospitality and a kind of mental theatre. From this perspective,

Shakespeare's plays supply readers, listeners, viewers, and performers of diverse backgrounds with equipment for living. Shakespeare solicits us to be more alert, more critically self-aware, more responsive to the texture of an encounter, whether in the intimacies of private bonds, the bustle of social life, the tangled arenas of political action, or the turbulent eddies of ethical decision.

Just as the conceit of entertaining carries diverse accents, so too the semantic range of the aesthetic "idea" harbours complex legacies that are variously reactivated on Shakespeare's stage. Erwin Panofsky's landmark study *Idea: A Concept in Art Theory* remains a touchstone guide to the dominant philosophical and aesthetic theories of the idea, from Greek antiquity through the Renaissance, that percolated into Shakespeare's artisanal culture. From the perspective Panofsky unfolds, the lingua franca of the idea in Renaissance art theory turns in part on the generative tension and play between Platonic and Aristotelian perceptions of the origin and potency of the idea (and its semantic cognates, *disegno interno* and *concetto*), construed as both transcendently derived copy and humanly crafted rival, respectively, of metaphysical realities.[2] As Panofsky argues, "The concept of Idea as reinterpreted in the Renaissance ... secured freedom to the artistic mind and at the same time limited this freedom vis-à-vis the claims of reality."[3] In this body of thought, the limit at stake is less a milestone in the supposed march toward a purely immanent secular order than a threshold posture, engaging both the mind's observation of nature and the contemplation of metaphysical intuitions of reality as speculative exercises that continually test – and entertain – the permeable boundaries between the known, the unknown, and the realm of conjectural possibility.

In Shakespeare's era, the enveloping background to this dynamic of aesthetic energies entertained a vibrant traffic in ideas about the nature of the secular world that carried impressions inherited from Augustine's influential understanding of secularity. Augustine's *saeculum,* described in the *City of God,* denotes an inherently ambiguous "middle ground" poised between sacred and profane orders, a provisional composite of earthly and heavenly cities: "In truth, those two cities are interwoven and intermixed in this era, and await separation at the last judgment."[4] For Augustine, the secular dimension to human history meant that it contained "no signposts to sacred meaning, no landmarks to the history of salvation," no providentially guaranteed link between Roman Empire and Christianity.[5] "In declaring the *saeculum* to be largely opaque to human scrutiny," Peter Brown suggests, "Augustine protected the richness of human culture from the hubris of those who wanted to relate every aspect of the world around them directly to the sacred" – or to the political administration and cannibalization of the sacred.[6]

For Augustine, the autonomy of the *saeculum* was not, of course, an absolute title. Neither can it be viewed in hindsight as the direct harbinger of modern secular liberalism, with its imagined partition between private and public spheres of interest. Both the visible church (the community of believers) and the secular order, though distinct from each other, were co-implicated in the parenthetical and radically contingent time – Robert A. Markus calls this the "eschatological gap" – between the Christ event and the eschaton.[7] Augustine's proposed dilation of parenthetical temporality may well have helped protect the richness of late antique human culture for a time, precisely by holding a residual attachment to the "cosmopolitan and pluralistic" ethos of the Hellenistic-Roman *paideia,* even as it also opened a space for the eventual ascendancy of the institutional infrastructure of "sacral Christendom" in the medieval era.[8] However, Augustine's sense of the opacity of events unfolding in the parenthetical time of the *saeculum* may well have turned out to be the more enduring dimension of his thinking about the nature of human affairs on the stage of the world vis-à-vis their ultimate ends. Certainly, by Shakespeare's time the secular world conjured and embodied in theatrical performance presents an unevenly distributed terrain of insiders and outsiders, with shifting degrees of inter-confessional and transcultural accommodation, conflict, complicity, and literacy that call for – and entertain – a "hermeneutics of attentiveness" to the human condition of plurality.[9]

For four centuries Shakespeare's plays have invited directors, actors, audiences, and readers to entertain a startling range of ideas: succour, social discord, and states of nature in *King Lear* and *The Tempest*; self-disclosure through amorous role playing in *A Midsummer Night's Dream, Twelfth Night,* and *As You Like It*; habit and virtue as well as irony and anxiety in *Hamlet*; the force of cursing in *Richard III*; or acknowledgment, presence, wonder, and love in *The Winter's Tale,* to announce a few of the ideas welcomed and weighed in this volume. Written during the eventful reshuffling of sacred verities and the launching of political and economic forms that are with us still, Shakespearean drama is intimately concerned with what it means to act, speak, live, and listen in a world whose points of orientation must be continually re-established. The 2016–17 Clark Library Core Program at UCLA, "Entertaining the Idea," staged a series of rapprochements between performance and philosophy in Shakespearean drama, conversations designed both to illumine the plays in their poetic and theatrical amplitude and to explore what philosophy and performance might offer each other in twenty-first-century literary studies. In this volume, *performance* refers not to an archive of particular stagings but rather to the inherently enactive character of core ethical concepts such as acknowledgment, virtue, habit, love, judgment, and care. The resulting volume, which features some of the most inventive scholars working in philosophically oriented Shakespeare studies today, aims to take up drama's capacity to enhance experience, exercise discernment, test existential limits, and assert common bonds. Such actions occur within the historical horizons in which Shakespeare lived and wrote, but have been renewed in the recollective history of adaptation, translation, performance, and critical response, and our contributors are united by their attention to the rhythm of this renewal.

Walter Benjamin's *The Origin of the German Tragic Drama*, published in 1928, remains an exemplary work of philosophical criticism. Benjamin approached the drama of Shakespeare's age under the rubric of the Baroque *Trauerspiel* or mourning play, and he gives special prominence to the idea in his analysis of theatre: "In the sense in which it is treated in the philosophy of art the *Trauerspiel* is an Idea."[10] By dramatizing *Trauerspiel* (modern drama) as an idea, Benjamin was distinguishing his project from both *literary history*, which, he argued, relativizes and homogenizes real differences among works, and *aesthetic classification*, which elevates genres into standards that exclude exceptional works and leads to a flattening of artistic production. To entertain *Trauerspiel* as an idea is to stake out modern drama's animating conditions and goals, even and especially when, as in the case of Shakespeare, these works fall short of classical genre prescriptions. Herder was the first philosopher-critic to recognize the import of Shakespeare's movement beyond genre, a transit Herder then applied retroactively to classical drama, which he liberated from its own rules.[11] Benjamin is working within Herder's hermeneutic. It is in the spirit of Herder, for example, that Benjamin makes his famous declaration: "A major work will either establish the genre or abolish it; and the perfect work will do both."[12] In her project on "books of second chances," to which her chapter in this volume belongs, Sarah Beckwith treats *The Winter's Tale* as initiating its own distinctive line of ethical and aesthetic inquiry, one that cannot be confined to tragedy or romance and that includes works of fiction, cinema, and philosophy in its generous embrace. In these and other works, Shakespearean drama often finds itself *moving away from tragedy* – inhabiting tragedy's generic architecture only to sound impulses beyond the tragic – in a manner that you will see tracked in different ways throughout this volume. Anselm Haverkamp calls Hamlet "a post-tragic hero," Sanford Budick maps the redemptive flow between *Lear* and *The Winter's Tale*, and Paul Kottman argues that Shakespeare is not only moving beyond tragedy in works like *The Tempest*, he is also moving *beyond art*, an insight affirmed by theatre critic Charles McNulty in his Afterword, "On (Not) Performing *King Lear*."

Whereas Herder works primarily through the concept of historical genius, Benjamin emphasizes instead the condition of creaturely life (*kreatürliches Leben*) and the condition of being created (*Erschöpfungszustand*).[13] Both Benjamin and Shakespeare pursue the Idea as it passes through a series of scriptural temporalizations, devolving into what Benjamin calls natural history, in which the consequences of human action metabolize with the physical world and materialize as ruin, desire path, and labyrinth. In Shakespearean drama, sublunar beings seek, avoid, or respond to the idea-traces impressed in their souls, secreted by their somatic processes, mapped by their dwelling places, projected onto the heavens, and infiltrating their relationships with other creatures. These natural histories remind us of the etymological associations of the Idea, in ancient Greek and post-classical Latin, with the phenomenal emergence of forms – the play of image, likeness, and archetype – together with forms' entailment in the affective genres of hope, joy, dread, and grief.[14]

Shakespeare's ideas are elaborated over time as well as space, linking disparate moments of thought (classical, Hebrew, scholastic, humanist, Reformed) that take shape in landscapes sedimented by upheaval and distress: the carbuncled heath of *King Lear*, the crenelated ramparts of *Macbeth* and *Hamlet*, the deutero-Pauline Vienna of *Measure for Measure*. An Idea in transit, "care" precipitates from a Greco-Roman creation myth through the scrims of Christian theology, humoral psychology, and modern virtue ethics to form a resonant composite between medical humanities and Shakespeare studies, as Sheiba Kian Kaufman demonstrates in her contribution to this volume. The curse is another such thought-fragment, as Björn Quiring argues in his piece: originating in the ancient juridical and ritual procedures of the Jews, the curse as ban was retooled in Catholic rites of excommunication and then ambiguously appropriated and transformed by the Anglican Church. Shakespeare and his contemporaries, Quiring suggests, clarified the theatricality at the heart of the curse by adopting its dramatic modes of address and its de-creating fantasies on the public stage. In his chapter Budick focuses instead on the gestural, linguistic, and existential dynamics of the blessing in *King*

Lear and *The Winter's Tale*, where benedictions incapable of changing fate still grant palpable grace to those who give and receive them. Expanding this palette of theo-philosophical and liturgico-dramatic ideas, Kottman adds Immaculate Conception and Beckwith offers resurrection and incarnation, ideas re-approached for their existential wisdom rather than their doctrinal meanings.

Shakespeare's overcoming of tragedy enlists the resources of comedy in all of its theatrical variants, from the plots of New Comedy to the foolery of clowns, but he drew on other tools as well, including Stoic spiritual exercise, as noted by James Kuzner in this volume and elsewhere in his work.[15] The overcoming of tragedy is never accomplished once and for all because it represents an existential trial, like the testing of Job, Jacob's wrestling with the angel, Abraham's binding of Isaac,[16] Jonah's sojourn in the belly of the whale, or Christ on Calvary,[17] recurrent scenarios in Shakespeare's post-tragic Bible. We might conceive of tragedy here along the lines of Benjamin's contemporary, the Protestant theologian Paul Tillich (1886–1965), a friend of Adorno and Arendt. In *The Courage To Be*, Tillich associated the *anxiety of death* with the classical world; the *anxiety of guilt* with medieval and Reformation Christianity; and the *anxiety of meaninglessness* with the condition of secular modernity.[18] All three anxieties are relevant to Shakespeare, who integrated classical, Calvinist, and Machiavellian strains into a late medieval dramaturgy whose resilient motifs of saints and sinners on the pilgrimage of life were shaken to the limit by the tremors of new thought. Shakespeare's struggle with these foundational anxieties ultimately issued in what critics call the romances, but it is evident in all of his works insofar as they address the recurrent challenge of finding meaning, establishing trust, and sustaining relationships in situations of escalating scepticism. The repeated nature of the struggle with tragic anxiety, whether over a day, across a life, or among epochs, means that tragedy continues to throb within the corpus that creatively confronts and sublimates it. In Tillich's terms, the "courage to be" always occurs "in spite of" a negativity that it incorporates into its styles of existence.

Anxiety so sublimated moves through irony to something else: what Hegel called "objective humour," as Anselm Haverkamp argues in his contribution. Objective humour is not the same as comedy – but it is not tragedy either; its chop-fallen emblem is the skull of the jester Yorick, his vital laughter frozen in the new grimace of the death's head, which in turn is handled with a new freedom by the contemplating Hamlet. Budick makes a related argument concerning the way in which Shakespeare is present in his plays as an "unbodied onlooker" who doesn't simply know the action to come, but who understands the "forces of being" unleashed in his plays, by virtue of his own prior meditative exercises. Budick's Shakespeare is to his dramas as Haverkamp's Hamlet is to Yorick's skull: each manages a sublime distance, a creative interim, that opens a new relationship to the world without issuing in estrangement. Both Haverkamp and Budick place the advent in understanding initiated by Shakespeare beyond dramatic irony, since what the plays yield is a form of consciousness that transcends any technical achievement, and hence becomes philosophy.

King Lear is the most anxious, and the most tragic, of Shakespeare's plays, as Samuel Johnson registered in his historic response to the drama. *King Lear* runs through this volume, in pieces by Sanford Budick, Sheiba Kian Kaufman, and Charles McNulty. *King Lear* begins under the shadow of the curse, hurled by the king first at his daughter Cordelia in the form of disinheritance and the withdrawal of legal acknowledgment, and then at his daughter Goneril in the form of a rant against her physical integrity and her reproductive and parental potential. Lear's curses lead to his expulsion into a hostile environment of weaponized households and affective storms that eventually destroys not only the king but almost everyone who is near and dear to him. His sojourn in that landscape, however, also introduces an ethics of care and a poetics of benediction that imperfectly sutures the devastating wounds inflicted on bodies, organs, relationships, and institutions over the course/curses of the drama. In his plays after *Lear,* Shakespeare continues to elaborate the complex relationship between cursing, caring, and curing, in their liturgical, medical, therapeutic, and poetic dimensions. Yet even in *Lear,* which pushes what is emotionally bearable in art to its tragic limit, the highly Baroque image – in Benjamin's sense – of Cordelia's tears indexes the glittering extremes of affect that edge *Lear* from tragedy towards something else: "Those happy smiles / That played on her ripe lips [seemed] not to know / What guest were in her eyes, which parted thence / As pearls from diamonds dropped" (4.3). This portrait juxtaposes the petrified brilliance of gems with the flowing essence of weeping in a dialectical image that excites cogitation while arousing affect. Cordelia's sidereal visage commingles sense *and* sensibility, to cite Shakespeare's most influential and perceptive post-tragic heir, Jane Austen. The romances that follow from *King Lear* take flight from the contrasting emotions that illumine Cordelia's face.[19]

Sanford Budick reads *King Lear* and *The Winter's Tale* as pendant plays in dynamic exchange with each other. The mirroring operations of chiasmus, Budick argues, disclose a nothing at its centre that makes room for a transcendental yet embedded spectator: Edgar in *King Lear*, Paulina in *The Winter's Tale*, and Shakespeare in both. Budick's starting point is *Hamlet*, who moves through and beyond theatricalization from the very beginning of the play, disclosing purposiveness within vacillation. Sheiba Kian Kaufman's chapter on "Care" elaborates a similar continuum between *Lear* and *The Tempest*, conducted on a more intimate level of human succour and attention. *The Winter's Tale* is also featured in complementary offerings by Sarah Beckwith (on paternal love, following Stanley Cavell) and by Paul Kottman (on maternal love, in contrast with Cavell). In Shakespeare's romances, the tragic and the comic refract each other like the pearls and diamonds that brim from Cordelia's abyssal eyes, and terror, grief, loneliness, betrayal, and shame yield to a profane reconciliation that affirms mortality, guilt, and doubt as the conditions but not the ends of human being.

Whereas Budick emphasizes the transcendental onlooker, Jeffrey Knapp is interested in spectators who refuse to stay in their places, both within play worlds and in the theatre that houses them. Knapp's "Entertainment" begins with a number of prologues in which playwrights express aggression towards their audiences. Knapp then turns to Kyd's *Spanish Tragedy*, whose internal and external theatrics display a decidedly mixed relationship to entertainment as a form of pleasing, hosting, and considering. If Shakespeare overcomes tragedy through romance, where does comedy fall? In Shakespeare's fabricated worlds, comedy carves out the distance between the late antique and premodern scenography of metaphysically charged error that moves toward beatitude – Dante's *Comedia* – and the exuberant thoroughfares of secular life captured with encyclopedic verve in Honoré de Balzac's *Comédie humaine.* This is the region of irrepressible liveliness, unavoidable folly, and everyday role playing that is always generic in its sense of normative experiment, yet exceeds genre by becoming co-equal with life as a congeries of sustainable relationships and routines.[20] Entertainment as performance and entertainment as hospitality embrace this comic spectrum, as Knapp notes. Tzachi Zamir takes up role playing in the dramas, which he opposes to pretending: "To role play is not to pretend. It is to attain or maintain, to externalize or to share. To pretend is to be away from others; to role play can sometimes be the only way of being with them." His consummate examples are *As You Like It*, in which Rosalind-as-Ganymede-as-Rosalind amplifies her own being in conversation with Orlando, and *Twelfth Night*, in which Viola-as-Cesario-on-behalf-of-Orsino both verbalizes the intensity of her own feelings and expresses her pain at the impossibility of full disclosure. Zamir also touches on the tragedies and even the Sonnets, but one senses that his real interest lies in role playing as a tool for living, and hence as a comic instrument in an existential rather than a literary sense. This is very much the approach of James Kuzner as well, who takes up love as a "way of life" in *A Midsummer Night's Dream* and reads the play as a sceptical exercise, in the tradition of Sextus Empiricus. Initially caught in the brittle absolutisms of young love, the friends in the forest pass into a more resilient and realistic love that incorporates doubt, acknowledges the role of fantasy in desire, and relinquishes the certainties of possession. Such a love just might endure.

"Habit" composes the infrastructure of daily life and is the subject of J.K. Barret's contribution. Taking off from Aristotle, Barret explores the sustaining and flexible role of habit as a form of fiction that travels between theatrical training and daily existence. Habit in Shakespeare, she argues, never becomes fully automatic, but instead retains an element of deliberative reflection that makes it into a powerful ethical tool as well as a key feature of theatre as an art of rehearsal. Habit, in other words, never completely relinquishes its relationship to judgment, the subject of Kevin Curran's contribution. Judgment, unlike habit, involves a punctual and incisive intervention in the flow of life that distinguishes among actions and is itself an act. Reading judgment from Aristotle to Arendt, Curran argues that judgment as practised in Shakespearean drama is collective, physical, and inventive. For Aristotle, habit is the support of virtue, while judgment (phronesis) *is* a virtue; together, these two chapters, along with Kaufman's work on "Care," suggest the relevance of virtue ethics broadly conceived to Shakespearean drama. In the classical tradition, virtue and performance flow into each other, whether in Aristotle's emphasis on virtue as habit and praxis, or in the link between virtue and the virtual implicit in ideas of latency and dynamism, or in the figure of the virtuoso as an expert performer of multiple arts and specialized knowledges. As a playwright, dramatic poet, and person of the theatre, Shakespeare tests virtue as both creative practice and serious play, offering up the actions of his characters to our own community-building and thought-refining habits of judgment.

This volume is divided into two sections. We begin with a sequence of shorter pieces organized around keywords that connect philosophy and performance in the works of Shakespeare. This turn to keywords is inspired and enabled by projects like Raymond Williams' *Keywords*, Émile Benveniste's *Vocabulaire*, and the *Dictionary of Untranslatables*, sweeping works that excavate cultural and conceptual vocabularies.[21] The goal for this collection is more open-ended and epistemologically modest: to use keywords to create or discover or unlock conversational spaces in which philosophy and performance speak to and with each other. These brief exercises are designed to help readers think creatively about Shakespeare, philosophy, and performance by providing conceptual tools supported by exemplary readings of works by Shakespeare, his contemporaries, and his heirs. In "Role Playing," Tzachi Zamir shows how role playing in Shakespeare is both creative and melancholic and extends to the way that characters think as well as act. In "Habit," J.K. Barret argues that the iterative process of theatrical rehearsal and performance, borrowed from rhetorical exercises and Aristotelian ethics, contributes to Shakespearean character-formation as problem and project. In "Acknowledgment," Sarah Beckwith compellingly compares Shakespeare's *The Winter's Tale* and the film *L'enfant* as stagings of knowing and its avoidance in the tradition of Cavell and Wittgenstein. Jeffrey Knapp addresses the keyword *entertainment*, using Kyd's *The Spanish Tragedy* to explore the ambivalence of audience relationships in the drama of the period and beyond. Kevin Curran addresses *judgment* as a term shared by philosophical, legal, and theatrical scriptings of deliberation. James Kuzner takes up Pierre Hadot's definition of philosophy as a way of life to read Shakespeare's evaluative enactments of love in *A Midsummer Night's Dream*. Björn Quiring invokes *curse* as an inherently dramatic speech act with biblical and thaumaturgic foundations. An alternative and supplement to the world-shaking animus of the curse is *care*, the concept analysed by Sheiba Kian Kaufman as a mode of comportment that transforms individual concern into collaborative possibility in the social work of the stage.

These shorter pieces aim to be portable and teachable, sparking connections among texts and disciplines. This section is followed by a cluster of chapters that attend to and create moments in which Shakespeare and philosophy meet.[22] Sanford Budick provides a compelling account of the deep relationship between *King Lear* and *The Winter's Tale* in Shakespeare's unfolding philosophical project; building on Kant and Husserl, Budick links the "now" of performance to philosophy's transcendental perspective and he boldly discovers in Shakespeare a knowledge beyond theatricalization. Anselm Haverkamp argues for the centrality of *Hamlet* to the philosophy of Hegel; through a series of meticulous and revelatory readings, Haverkamp shows how Hegel derived from *Hamlet* a form of objective humour that conceived of the world as history. Finally, Paul Kottman turns to both Hegel and Cavell. Hegel's commentary on the passionless character of parental love, manifested above all by paintings of the Virgin Mary, re-centres *The Winter's Tale* on Leontes's refusal to acknowledge Hermione's role as a mother in the lives of their children. Whereas Beckwith zooms in on the challenge of acknowledging paternity that animates Cavell's foundational reading of *The Winter's Tale*, Kottman draws our attention to maternal love as a form of self-relation upon which fathers, including God the Father, depend.

The volume concludes with an afterword by Charles McNulty, award-winning drama critic for the *Los Angeles Times.* McNulty has seen and reviewed many of the major productions of *King Lear* staged in the past two decades and has read deeply in earlier Shakespeare criticism from Jonson to Bradley. McNulty brings a performance perspective to the debate about page and stage that the great nineteenth-century readers of *King Lear* took up with such intelligence and evaluative insight, demonstrating in his writing what dramatic criticism can be today.

Although all of the contributors to this volume seek ideas in Shakespeare and honour Shakespeare's own intellectual questing, our interlocutors resist placing ideas "behind" or "beneath" the text, striving instead to show how wisdom, judgment, and consciousness are pursued through action and exercise in the medium of drama as it overlaps with the conduct and adventure of life. To entertain an idea is to care for it, to consider its intentionality, history, rhythm, and emergent organization with the kind of attention that an actor devotes to a part, or teachers devote to the learning of their students. As philosopher Milton Mayeroff argues in his classic essay *On Caring*, "In working out a philosophical concept the need to reflect on it again and again from similar and dissimilar points of view is not a burden forced on me; I am simply caring for the idea."[23] From Aristotle and the Stoics through Tillich and Mayeroff, philosophy's commitment to the formation and transformation of persons through spiritual exercise and the ethical and cognitive work of trust, care, and courage/encouragement finds its neighbour in drama's arts of action, audition, and acknowledgment. Shakespeare's plays entertain an idea of drama that constellates the material and the transcendental, the familiar and the unexpected, the actor and the onlooker, in an uneasy stand-off, at once duel and duet.[24] Shakespeare pushes comedy and tragedy towards each other and beyond themselves, emancipated from generic distinctions yet continuously re-prompted by inherited formulae, such as the blessing and the curse. Shakespeare's eclectic philosophy of theatre convenes various forms of performance, including Aristotelian habit, sceptical exercise, Socratic dialogue and role playing, and experiments in phenomenological bracketing that continually restage occasions to welcome the arrival of new forms, new ideas, of how to live together.

NOTES

1 All citations from Shakespeare are from the Oxford Scholarly Editions Online, http://www.oxfordscholarlyeditions.com/nos/.

2 Erwin Panofsky, *Idea: A Concept in Art Theory*, trans. Joseph J.S. Peake (New York: Harper & Row, 1968), 85–95, 119.

3 Panofsky, *Idea*, 68.

4 Augustine, *City of God* [1.35], trans. Henry Bettenson (New York: Penguin Books, 1972), 46. As Robert A. Markus has argued, Augustine's innovative interpretation of the *saeculum* was to a large degree designed to stave off what he viewed as the corrosive proprietary claims on the meaning of secularity by prevailing millenarian and imperializing habits of thought in contemporary, early fifth-century Christian culture. See Robert A. Markus, *Christianity and the Secular* (Notre Dame, IN: University of Notre Dame Press, 2006).

5 Markus, *Christianity and the Secular*, 36.

6 Peter Brown, "Introducing Robert Markus," *Augustinian Studies* 32 (2001): 184, qtd. in Markus, *Christianity and the Secular*, 37.

7 Markus, *Christianity and the Secular*, 15.

8 Markus, *Christianity and the Secular*, 78. The phrase *sacral Christendom* is Jacques Maritain's and refers to the format of medieval Christianity that Maritain saw being superseded in modernity by a "secular" (i.e., modern) Christendom; see Jacques Maritain, *The Range of Reason* (New York: Scribner, 1952), 193–4.

9 The expression is Nicholas Davey's, in "On the Polity of Experience: Towards a Hermeneutics of Attentiveness," *Renascence: Essays on Values in Literature* 56, no. 4 (Summer 2004): 217–34.

10 Walter Benjamin, *The Origin of the German Tragic Drama*, trans. John Osborne (London: Verso, 1988), 38.

11 Kristin Gjesdal, "Literature, Prejudice, Historicity: The Philosophical Importance of Herder's Shakespeare Studies," in *The Insistence of Art:*

Aesthetic Philosophy after Early Modernity, ed. Paul Kottman, 91–115 (New York: Fordham University Press, 2017).

12 Benjamin, *Origin of German Tragic Drama*, 44.

13 Eric Santner, *On Creaturely Life: Rilke, Benjamin, Sebald* (Chicago: University of Chicago Press, 2006).

14 *Idea*: "(in Platonic philosophy) eternal archetype, in post-classical Latin also form, image, likeness (from 8th cent. in British sources), image existing in the mind (13th cent. in a British source) < ancient Greek *ἰδέα* form, appearance, kind, sort, class," *OED*, idea, n.

15 James Kuzner, *Shakespeare as a Way of Life: Skeptical Practice and the Politics of Weakness* (New York: Fordham University Press, 2016).

16 See Tzachi Zamir in this volume on Dover Cliff as a version of the *Akedah*.

17 See Anselm Haverkamp in this volume on Hamlet and Calvary.

18 Paul Tillich, *The Courage To Be* (New Haven, CT: Yale University Press, 2014).

19 See Kottman, "What Is Shakespearean Tragedy?" on the post-generic quality of Shakespearean drama. *Oxford Handbook of Shakespearean Tragedy*, ed. Michael Neill and David Schalkwyk (Oxford: Oxford University Press, 2016), Oxford Handbooks Online, DOI: 10.1093/oxfordhb/9780198724193.013.1.

20 On Shakespearean comedy as the scene for the creative exploration of norms, see Lars Engle, "Shakespearean Normativity in *All's Well That Ends Well*," *Shakespeare Yearbook* 4 (2005): 264–78.

21 Raymond Williams, *Keywords: A Vocabulary of Culture and Society* (London: Fontana, 1976); Émile Benveniste, *Indo-European Language and Society*, trans. Elizabeth Palmer (London: Faber & Faber, 1973); *The Dictionary of Untranslatables: A Philosophical Lexicon*, ed. Barbara Cassin (Princeton, NJ: Princeton University Press, 2014).

22 *Entertaining the Idea* follows in a long tradition from antiquity forward that attempts to bring drama and philosophy into dialogue with each other. Theatre historian Freddie Rokem stages a series of such encounters and exchanges in his remarkable *Philosophers and Thespians: Thinking Performance* (Stanford, CA: Stanford University Press, 2010). Influential recent voices from the philosophical side of this tradition include Stanley Cavell, Bernard Williams, and Martha Nussbaum. See especially Cavell, *Must We Mean What We Say? A Book of Essays* (Cambridge: Cambridge University Press, 1969); and Cavell, *Disowning Knowledge: In Six Plays of Shakespeare* (Cambridge: Cambridge University Press, 1987); Williams, *Shame and Necessity* (Los Angeles: University of California Press, 1993); and Williams, *The Sense of the Past: Essays in the History of Philosophy* (Princeton, NJ: Princeton

University Press, 2006); Nussbaum, *The Fragility of Goodness: Luck and Ethics in Greek Tragedy and Philosophy* (Cambridge: Cambridge University Press, 1986); and Nussbaum, *Love's Knowledge: Essays on Philosophy and Literature* (Oxford: Oxford University Press, 1990).

23 Milton Mayeroff, *On Caring* (London: Harper and Row, 1971), 11.

24 See Paul A. Kottman, "The Duel," in *Theatricality*, ed. Henry Turner (Oxford: Oxford University Press), 402–22; and Lawrence Manley, "Folie à Deux," in *Face-to-Face in Shakespearean Drama*, ed. Matthew J. Smith and Julia Reinhard Lupton, 52–76 (Edinburgh: Edinburgh University Press, 2019).

SECTION I

KEYWORDS

chapter one

Role Playing

TZACHI ZAMIR

Anyone reading a chapter on role playing in a book such as this will already know that Shakespeare's plays are fraught with deviations from identity: disguises, forays into cross-dressing, elaborate acts of pretence and of calculated deceit. Yet the blurring of the differences among these deviations may lead to overlooking some of the most rewarding insights into Shakespeare's works. *Role playing* will be the notion I will probe. Role playing will be set apart from overlapping motifs, such as pretence, lying, or acting. I will then turn to some episodes – in the plays as well as in the sonnets – in which role playing is revealed as a formative process of self-realization, but also as entailing unhappy disquiet.

First scenario: I inform my wife that I have just returned from murdering a man who slept in another room, knowing that I did nothing of the kind.

Second scenario: I run to my wife, panting. I have splashed ice water on my face, so I appear pale. I anxiously mumble to her that I have just murdered a man who was sleeping in the next room, knowing that I did nothing of the kind.

Third scenario: I am acting Macbeth and have just returned to my wife's company from Duncan's room, shaken after murdering him.

Fourth scenario: I am investigating a murder in which the alleged killer has returned home to confess to his wife about the murder. I ask my wife to help me visualize how this conversation might have transpired. I enter the room where she sits, trying to imagine what I have committed. I sense that I am unsure of my stride. My knees buckle. Noting my distress, she offers me a glass of water. My hand shakes as I lift the glass to my lips. Water spills on the carpet.

In the first scenario I am lying, intentionally giving my wife wrong information. In the second scenario I am lying to my wife, but also *pretending*: I am not merely conveying wrong information, but also embodying my sense of what has come to pass. I am living *as if* the information were true, responding and talking *as if* I were undergoing what I know to be untrue. In the third scenario, while I am unfaithful to the truth, I am neither lying nor pretending. I am *acting*. I imagine my way into being Macbeth as part of an *aesthetic* offering to an audience. What this means is that while acting, I try, for example, to be deep, or complex, or original, or vivid. These are all aesthetic qualities that are potential constituents of an artistic achievement for which I can be praised or faulted. In the fourth scenario I am not lying, pretending, or acting. Rather, I am *role playing*, trying to embody what it would be like to live through a situation that is not a part of my reality.

Because acting and pretending are both embodied shifts away from what is known to be really occurring and because acting includes episodes of pretending, it is easy to miss the differences between them. To begin with, pretending is not governed by aesthetic considerations; when pretending, the focus is not on my art. Second, pretending is instrumental: my pretending succeeds if you accept what I want you to believe (so if a colleague pretends to be ill to avoid a meeting, the objective is solely to get others to believe that such is her situation). In acting, though, your beliefs are only my starting point. I fail as an actor if I make you believe that I am Macbeth and that I have murdered Duncan but prove unable to engage your emotions. On its own, your deep response is also insufficient to validate my acting: I can be dissatisfied with my own performance even if you are moved by it (for example, I may suspect that my performance prompted your response in a cheap manner). Third, pretending aims to instil false beliefs; acting plants fictional ones (which also explains why acting is not a form of deception).[1]

Turn to role playing. Because acting and role playing are both embodied departures from known truths, and because, like acting, there is also an exploratory dimension to role playing, an inquisitiveness relating to finding yourself existing in some other context, it can be easy to overlook their differences. Acting is an aesthetically controlled imaginative transformation, an attempt to be in another way. *Role playing* also entails the attempt to be otherwise, but without this being aesthetically controlled. In the fourth scenario above, as I roleplayed my way into the world of the murderer, I was not trying to avoid clichés or looking for unpredictable ways to convey my nervousness, which I would have done had I acted, in other words, had this been an aesthetically controlled undertaking. What I was focusing on was my inner state: what I saw or felt or did when trying to become the murderer.

Role playing is an attempt to imagine your way into realizing an alien possibility. It can be a form of existential amplification in which you momentarily step outside the prescribed limits of your identity, actualizing a potential to be other than you are. Role-playing games, sexual role playing, masquerades, exploratory metamorphoses – these are all committed imaginative embodiments that are unrelated to art and hence are not forms of acting but of being other.[2]

Because this is a chapter about imaginative movements away from identity rather than about strategies of deception, it would be expedient to set aside pretending and lying. Some of Shakespeare's characters lie or pretend, but this will not be my focus. As for acting, what is riddling about Shakespeare's attitude to it, is that if you glean his plays for insights on acting, you will be squeezing a rather dry lemon. Yes, Hamlet admires actors, warning Polonius that they may soil reputations. There are also scenes in which characters are moved by acting. Sometimes bad acting is geared as a trope for something. Once or twice the image of an actor forgetting his lines is employed. Disappointingly, that's about it. Such an outcome is puzzling in light of Shakespeare's own acting career and his ongoing interactions with fellow actors throughout his creative life. It is striking that a man who writes his way so perceptively into the minds of kings and war heroes, braggarts and servants, into the psyche of a Cleopatra, or a baptized Moor, a stigmatized Jew or a raped woman, says so little when writing about acting, a subject matter so near to his heart.

All acting students are treated, at least once, to Hamlet's admonition to actors: avoid exaggerations; be faithful to nature; fit words to actions. These are hardly profundities. What they reveal is that Shakespeare regarded acting merely as a craft. Like other crafts – even those more reputable than acting – acting was for him no more than a financially motivated activity. His pen was drawn to the underlying currents, not to their superficial manifestations. Of acting, that underlying current is role playing. And – unlike his characters' hackneyed comments on acting – when it came to role playing, Shakespeare gave us gold.

Shakespeare wrote in a period for which the identification of living with role playing was already a platitude. *Theatrum mundi*, the perception of the world as a theatre, beheld (or not) by bemused overseers, was ubiquitous. That Shakespeare puts it in the mouth of tedious Jacques suggests that he did not enthusiastically endorse it. "All the world is a stage, and men and women are merely players," says this caustic man, who loves nothing more than the sound of his own voice. It is remarkable how often one is subjected to this line along with the "Seven Ages of Man" speech (*As You like It*, 2.7.138–65), as if it conveyed the Bard's own view. It matters not that no one in the play takes Jacques seriously, least of all the impressive characters, who dismiss him and his wisdom as idiotic irrelevancies as soon as they meet him.

In fact, one of the most subtly touching moments in Shakespeare is Orlando's stage entry carrying Adam upon his back just after Jacques completes his description of living as performing. Old age, Jacques has just confidently declared, is nothing but a second childhood: squeaking old voices, trousers that have become oversized, the decline into an unappealing baby. Yet just as he says this, in comes Orlando with his unquestioning commitment to an old servant.[3] Orlando demonstrates how the dependency of old age need not be mere disempowerment. The weakness that comes with age affords an opportunity to experience gratitude, the rewards of the good done by others in the past. You gave. Now something is given to you, not as repayment, but as the reciprocation of a loving gesture. Does Jacques see this? No. Does he hear it? No. His myopia – perceiving merely ugly caricatures around him, his theatricalization of life – are all dregs floating in the same muddied pond that he mistakes for disenchanted wisdom.

I believe that Shakespeare cannot share Jacques's version of *theatrum mundi* because Jacques is unaware of the distinction between role playing and pretending, a distinction time and again dramatized in Shakespeare's work. Jacques talks of acting and equates acting with pretending. This means that when existence is a serialization of roles performed, life amounts to variations on an embodied aping of something other. Jacques misses the overlap between acting and role playing. By contrast, what Shakespeare finds is that embodied make-believe, role playing, can be a gateway into touching reality, not just a vehicle for its avoidance. This insight is repeatedly realized in episodes in which his characters are role playing. (That such role playing is itself set in motion as part of acting - a real actor's enactment of a fictional character immersed in role playing – amounts to a reframing, which does not alter what such episodes show about role playing as such.)

The very play featuring the "Seven Ages of Man" speech presents the capacity of role playing to establish love. Rosalind, role playing as

Ganymede, tutors Orlando into wooing a woman in the most effective way. Ganymede voices dimensions of Rosalind's being – vulgar humour, sexuality, wit – that ought to be suppressed in her cultural context. Rosalind is aware, too, that apart from violating expected norms, these sides of her will prove unpalatable to Orlando. She is cognizant of this because she has taken a look at his sonnets, Orlando's graffiti on Arden's trees, recognizing that an angel is what he pines for. The Rosalind of Orlando's dreams is a meek being serenely accepting his honourable courtship. Perhaps, after months of timid wooing, she would guardedly grant him a lock of hair. Alas, Rosalind is no Juliet. She is more of an adolescent version of a Cleopatra, envisaging bedding him after tying his arms with her scarves. "My Rosalind is fair," he whispers in devotion. "I would have you out of your apparel," she dryly tells him as Ganymede. She, for him, resembles a sublime idol. He, for her, resembles a Chippendale performer.

This experience of being released into a fuller subjectivity is no private affair, but an interpersonal feat. Rosalind is not merely expressing sexual desire or an unbridled sense of humour that happen to disagree with norms of femininity. She does so while conversing with Orlando. The self is not only a ready-made entity coming into contact with other selves, like interacting billiard balls. Rather, the self is, to an extent, a cluster of occurrences. You are not just a you, but a happening. You happen in and between other self-happenings. And some of these self-happenings require an imaginative embodiment whereby you work yourself into being other.

Another example for such self-happening within a role is how loyalty, friendship, and filial gratitude intersect with role playing in *King Lear*. Kent's very being consists of his fidelity to Lear. Yet when, through becoming Caius, Kent's unwavering allegiance becomes an extended taxing gift to Lear, a gift that will not be reciprocated or even acknowledged, something in Kent's essence gets distilled even further. His loyalty becomes prodigal, ripening into the unconditional love Lear was yearning for. Edgar, too, chooses to remain undisclosed to his blind father. He leads him on while succeeding in remaining a son. Perhaps Edgar realizes that nothing being said could rectify what has been undone by his father. "How could Isaac go on living with Abraham after what elapsed between them?," Edgar may have wondered, deciding to role play his way into preserving something of the son. To role play is not to pretend. It is to attain or maintain, to externalize or to share. To pretend is to be away from others; to role play can sometimes be the only way of being with them.

Need we speculate about Shakespeare's own homoerotic tendencies, about the particular attraction of theatre for him and the appeal of a mask-enabled acting of same-sex love in public settings? Could this safe-zone also be the wellspring of his ability to recognize and vividly linger upon how theatricalizing a life can amount to not merely an evasion, but self-realization? We may ponder this; we are not compelled to, though. When writing words daily intended to assume the flesh and blood of actors, the manner whereby some lines bring out more than play cannot be missed.

Macbeth's lament over his wife is a potent example. Commenting upon one of the lines – "Life's but a walking shadow, a poor player / That struts and frets his hour upon the stage / And then is heard no more" – Ian McKellen notes how the text drives the actor delivering the lines to no longer speak in character. If life is a poor player that will all too soon vanish, and if that is what I am doing now, as actor, Shakespeare's words force me to face not my in-character experience, but my real one. What the line points to is the ephemeral nature of the genuine focus, now bestowed upon the genuine me – how it, how all of it, signifies nothing. When writing for actors, it is possible to configure a fictional context of role playing in which a truth that transcends the role playing is being encountered and then channelled back into the role played, animating the performance.[4]

Regardless of where and how Shakespeare discovered life's interlacing with role playing, it is important not to overlook how such episodes are not only celebrated as indubitable positives. Apprehension, or some sense of lack, always shadows such moments.

Shakespeare could have been cheerful through and through: people sometimes become who they are by virtue of what they imagine through acts of role playing. Instead, the processes he depicts involve characters growing into their identities, *but also foregoing something*. Characters may lose their way because of a role. This happens to Rosalind, who fails controlling Ganymede. It may also be occurring to Hamlet, who puts on an antic disposition but suspects that he is genuinely losing his sanity. Characters may also be endangered by the roles they play. This transpires when others mistake them for someone other. Such is exemplified by Viola, who is challenged to a potentially mortal duel. Characters may unwittingly harm others because of their role playing: women undergo the torments of love after falling for Viola and for Rosalind, mistaking them for men. Role playing causes characters to discover hurtful information that they would rather avoid. Such is Portia's lot when Bassanio tells her that his love for his wife is merely skin deep. Characters can intentionally demean each other through role playing, as when Hull and Falstaff pretend to be father and son, and the would-be king exploits the opportunity to shift from friendly ridicule to cruel abuse by insisting that Falstaff is a nothing. Even when characters experience love in and through role playing, they are evading some other contact: such is evident in the relationship between Rosalind and Orlando when, because Rosalind's role playing is shared with the audience and Celia but not with Orlando, the romance as a whole assumes the quality of an affair.

Role playing is an attainment. It is also, however, a danger and a loss.

When thinking of Shakespearean role playing, it is confining to consider merely masks, disguises, and donned personas – the Duke of Vienna as Friar Lodowick, Portia as Balthazar, Falstaff as the fat woman of Brainford. We ought to think in broader terms, of episodes in which role playing is mentalized. At such moments, role playing is vocalized, but not embodied.

Consider the first words spoken between Romeo and Juliet, that mutual plunge into a game of make-believe in which she becomes a holy statue and Romeo her devoted pilgrim. The exchange is too brief to amount to role playing, even less to a role playing that another is meant to be taken in by. Coordinates of an imaginary situation get borrowed, but the players are not immersing themselves in roles. Rather, they are improvising, indicating what they *might* say or do. This game of make-believe is fleeting; it is delicate – the purpose is to give structure to love; and it differs from imagining another as something else, as, say, when Romeo imagines Juliet's face to be a battlefield upon which death is advancing, or when Juliet imagines cutting Romeo up into little stars. This is not to see X as Y, but to momentarily *perform* as if X were Y, to speak to X *as if* he were Y, to fancy how X would relate to you were she Y. Three centuries later, Stanislavski will write that this *as if* is the heart of acting.

Because what we are presently considering are examples not merely of disguised characters, but of brief yet intense forays into a mindscape in which a role is playfully adopted, the threshold between drama and poetry becomes blurry. Consider sonnets that involve such imaginary odysseys into what the speaker would do or feel if he were someone other, for example, Sonnet 57:

> Being your slave, what should I do but tend
> Upon the hours and times of your desire?

I have no precious time at all to spend,
Nor services to do, till you require.
Nor dare I chide the world without end hour
Whilst I, my sovereign, watch the clock for you,
Nor think the bitterness of absence sour
When you have bid your servant once adieu.
Nor dare I question with my jealous thought
Where you may be, or your affairs suppose,
But, like a sad slave, stay and think of naught
Save, where you are, how happy you make those.
So true a fool is love that in your will,
Though you do anything, he thinks no ill.

The sonnet does more than to invoke the conventional courtly trope of the beloved as a detached mistress (and not just because the mistress may well be a master). What the speaker insists on doing is to eroticize the beloved's absence by imagining his way into the role of an awaiting slave. To be neglected would have been offensive, had I not been your slave.

I have elsewhere argued that unlike the purely sexual quality of sadistic theatricality, masochistic role playing may revolve around love and intimacy.[5] For some of us, love is not found when restricted to set identities but is located in the to-and-fro of gravitating into a role. Sonnet 57 brings out the mental operation being mobilized. We note that the speaker's identity does not disappear through such role playing. He is not *a* slave but *like* a slave. The concluding couplet bitterly comments upon his awareness of rationalizing something. He moulds the experience of being abandoned into a bearable form, while aware that it is a self-serving trick. The transition to the next sonnet, in which the speaker is not *like* a slave but is one, coupled to the disappearance of the self-mockery, becomes moving precisely because the speaker is no longer sure of role playing.

My first point is that something is being achieved – a ripple of comfort, a flutter of arousal – by entering a slave's role, even if the role playing takes place in thought alone. To find role playing in the sonnets is to appreciate how imagining oneself into otherness begins in the mind and how it sometimes lingers there. A word, *slave*, may function like a prop, may be as potent as a costume being donned. So if Shakespeare associates role playing with a birth of something that is otherwise unavailable, we should look for such surfacing of being other not only in his disguised characters. My second observation is that in many of these mental forms of role playing, too, it is possible to hear the murmurs of a not wholly positive experience, that, once again, the role playing orbits around some locus of pain. The transformed speaker resorts to imaginary role playing not because it is uplifting or pleasurable, but because it is the lesser of two evils.

The cue for acting is not just some visible mask. It is a willingness to be teleported to the realm of "what if." This holds true even for the disguised characters, who are already role playing. For them, too, there is role playing and there is *role playing*. Here is Viola being prompted by Olivia to tell her what she (as Cesario) would do were she rejected by Olivia. Viola's response is sufficiently mesmerizing to get Olivia to fall in love with her:

> Make me a willow cabin at your gate
> And call upon my soul within the house.
> Write loyal cantons of contemned love
> And sing them loud even in the dead of night.
> Halloo your name to the reverberate hills
> And make the babbling gossip of the air
> Cry out "Olivia!" Oh, you should not rest
> Between the elements of air and earth,
> But you should pity me.

After you shake away the dizziness suffered by sorting out the many levels of role playing (a male actor is playing a woman, Viola, pretending to be a man, Cesario, invited to imagine how he would act if he were her rejected lover), you will feel for Viola's capacity to take advantage of the opportunity to encode a genuinely suppressed desire into the role of an unreciprocated lover. Viola's actual predicament is her painful love for Orsino, a love she must hide. How apt, then, that the conceit shot through the lines above is all about giving voice, about shouting the beloved's name day and night, about publicly announcing one's love. Once again, role playing is a means to both touching and projecting what is real, but also expresses the pain that making this very choice entails.

While I do not think that the reflections advanced here depend too much upon Shakespeare's own love preferences, it is difficult to resist intuiting, here too, how the power of Viola's lines is driven by extensive familiarity with clandestine love, a love that must remain coded. "No longer mourn for me when I am dead," says the speaker in Sonnet 71, "Lest the wise world should look into your moan / And mock you with me after I am gone." The loss of some lovers cannot be mourned as such. If the world suspected, the world would mock you for it. One wonders about the degree to which Shakespeare's love writings are, ultimately, informed by extensive transitions into the world of "what if."

NOTES

1 For a more detailed analysis of these differences, as well as discussions of rival definitions of acting, see Tzachi Zamir, *Acts: Theater, Philosophy, and the Performing Self* (Ann Arbor: University of Michigan Press, 2014), 33–8, 161–3. Acting may involve episodes of pretending. I may, for instance, act a character that is pretending. It has also been suggested that some onstage work relating to states, such as being asleep or dead, constitutes pretending rather than acting: see Declan Donnellan, *The Actor and the Target* (London: Nick Hern, 2002). When I am lying dead on stage, I am not really acting, but pretending. Here, too, the difference between acting and pretending lies in the instrumental nature of the act: when lying dead on stage, my purpose is no more than encouraging the audience to believe that my character is dead. I am not attempting to be dead in some original or rich way.

2 For examples of role playing as a prolonged imaginative metamorphosis that is not acting, see Thomas Thwaites, *GoatMan: How I Took a Holiday from Being Human* (New York: Princeton Architectural Press, 2016).

3 Ruth Nevo, *Comic Transformations in Shakespaere* (London: Methuen, 1980), 185.

4 Kirk Browning, dir., *Ian McKellen: Acting Shakespeare* (New York: Entertainment One, 1982).

5 See Zamir, *Acts*, 175–92.

chapter two

Habit

J.K. BARRET

Habit is a hard word. Its roots reach back, via the Latin noun *habitus,* to the verb *habeo, habere,* which can mean "to hold" as well as "to have as a habit, peculiarity, or characteristic."[1] As the *Oxford English Dictionary* documents, *habit*'s definition includes clothing as well as the way a person "holds oneself," demeanour, disposition, character, "personal custom, accustomedness."[2] *Habit* collects in one word a range of meanings that its sometimes-synonyms split into two: custom and costume. John Bullokar offers a lengthy entry in his *An English Expositor: Teaching the Interpretation of the Hardest Words in Our Language* (1616):

> The outward attire of the bodie, whereby one person may be distinguished from another; as the habit of a Gentleman, is different from the habit of a merchant, and the habit of a Handi-crafts man differing from them both. Sometime it signifieth a qualitie in the bodie or minde, not natural, but gotten by long custome, or infused by God: as an Orator still exercised in making orations, hath gotten a habit of eloquent speaking; and the holy Apostles had a habit to vnderstand and speake languages without studie.[3]

His definition elaborates certain cruxes: not just clothing, but the capacity for that "outward attire" both to individuate and communicate recognizable social position; not just a "qualitie in the bodie or minde" – an indication of character or personality – but the source of that quality (whether acquired over time or divinely injected).

Bullokar's inclusion of a "qualitie in the ... minde, not natural, but gotten by long custome" situates his definition in a tradition that reaches back to Aristotle's influential account of ethical cultivation. In the second book of the *Nicomachean Ethics,* Aristotle explains that "moral virtue comes about as a result of habit, whence also its name [*ethike*] is one that is formed by a slight variation from the word ethos [habit]" (1103a.16–21).[4] Aristotle's attention to the etymological links between habitual action and the development of character underscores how habit shapes and trains the person who repeats an action into the kind of person who exemplifies the characteristic for which that action is typical.[5] In this chapter I approach Shakespeare's plays in terms of habit to show how the playwright uses the exigencies of stage performance to investigate such philosophical models. The implications for character development – onstage and off – resemble the challenge that arises, as William Gillette puts it in his well-known manual *The Illusion of the First Time in Acting* (1915), in trying to make a (thoroughly rehearsed) performance seem fresh and spontaneous to "each successive audience" rather than "one of a thousand weary repetitions."[6] I argue that Shakespeare not only critiques the assumed stability of "outward attire," but also innovates longstanding approaches to habit by entertaining the possibility that its hold might be temporary. In so doing, he advocates for an ethics predicated not on training or performance that boasts staying power, but rather on the creative potential of a habitual practice that demands active and deliberative choice.

Clothes and the Man

Of the fifty-odd appearances of the word *habit* in Shakespeare's plays, fewer than ten refer to something besides clothing. In most instances, Shakespeare's *habit* means "dress": in *King Lear*, to cite just one example, Edgar adopts "a madman's rags, to assume a semblance / That very dogs disdained" and helps his father, undetected, "in this habit" (5.3.184–5).[7] If, in the early modern period, it was the "putting on of clothes, that quite literally constituted a person … the means by which a person was given a form, a shape, a social function, a 'depth,'" theatre challenged the stable social identities that attire (and its regulations) aimed to fashion.[8] Clothing may operate like so many uniforms to establish and reinforce social position, but the very fact that Shakespeare's habits can be mere "semblance" – the basic building blocks of disguise – unsettles the force of the link.

Shakespeare's employment of the word *habit* in *Measure for Measure* structures Duke Vincentio's plan to get new perspective on Vienna by visiting it in disguise. As he prepares, he implicitly invokes a well-known saying, which cautions that the hood does not make the monk:

"Supply me with the habit, and instruct me / How I may formally in person bear / Like a true friar" (1.3.46–8). He underscores the proverb's meaning by admitting that clothing is necessary but not sufficient to pull off the charade he has in mind. His formulation, in other words, severs habit, meaning "clothing," from habit's potential to mean "manner" or "demeanour". Vincentio's request implies that the "outward attire" aspect of habit does not extend to a person's formal "bear[ing]," even as it communicates that such demeanour can be taught ("instruct me").[9]

The Latin form of the proverb that lurks behind Vincentio's words appears verbatim in *Twelfth Night*, where Shakespeare comes at the question of dress from a slightly different angle:

OLIVIA: Take the fool away.... Sir, I bade them take away you.
FESTE: Misprision in the highest degree! Lady, *cucullus non facit monachum* – that's as much to say as I wear not motley in my brain. (1.5.36–7, 52–5)[10]

It's not quite right to say that Feste's liberal gloss translates the proverb's point rather than its Latin words. Though he maintains the distinction between clothes and the person who wears them, his approximation alters the inflection. On his account, attire is not aspirational. Rather, motley – a jester's multi-coloured outfit – guarantees nothing about its wearer's mental faculties, nor, presumably, interior state. Feste insists on a distinction between a person's costume and essence. In rejecting the idea that he can be reduced to and limited by his outfit, he takes aim at the hierarchizing power implicit in the sumptuary laws operative in Shakespeare's England, what Bullokar's definition claims habit is good for – distinguishing between kinds of people. *Twelfth Night*'s alleged fool showcases how drama might guide an examination – and even an unstitching – of the seams that join habit's meanings together. The pointed rewriting accomplished by his paraphrase questions outward attire's function as shorthand for sorting people into types.

How to Breed a Habit

Feste employs a proverb to challenge the assumption that we are bound or defined by the clothes we wear; Vincentio refers to it to signal that threads alone cannot animate a costumed type. Their perspectives highlight tensions that separate habit's range of meanings; they also invite us to push beyond a critique of sartorial limitations to consider Shakespeare's revision of the other aspect of the definition – those qualities of mind "not natural, but gotten by long custome." In *Two Gentlemen of Verona*, Valentine succinctly articulates that meaning of the word without any mention of clothing: "How use doth breed a habit in a man!" (5.4.1). His description roughly accords with the explanations of habit formation offered by twenty-first-century psychological and neuroscientific research. Forming a habit, one such study claims, takes between 18 and 254 days (the average is 66).[11] To hear contemporary neuroscience tell it, "use" establishes "habit circuits" in the brain. The litmus test is "automaticity" – habit is what you do often, without thinking. This approach to habit highlights the "experience-dependent plasticity" of the brain – repetition establishes habit because the brain is adaptable, shaped by our encounters.[12] From a neuroscientific perspective, habits emerge as a kind of resource management: "Fully acquired habits are performed almost automatically, virtually nonconsciously, allowing attention to be focused elsewhere."[13] By this account, habitual actions and behaviours stand distinct from deliberate ones.[14]

After *Othello*'s Iago has nudged Cassio into the drunkenness that will lead him into personal and professional peril, Cyprus's governor asks, "But is he often thus?" (2.3.111).[15] Montano's question assumes the success of "experience-dependent plasticity"; habits might take time to form, bred by "use" and "long custom," but eventually they indicate defining features. Parsing this trajectory takes on an almost forensic cast in the play.[16] After Othello strikes Desdemona, Lodovico floats two explanations: "Is it his use / Or did the letters work upon his blood, / And new-create this fault?" (4.2.267–9). In asking his charged question – is Othello always abusive or were there extenuating circumstances? – Lodovico, like Montano, assumes that identifying an action as singular or signature makes a difference. In this regard, both men employ the logic of the Aristotelian tradition – that habit entails character – on terms that activate a discourse that fears the dangerous potential of "use." Custom's insidious capacity to breed shows up frequently in the period's extensive anti-addiction literature, which tethers bad habits to vice.[17] Richard Younge writes at length about alcohol's deadly power to incite "desperate custom" in *The Drunkard's Character* (1638). He cautions against the dangers of

> habituat[ing] errors into manners.... Custome brings *sinne* to be *familiar*, that the *horror* of it is turned into *delight*; and as men doe at first lesse like sinne, so with continuance they doe lesse feele it: *frequency* in *sinne*, takes away the *sense* of sinne.[18]

Younge's warning adds another pervasive view of habit to the repetition that takes hold as automatic: habit dulls perception. In this case, "drunkards" grow so accustomed to sin that they can no longer recognize drinking as a vice.

Is habit so corrupting that, far from forming ethical character, it can pervert the very ability to identify sin as such? Hamlet takes up this question explicitly in a heated address to his mother:

> Assume a virtue if you have it not.
> That monster custom, who all sense doth eat
> Of habits evil, is angel yet in this:
> That to the use of actions fair and good
> He likewise gives a frock or livery
> That aptly is put on. Refrain tonight,
> And that shall lend a kind of easiness
> To the next abstinence, the next more easy;
> For use almost can change the stamp of nature,
> And either shame the devil or throw him out
> With wondrous potency. (3.4.157–67)[19]

Hamlet's prominent sartorial metaphor highlights a core tension – Denmark's prince recognizes the potential for "habits evil" to lose their visibility as sins ("custom ... all sense doth eat"), but, unlike Younge, Hamlet approaches the acquisition of virtue and vice with notable evenhandedness; they are equally "easy" to "assume."[20] The "use of actions" that "lend[s]" increasing ease to successive iterations recasts habit's automaticity as ever-diminishing resistance. However, even if the ease of repetition that Hamlet advocates blurs the line between rote performance and sleepwalking, he notably never goes so far as to claim that habitual action will become automatic.

In a published piece of fatherly advice, John Basire enlists a commonplace beloved by the writers who warn against drinking: "Custom turns into an Habit. *Est enim Consuetudo altera Natura*: For Custom is a second Nature."[21] Although the Latin *alter, altera, alterum* can be employed in a number of ways – "second" (whether as a numeral or as an indication of quality); similarity (a "second self"); contrast ("another"; "different") – the early modern tendency to English this popular saying as "second nature" still resonates.[22] We retain that interpretation of the phrase in current idiomatic speech – to call a behaviour or an action "second nature" is to highlight how effortless and ingrained it is. We don't invoke second nature to set our inclinations apart from nature, but rather to affirm them as natural. Our own usage bears witness to a strain in which similarity registers as sameness. Put another way, the "second nature" rendering smoothes over any worry that *second* means "lesser"; more importantly, it sidesteps habit's potential to be alien, for *altera* to signal difference. Approaching the commonplace with this fuller range of options in mind reveals a subtle split – not all writers equate custom and second nature.[23] For example, Cicero's version reads: "consuetudine quasi alteram naturam effici" (5.25).[24] His inclusion of a qualifier (*quasi*) resonates with remarks in Aristotle's *Rhetoric*: "As soon as a thing has become habitual, it is virtually natural; habit is a thing not unlike nature; what happens often is akin to what happens always, natural events happening always, habitual events often" (1.11.1370a).[25] In the *Nicomachean Ethics*, no one is effortlessly good (2.5.1105b.10–11). In the *Rhetoric*, habit comes indescribably close to nature without ever merging into it. Yet unlike the emphasis that neuroscience places to splice habitual and deliberative actions, the tradition that retains the difference between a second nature and *almost* a second nature, between *always* and *often*, defines *habit* as the crucially deliberative side of the coin. In Hamlet's outburst, the word *almost* provides the only protection on the slippery slope down which "monster custom" slides.[26] Without it, habit's amorality provides no safeguards to prevent casting off with equivalent "ease" what anyone might "put on." For Hamlet, habit comes close to "chang[ing] the stamp of nature" without actually effecting a lasting alteration. By invoking ease, by invoking good and bad habits, by remembering that often is not always, he admits that habit's hold might be temporary. In signalling this qualification – almost a second nature as an other nature – he implicitly urges a re-evaluation of experience-dependent plasticity, and gives voice to theatre's potential to disrupt habit's circuitry. Habit's flexibility, in turn, becomes an ethical resource by retaining a continual need for conscious choice.

Theatre's Dual Natures

Hamlet's diatribe highlights the intersection of habit's putative ability to shape ethical character and the discourse that surrounds acting: as theatrical device, clothing functions like the actor's mask; it aids impersonation.[27] According to a logic compatible with Aristotle's ethical interest in habit, early modern pedagogy, following the rules of ancient rhetorical training, operates on the assumption that donning a mask has lasting consequences for the face that bears it.

Critics of the stage shared this belief. According to the anti-theatricalist John Rainolds, the "inconvenience and hurt which [playing] breedeth, [is] principally to the *actors*, in whom the earnest care of liuely representing the lewde demeanour of bad persons doeth worke a great impression of waxing like vnto them; next, to the *spectators*, whose maners are corrupted by seeing and hearing such matters so expressed."[28] If Rainolds believes that the "inconvenience and hurt" to which actors are subjected develops incrementally, just as Gertrude's assumed virtue would "lend a kind of easiness" to each successive "abstinence," he keeps that opinion to himself. For both actor and spectator, the "great impression" and "corrupt[ion]" of "maners" works as instantaneously as Medusa's gaze. Yet Rainold's own metaphor works against his point. He might intend to communicate that "lively" representation grows into or becomes an impression "great" because indelible, but his word choice – "waxing" – retains a potential for alteration and malleability through the very material it invokes. As Shakespeare puts it in *Venus and Adonis*, "What wax so frozen but dissolves with tempering, / And yields at last to every light impression?" (586–7). Unlike its critics, practitioners of theatre, in Shakespeare's time and after, keep pressure on the temporary, deliberative side of the process of "waxing like."

To be sure, learning lines might require actors to engage their "mere imitative echo faculty" in order to "jabber [a theatrical part] as a street piano forces you to hum a tune that you positively dislike," as George Bernard Shaw once advised.[29] The link between repetition and involuntary delivery in theatrical rehearsal and performance informs Constantin Stanislavski's concern that the actor who doesn't "experience his role" by using "his own living desires" will "execute" his part "mechanically."[30] He returns repeatedly to habit, second nature, and the threat of mechanical performance to discuss the careful middle ground an actor must tread in preparing a part. In the best-case scenario, the actor "completely dominated by passion" will be able to forget "physical objectives, he executes them mechanically, oblivious to them.... The body lives its own habitual, motor existence and the soul lives its deeper psychological life."[31] Since it is the automaticity of "motor existence" that frees the actor to engage the "soul" and "passion" necessary for performance, managing that "mere imitative echo faculty" allows performance to draw on habit without stopping there. In Stanislavski's version, the actor's own life experiences inform the character that the actor plays, which flips the prescription for shaping character upon which the rhetorical tradition relied and against which early modern anti-theatricalists warned while still retaining its lexicon. Stanislavski claims that "everything must be done through habit, which turns what is new into something that is my own, organic, into second nature."[32] If we read the expanded terms this approach to habit contributes to character development back into Shakespeare, Hamlet's "almost" engages a flexibility inherent to habit and also serves as a reminder that onstage habit was never limited to the assumption of "outward attire," metaphorical or otherwise. When, however, Shakespeare opposes calculated recurring behaviour to supposedly signature repetition, he also relocates the force of habit's potential to "new-create" another nature.

Repetition's Uses

When Emilia finds Desdemona's "napkin," she notes that her "wayward husband hath a hundred times / Wooed me to steal it" (3.3.296–7). Her adjective registers a tension between Iago's erratic tendencies – "wayward" as "capricious" – and the steadiness of his interest in Desdemona's handkerchief.[33] Emilia emphasizes his consistency when she presents it to him: "which so often you did bid me steal" (3.3.309). In the exchange that follows, Emilia claims she seized an opportunity: "[Desdemona] let it drop by negligence. / And to th'advantage I, being here, took 't up" (3.3.311–12). As she hesitates to hand it over, Emilia implicitly contrasts her happenstance encounter to Iago's "hundred" requests, voiced "often," a point she makes a third time as she tries to assess what he wants with it: he was "so earnest / To have me filch it." Despite being attuned to his repetitions as she produces her own, she fails to hear the language of habit in his oblique reply: "I have use for it" (3.3.319).[34]

It is not until the play's final act that Emilia comes to a realization about Iago's frequent request, one that shifts the terms of habit. Over Desdemona's dead body, Othello rants that his wife "was as false as water," that "Cassio did top her." "Ask thy husband else," he tells Emilia. "Thy husband knew it all" (5.2.137–40). This exclamation takes Emilia by surprise. "My husband?" she asks. After she has asked this same question three times, Othello remarks, "What needs this iterance, woman? I say thy husband." When she utters a fourth version of the query, Othello voices his exasperation: "He, woman; / I say thy husband: dost understand the word? / My friend, thy husband, honest, honest Iago" (5.2.145–59). Othello defines *husband* through a series of referential links – Emilia's husband is Iago. How might she recognize him? Because he is Othello's friend; because he is "honest, honest." Emilia's repetition marks a dissonance she herself does not yet understand. It is not until Othello explains that he knew about his wife's infidelity because of the handkerchief that Emilia identifies a pattern that can explain the incredulity underwriting her earlier "iterance":

> I found [the handkerchief] by fortune and did give my husband,
> For often, with a solemn earnestness
> – More than indeed belonged to such a trifle –
> He begged of me to steal't. (5.2.223–7)

This is Emilia's fourth version of the same information. This time, however, rather than a sign of caprice or wooing, she retrospectively reads Iago's earnestness as "solemn" and out of step with "such a trifle."

If Iago's "hundred" requests were meant to power a terrible scheme, then they conflict with his wide-circulating reputation as an honest man.[35] Although Emilia's initial account shared the hyperbolic math evident in Othello's claim about Desdemona's infidelity – "she with Cassio hath the act of shame / A thousand times committed" (5.2.217–18) – she did not understand Iago's request via Lodovico and Montano's forensic principle, which assesses "use" and behaviour repeated "often."[36] Their account relies on a world view that naturalizes unthinking iterations – the habits bred by use – as stable, defining features. It imagines habit inseparable from repetition (verbal or behavioural). By contrast, Emilia's own repetitions attempt to make sense of discomfiting suspicions. The subtle shifts in phrasing across her four versions of Iago's entreaties chart her emerging recognition of the habitual nature of his request. Remarkably, that realization occurs because she finally understands Iago's "wooing" in the light of premeditation. Put another way, when Iago said he had "use" for the handkerchief, he was clarifying that his "often" and "hundred" requests signalled the deliberative logic of habit. Emilia discovers that automaticity provides a limited guide to character, because Iago treats habit as a kind of making. His version of cultivating a habitual practice brings fiction into the world.

Yet Another Nature

Viewed in a certain light, Stephen Gosson's complaint that when we play theatrical parts we "declare our selues by wordes or by gestures to be otherwise then we are," and are thus guilty of lying, takes the worlds that fiction builds incredibly seriously.[37] Although he would classify it as benefit, not threat, Stanislavski might mostly agree. He posits that "daily, systematic work in imagining the given circumstances of a role can create *habit* in the imaginary life which becomes nature, a second imaginary actuality."[38] Stanislavski introduces seismic shifts into a familiar vocabulary; not only does he stress the real impact habit can have on "imaginary life," but he also replaces second nature with "second imaginary actuality" – what we would call fiction, and what Philip Sidney would call poetry. In his *Defense of Poetry*, Sidney, like Aristotle, foregrounds ethical cultivation: it is exclusively poets who "deliver a golden" world – one that compares favourably with nature's "brazen" world – that can, in turn, better its readers. As he puts it, the "poet doth grow in effect another nature."[39] In Sidney's case, "another nature" describes the creation of a fictional world that imagines things (and the readers who encounter them) to be "otherwise," but inoculates it from the charge of lying.[40] Shakespeare shows how we might turn to the resources and limitations of habit, but not as a tactic for grounding "imaginary life." Instead, his art creates "another nature" that investigates the deliberative possibilities we might both assume and discard. Shakespeare recasts habit as its own kind of poetry, which can give shape to a world that is otherwise without necessarily striving to be golden. Rather than relying on an ethics entailed in the dependability of habit's circuits, he retains the temporary, malleable starting point assumed by both ancient virtue ethics and contemporary neuroscience. In associating habit with an ongoing process of deliberation and judgment that concerns virtue in an extramoral sense, he recuperates habit's creative potential to imagine other worlds or to imagine the world otherwise. In so doing, he incorporates habit's amorality into an ethics predicated on the deliberative demands of active choice, which showcases habit's capacity to become an embodiment of a modality of fiction. Attending to habit in Shakespeare's plays enables us to examine how fiction furnishes alternatives without simultaneously presupposing a reliable vision – akin to the easy shorthand that habit as clothing supposedly provides – of how things might be other than they are.

NOTES

1 William Smith and John Lockwood, *A Smaller Latin-English Dictionary*, 3rd ed. (London: John Murray, 1933), 302–3.

2 "habit, n.," OED Online. July 2018. Oxford University Press.

3 John Bullokar, *An English Expositor: Teaching the Interpretation of the Hardest Words in Our Language* (London, 1616), H4r.

4 Aristotle, *Nicomachean Ethics*, trans. David Ross (Oxford: Oxford University Press, 1980). Some scholars dispute the translation of *hexis* as "habit," but I am tracing the foundational tradition that translated Aristotle's *hexis* into Latin as *habitus*, which made its way to writers and thinkers in early modern England.

5 In Aristotle's terms, "It is by doing just acts that the just man is produced, and by doing temperate acts the temperate man" (2.5.1105b.9–10).

6 William Gillette, *The Illusion of the First Time in Acting* (New York: Dramatic Museum of Columbia University, 1915), 43.

7 Unless otherwise specified, all references are to William Shakespeare, *The New Oxford Shakespeare: The Complete Works*, ed. Gary Taylor et al. (Oxford: Oxford University Press, 2016).

8 Ann Rosalind Jones and Peter Stallybrass, *Renaissance Clothing and the Materials of Memory* (Cambridge: Cambridge University Press, 2000), 2. As they later point out, "The professional theaters were founded upon the flouting of the sumptuary laws and upon the circulation of clothes from aristocrats to commoners" (187).

9 Notably, he does not request spiritual instruction. For discussion of Shakespeare's use of this anticlerical proverb more broadly, see Jones and Stallybrass, *Renaissance Clothing*, 6.

10 All references are to William Shakespeare, *Twelfth Night, or What You Will*, ed. Keir Elam (London: Arden Shakespeare, 2008).

11 Phillipa Lally, Cornelia H.M. Van Jaarsveld, Henry W.W. Potts, and Jane Wardle, "How Are Habits Formed: Modelling Habit Formation in the Real World," *European Journal of Social Psychology* 40 (2010): 998–1009.

12 Ann M. Graybiel, "Habits, Rituals, and the Evaluative Brain," *Annual Review of Neuroscience* 31 (2008): 359–87.

13 Graybiel, "Habits," 361.

14 See Ann M. Graybiel and Kyle S. Smith, "Good Habits, Bad Habits," *Scientific American* 310, no. 6 (2014): 39–43. For an interesting account of neuroscience's debt to William James's conception of habit – as well as a proposal to incorporate Aristotle's outlook – see Javier Bernacer and Jose Ignacio Murillo, "The Aristotelian Conception of Habit and Its Contribution to Human Neuroscience," *Frontiers in Human Neuroscience* 8 (2014): 1–10.

15 All references are to William Shakespeare, *Othello*, ed. E.A.J. Honigmann (London: Arden Shakespeare, 1997).

16 For an analysis of causation, which highlights the prosecutorial tenor of *Othello* and its editorial history, see Dennis Kezar, "Shakespeare's Addictions," *Critical Inquiry* 30 (2003): 31–62.

17 See, for example, Rebecca Lemon's discussion of the consideration of habit's transformation into a need in the consideration of voluntary acts in early modern legal discourse in *Addiction and Devotion in Early Modern England* (Philadelphia: University of Pennsylvania Press, 2018), esp. 84–6 and 103–9.

18 Richard Younge, *The Drunkard's Character* (London, 1638), H2v. Younge's treatise furnishes a useful case study for navigating between "custom" and "habit": unlike habit, custom sometimes refers to social norms, as in the "usuall custome of the place, and the common practice of the people" and "publique custome" (M1v, M2r).

19 Some modern editions, following Theobald-Thirlby, replace *evil* with *deuill.*

20 As Jones and Stallybrass note, in this speech "virtue is figured as a garment that can be put on.... The costume of custom habituates one to the habits (both dress and customary behavior) of good and evil alike" (267). In *Common Prayer: The Language of Public Devotion in Early Modern England* (Chicago: University of Chicago Press, 2001), Ramie Targoff points to this speech in her claim that rather than "a cynical indifference to the worshipper's inner state," Hamlet's advice is consistent with the incorporation of Aristotle's "behaviorist philosophy" into the strategies of the "religious establishment": "What appears to be a simple request for an untaxing and potentially unmeaningful participation in a weekly service turns out to be a strategy to transform the worshipper's soul" (4). Kezar ("Shakespeare's Addictions") notes that, despite the frequency with which "vaguely materialist accounts" discuss this passage, they ignore "the conditional *almost*" (60n69). He does not elaborate about the analysis that restoring attention to *almost* would enable. See also Paul Cefalu, "'Damnéd Custom ... Habits Devil': Shakespeare's *Hamlet*, Anti-Dualism, and the Early Modern Philosophy of Mind," *ELH* 67, no. 2 (2000): 399–431.

21 John Basire, *An Excellent Letter from John Basire Doctor of Laws, to His Son Isaac Basire* (London, 1669) A6r. The phrase, which appears in various forms, dates back to antiquity.

22 Smith and Lockwood, *Smaller Latin-English Dictionary*, 38.

23 For a more comprehensive survey of writers who have meditated on the implications of *second nature*, as well as a valuable introduction to philosophical approaches to habit, see Clare Carlisle, *On Habit* (London: Routledge, 2014).

24 Cicero, *De Finibus Bonorum et Malorum*, ed. T.E. Page and W.H.D. Rouse, trans. H. Rackham. Loeb Classical Library (London: William Heineman, 1914), 476. Rackham renders it as "habit produces a sort of second nature" (477).

25 Aristotle, *Rhetorica*, in *The Works of Aristotle*, vol. 11, ed. W.D. Ross and trans. W. Rhys Roberts (Oxford: Clarendon, 1924), 1.11.1370a.5–10.

26 See Graybiel for a discussion of experiments that aim to rewire neural pathways and attest to habit's almost palimpsestic traces.

27 For discussions of rhetorical impersonation exercises in the early modern schoolroom, see, for example, Joel Altman, *The Tudor Play of Mind: Rhetorical Inquiry and the Development of Elizabethan Drama* (Berkeley: University of California Press, 1978); Lorna Hutson, *Circumstantial Shakespeare* (Oxford: Oxford University Press, 2015); Carol Chillington Rutter, "Learning Thisby's Part – or – What's Hecuba to Him," *Shakespeare Bulletin* 22, no. 3 (2004) 5–30; Lynn Enterline, *Shakespeare's Schoolroom: Rhetoric, Discipline, Emotion* (Philadelphia: University of Pennsylvania Press, 2012); John Parker, "Persona," in *Cultural Reformations: Medieval and Renaissance in Literary History*, ed. James Simpson and Brian Cummings, 591–608 (Oxford: Oxford University Press, 2010); Gavin Alexander, "Prosopopoeia: The Speaking Figure," in *Renaissance Figures of Speech*, ed. Sylvia Adamson, Gavin Alexander, and Katrin Ettenhuber, 97–112 (Cambridge: Cambridge University Press, 2007).

28 John Rainolds, *Th'overthrowe of Stage-Playes* (London, 1599), O4v.

29 Christopher St. John, ed., *Ellen Terry and Bernard Shaw: A Correspondence* (London: Reinhardt and Evans, 1931), 38–9.

30 Constantin Stanislavski, *Creating a Role*, ed. Hermine I. Popper, trans. Elizabeth Reynolds Hapgood (London: Eyre Methuen, 1981; repr. London: Bloomsbury, 2013), 50.

31 Stanislavski, *Creating a Role*, 66.

32 As qtd in Rose Whyman, "The Actor's Second Nature: Stanislavski and William James," *NTQ* 23, no. 2 (2007): 117.

33 See, for example, the gloss in the Longman edition, *William Shakespeare's The Tragedy of Othello, the Moor of Venice and Elizabeth Cary's The Tragedy of Mariam, The Fair Queen of Jewry*, ed. Clare Carroll (New York: Longman, 2003), 76n113. By contrast, the Arden offers "self-willed; wrong-headed; perverse" (227n296), the New Oxford "unaccountable" (2157n3.3.286).

34 *Othello*'s handkerchief in particular, of course, affords consideration of habit as clothing. A wealth of important recent criticism has reconsidered the infamous prominence of the handkerchief, especially in terms of its circulation, symbolic signification, and conditions of its material production. See, for example, Lynda E. Boose, "Othello's Handkerchief: 'The Recognizance and Pledge of Love,'" *English Literary Renaissance* 5, no. 3 (1975): 360–74; Dympna Callaghan, "Looking Well to Linens: Women and Cultural Production in *Othello* and Shakespeare's England,"

in *Marxist Shakespeares*, ed. Jean E. Howard and Scott Cutler Shershow, 41–57 (London: Routledge, 2001); Susan Frye, *Pens and Needles: Women's Textualities in Early Modern England* (Philadelphia: University of Pennsylvania Press, 2010); Natasha Korda, *Shakespeare's Domestic Economies: Gender and Property in Early Modern England* (Philadelphia: University of Pennsyvlania Press, 2002); Ian Smith, "Othello's Black Handkerchief," *Shakespeare Quarterly* 64, no. 1 (2013): 1–25; Paul Yachnin, "Magical Properties: Vision, Possession, and Wonder in Othello," *Theatre Journal* 48, no. 2 (1996): 197–208.

35 Notably, when Cassio laments his lost reputation, he calls it the "immortal," rather than iterative, part of himself.

36 A longstanding critical tradition has noticed *Othello*'s "double time." The play, so the observation goes, seems to take place in the course of an eventful thirty-six hours, but it also seems that the unfolding of the plot's action would require that months, not mere minutes, pass within the fiction. On these terms, my argument understands the "second" time of "double time" as a theory of habit, not a record of literal duration.

37 Stephen Gosson, *Playes Confuted in Five Actions* (London, 1582) C5r. Gosson dedicated his earlier *Schoole of Abuse* (1579) to Sidney, whose *Defense of Poetry* can be viewed as a response.

38 As qtd in Whyman, "Actor's Second Nature," 119.

39 Katherine Duncan-Jones and Jan van Dorsten, eds., *Miscellaneous Prose of Sir Philip Sidney* (Oxford: Clarendon, 1973) 78. For an interesting discussion of the single textual variant that adds the word *into* to render Sidney's phrase "grow in effect into another nature," see Catherine Bates, *On Not Defending Poetry: Defence and Indefensibility in Sidney's Defence of Poesy* (Oxford: Oxford University Press, 2017), 30–1.

40 Sidney famously writes that the poet "nothing affirmeth, and therefore never lieth."

chapter three

Acknowledgment

SARAH BECKWITH

In this chapter I explore the path-breaking, wide-ranging, and profound concept of acknowledgment in the work of Wittgenstein and Cavell, and I exemplify the practice of acknowledgment in Shakespeare's *Winter's Tale,* and in an astonishing film by the Dardenne Brothers called *L'enfant.* Finally, I investigate the implications of acknowledgment for the task of criticism.

Acknowledgment in Wittgenstein and Cavell

Wittgenstein's Remark 244 (*PI,* ¶244) gives voice to a philosophical problem and invites us to imagine a possibility: "How does a human being learn the meaning of names of sensations? For example, of the word 'pain.' Here is one possibility: words are connected with the primitive, natural, expressions of sensation and used in their place. A child has hurt himself and he cries; then adults talk to him and teach him exclamations and, later, sentences. They teach the child new pain-behaviour."[1]

Stanley Cavell first develops his idea of acknowledgment in relation to Wittgenstein's numerous remarks and examples about pain in the *Philosophical Investigations.* The idea of acknowledgment first emerges in "Knowing and Acknowledging," an essay paired with his more famous "King Lear and the Avoidance of Love," both published in *Must We Mean What We Say?* in 1969.[2] From the beginning, acknowledgment and avoidance are bound up together: avoidance turns us away from knowledge we have, distorting our relation to ourselves and the world. That relationship is most developed in part 4 of the great *Claim of Reason,* which takes up "Skepticism and the Problem of Others."[3] It takes Cavell some 167 pages of densely imaginative philosophical writing to explore the idea that we live, in his words, "between acknowledgment and avoidance," which is also the title of the final chapter, chapter 13. Here by exploring Wittgenstein's extraordinary thought experiments – the parable of the water boiling in the pot *(PI,* ¶297), the brilliant beetle in the box *(PI,* ¶293), the imagination of a race of men and women who don't express pain when they have it, smiling babies (*PI,* ¶249) and dogs simulating pain *(PI,* ¶250), the would-be private diarist trying to impress upon himself the sign *S* onto his supposedly recurrent sensation *(PI,* ¶258), or the invitation to see if we could possibly imagine a language that we alone could use *(PI,* ¶243, 256) – Cavell claims that the moral of the *Investigations,* and the heart of its philosophical cure, was to diagnose our false pictures of the inner and the outer. Such pictures, in denying our *actual* separation from each other, all but obliterated the precise ways in which we know each other, that is, by virtue of our expressions. In Cavell's reading of Wittgenstein, language, gesture, and the entire intricate world of our responsiveness are the way, the only way, we reveal ourselves to each other. This basic feature of our encounters is distorted in false pictures of inner and outer where our bodies and gestures, words and expressions are pictured as a veil, a mask, a *superficies,* that covers over, disguises, or hides our true inner-ness, rather than the only way it is humanly revealed.

The idea of acknowledgment comes as an alternative to the philosophical habit of mind that worries over the *gap* between word and world, between the expression of pain and pain itself. There is no need to get *between* pain and its expressions because our callings out of pain and our responses to each other's pain in comforting, succouring, healing, are expressions of pain, not something that gets in the way of it. "Between," Cavell suggests, is a picture, an attempt to wedge language between our inner lives and our outward expressions.[4] "The dependence of reference on expression in naming our states of consciousness, is, I believe, the specific moral of Wittgenstein's inventions containing the so-called private language argument."[5] What it reveals is the depth to which language is shared.

Cavell had begun his analysis of the *Investigations* with the idea that criteria in Wittgenstein are invoked not so much for, say, entrance qualifications, or dog competitions, where there were specific guidelines, and rules set by experts and umpires, but rather for things such as sitting on a chair, having a toothache, reading, thinking, pointing to something. These are things we are all in a position to know, that need no expertise. How do we learn pain then? Well, we learn how to talk, says Wittgenstein – suggesting that our learning is not best described as a process of attaching a name to a thing, but rather an initiation in all the complex modes of life, habits, practices, and ways of doing things that give us a world at all. "You learned the *concept* pain when you learned language" *(PI,* ¶384; Wittgenstein's italics). Furthermore these criteria for things being what they are – which is what Wittgensteinian criteria elucidate *(PI,* ¶371, ¶373), why Wittgensteinian grammar shows us what kind of object anything is, can tell us only of the identity of something, not whether it actually exists. They are criteria for things being *so,* but not for their *being* so, as Cavell so felicitously puts it.[6] (This is why scepticism is a permanently available possibility, why criteria are fully open to scepticism.) Criteria are disappointing in this respect: they can't tell us whether that man over there is only feigning pain or actually having it, only that it is pain at issue. And they are doubly disappointing because they depend on our voicing of them to do the work they actually do, on our counting this as something here and now in this instance, for this occasion.

Cavell thinks that the idea that there could be a language known only to me, which he calls the "fantasy of necessary inexpressiveness," would mean that I did not have to take the responsibility for making my desires, needs, dreams, feelings known to others, because in the fantasy I could not do so, and I could escape myself and my own self-knowledge.[7] If the word and the world could somehow be stamped on each other without my intervention I would also not have to take a role in the voicing of criteria, and so I would not be exposed to you and all the others who make up my world. The fantasy maintains my autonomy; it denies the depth of my dependence on others. In exploring the terrain of acknowledgement Cavell shifts the entire terrain of our knowledge of others from the realm of epistemic failure to the harder terrain of response and responsibility.[8] But in so doing he confronts our deep and pervasive disappointment with what criteria can do. To do what they do, we have to give voice to criteria – we have to decide whether what you are showing me now is pain, and it seems as if I may have nothing to go on but my sense of your wince or moan. Would it not be better that I knew you were in pain by some more sure means that your giving voice to it, and that I could know your pain by something other than my response. My response, my acknowledgment *is* the way I know your pain, the way I respond to your expressions that are your criteria for pain, and this seems so vulnerable and precarious, so small and unreliable a thing to bank on.

Cavell suggests that when we imagine some better way of knowing each other than humanly, through our bodily expressions and responses, we exit our mutual attunement and threaten the ways in which we are intelligible to each other at all. That is why these sections and others of the *Investigations* lead on to remarks such as "What gives us so much as the idea that living beings, things, can feel?" *(PI,* ¶283), or "How am I filled with pity for this man?" *(PI,* ¶287).

Cavell's elucidation of the concept of acknowledgment makes our responses towards each other the crux of the matter, as Edward Minar has recently affirmed.[9]

When Regan sees Gloucester gripping the sides of the chair on which he is bound, in helplessness, in impotent defiance, in terrified anticipation of whatever is to come, when he howls at the pain and horror of his blinding, both the inestimable pain of it and the terror of the fact of it, Regan surely knows it is pain Gloucester is in. She knows his pain as a dimension of her power; her pleasure means that her acknowledgment of it is wrenched out of the natural ways in which we learn about pain from being comforted, succoured, and cared for (if indeed we are). Regan knows Gloucester's pain through her power and pleasure, just as the servant acknowledges Gloucester's pain by trying to put a stop to it, or by fetching poultices for his bleeding rings. We are being asked to see the role such knowledge plays in their lives, and the claims such knowledge makes on them and us here and now. We know Gloucester's pain through his expression of it *and* our responses: Regan and the rebellious and faithful servant will reveal what counts for them. That will be part of Gloucester's knowledge of it too. Our criteria thus show what pain is, and they show *us* too, they reveal who we are by virtue of our responses.

John Gibson has helpfully suggested that there is something dramatic about acknowledgment in the sense that "an act of acknowledgment is a way of giving life to what it is that we know, of bringing it into the public world.... Understanding, if fully possessed, establishes a type of dramatic relation between knower and the world. It places us in the world as agents who are responsive to the range of values and experiences that are the mark of human reality."[10]

Cavell's reading of Wittgenstein shifts the entire terrain of knowledge from the false terrain of the internal objects transparently and naturally known to me by introspection. It is by means of acknowledgment (which of course includes knowledge, being a dimension of it) that we as humans know each other and come to know our selves. Are there implications for criticism?[11]

I can't encounter works of art without asking what counts for me, and struggling to give voice to why it matters and how, so that you might be able to see it too.[12] Cavell's idea that criteria are criteria of judgment – that they are both predications of judgment – that this is judged to be *X*, and proclamations (hence expressions) of judgment – that it counts as *X* for us now and in this instance – extends to the entire terrain of language and judgment what Kant had articulated for the specific terrain of aesthetic judgment alone.[13] When I tell you what I see in this film, I want you to see it too. I am not at all content to let you rest in your wrong opinion of this film but will strive to become clearer and more articulate about what it is I do see. My judgment of this film is my acknowledgment of it, it is how I come to know it. My acknowledgment encompasses self-knowledge, for I will have revealed to you and to myself what counts for me.

Part 2: *L'enfant* and *The Winter's Tale*

I have been teaching a new Shakespeare class recently under the loose and capacious rubric, "Shakespeare Now and Then." Most of the materials we study are versions of *The Winter's Tale,* beginning with one source, Robert Greene's *Pandosto.* Eric Rohmer's beautiful film *Conte d'hiver* (1992) is an evident homage to Shakespeare's play. Rohmer shows us Félicie watching entranced as the "statue" comes to life in a performance of *The Winter's Tale,* and we come to understand that the play confirms and helps articulate her self-understanding. George Eliot's *Daniel Deronda* (1876) features the statue scene in *The Winter's Tale.* There Gwendolyn shows herself to great effect in her alluring costume, and it is an instance of her painful ignorance of herself and the world. But the other films and novels we examine, such as Jane Austen's lovely and late novel, *Persuasion* (1818), perhaps as much a tale of autumn as of winter, or the Dardenne Brothers' haunting film, *L'enfant* (2005), and Pedro Almodóvar's scintillating melodramas, *Talk to Her* (2002) and *Volver* (2006), never explicitly reference Shakespeare's play. But they are Winter's Tales: that is my claim. They share the promise and the terror of those words that sound and resound the idea of return (coming back, *volver*), recovery, renewal, but too remembrance, repentance, resurrection, remorse, recognition, redemption. They are all books of second chances. When read together they mutually illuminate each other, interweaving strand on strand of the themes of childhood, forgiveness, remarriage, the role of art, and the relation between the past and the present. To our class *The Winter's Tale* seemed so deep and generative in these works that the vocabulary of source, influence, analogue, adaptation, homage, or re-creation gave way to words such as *incarnation, resurrection, echo, haunting.*

After 1996 when the Dardenne Brothers made their breakthrough film *La Promesse*, they went on to make a series of stunning films that renovate filmic realism. Hand-held cameras and, at least at the beginning of their film careers, unknown amateur actors were used. The films stay very close to the grain of life of their largely impoverished and marginalized characters, inarticulate in words but extraordinarily expressive. The protagonists are depicted with no condescension, and because there is no moralism in the way we are asked to encounter them, the films open up an astonishing ethic of acknowledgment. In the context of my class, what emerged in rich association with *The Winter's Tale*, was the disowning of childhood, and the fundamental theme of the second life of forgiveness.

In the Dardenne Brothers' searing 2005 film, *L'enfant*, *The Child*, a young grifter called Bruno, played by Jérémie Renier, sells his child, Jimmy, newly delivered to his partner, Sonia. Asked to look after Jimmy for the afternoon while Sonia signs on to the Social Services in the dismal and decayed post-industrial outskirts of Liège, Bruno, as if on impulse, arranges to exchange Jimmy for five thousand euros. He has learnt about a so-called adoption service, a thinly veiled front for human trafficking, from the woman who buys his stolen goods. When Sonia asks Bruno where Jimmy is, in a scene that takes place near the polluted river in which he has an utterly makeshift shelter, he says in a matter-of-fact way, "I sold him" and "I thought we could have another." At this news Sonia, like Hermione, faints. We next see her in hospital refusing to speak to Bruno and cutting off all relations with him.

The transaction with the traffickers is depicted in the most painstaking detail. We follow closely behind Bruno, the hand-held camera never far from him as he takes Jimmy to a derelict apartment on the outskirts of the town and leaves him there, as he receives the money, counted note by note. What *counts* for Bruno is very much at issue in this film, and counting here has the full force of accounting both in its financial and fully ethical sense.[14] Every transaction is in cash, as Bruno lives in an entirely cash economy, made up of pawnshops, fences, impulse buys, and surviving for the day: work is for losers. In the transaction we see only the trafficker's hands counting the notes, and not his face.

At almost every moment we are aware of Jimmy's extraordinary vulnerability and about what it means to be born into such a world. The film opens with Sonia's search for Bruno to show him his child when she is released from hospital after giving birth. (He has sublet her flat while she is in hospital without her knowledge.) As she crosses the busy highway holding the newborn Jimmy to reach Bruno in his shack by the river, we are made aware of the smallness and fragility of the child in the harsh world he is born into. The Dardenne Brothers used twenty babies to shoot the scenes with Jimmy, although it is a relief to know that dolls were used for the scenes in which Jimmy rides on the back of a motorbike with Sonia and Bruno.

Now it is important to say that the intense human drama of the film is not in the merciful return of Jimmy – which happens very quickly. Bruno recovers Jimmy but is then beaten up and taken for the sixteen euros he has on him and told now to steal for the traffickers to repay the money lost on the transaction. Since Jimmy is quickly recovered, most of the film depicts the aftermath of the sale, and chiefly, as I see it, the possibilities of Bruno's acknowledgment of Jimmy as his child, that is, of himself as a father. This is to say, as Cavell says of Hermione to Leontes, that Jimmy is not empirically lost, but transcendently lost to Bruno.[15]

The film has four main protagonists, all of whom are contenders for the title: Jimmy, is l'enfant, whose loss and recovery drive the plot; but Bruno and Sonia are children, playing like puppies nuzzling, fighting and joshing around with each other in affection, playful rivalry, and as children seemingly unaware of the responsibilities, implications, and commitments of parenthood. The last contender for the film's title is the boy Steve who works for Bruno as his main accomplice and child thief. It is with Steve that Bruno is first awakened into a different way of being.

Steve and Bruno embark on a bravura theft – Steve grabs a woman's handbag while on the back of a motorbike with Bruno. It seems foolproof, but the victim of the theft is surprisingly persistent and she commands a nearby car to set off in hot pursuit. The car chase ends with Steve and Bruno parking the moped near the river and submerging themselves under a jetty in its stinking, cold, polluted waters. (The actors had to be hospitalized after shooting this scene.) Steve, terrified with cold and the fear of discovery, loses his grip on the jetty. He panics and flails around in the water, looking as if he might drown. Bruno immediately saves him from the waters, and afterwards we seem him trying to warm Steve's poor frozen feet back into life and feeling. But the cops come, and while Bruno makes a run for it, Steve is carted off for his first arrest.

Steve has grabbed onto him, and Bruno has – almost inadvertently – "rescued" him. He turns himself in to the police to save this boy. "It was me," he says, performing an act bound to lead him to prison.

It is important to see that Bruno's responses to the boy are fully natural and instinctive. I once heard a story like this. In London in the 1980s, a friend of mine had been raped by a man who, it appeared, was a serial rapist, sometimes acting alone, and sometimes with another man. In the attempt to prosecute these men – who wore masks and were hard to identify, the police brought together the women who had been raped over a number of preceding years. There were nearly thirty women in the room, and it was apparent that these men had been operating all over the city. One girl told my friend that she was attacked on Hampstead Heath, but that as the two men dragged her down into a copse where they could rape her out of sight, she tripped over a root in the copse. She instinctively put out her hand to the younger man standing next to her to prevent herself from falling and he, instinctively too, held her hand to steady her. This man was unable to rape her. For a moment he had – by the purest instinct – acted to save her from the simple harm of falling down. He was now, for that moment, in a flash able to experience himself as a helper, not a harmer. The two men started arguing and they let her go.

At each point, and minutely, variously, precariously, we take up positions in relation to each other, we figure out where we stand in that relation, what we are prepared to take responsibility for. Of course, that young man assumed a different responsibility in relation to his instinctive response to the girl. Another man might have done something different – he might have hardened himself more decisively against the girl, wanting not to appear weak in front of his fellow rapist.

Bruno's responses to the boy in the water are like this: he rescues the boy who is terrified of drowning. He helps him get to the shore and then he rubs his feet to warm him up. He has not suddenly become kind but he has *responded,* and the later events of the film show that something has shifted in him, because he knows himself to be capable of such a response. When he turns himself in to the police, he is trying to save the younger boy from getting into the hands of the justice system. The film shows us no struggle of conscience. It is simply something he does. In taking on this action, which grows out of his response to the boy, he is building on something instinctive and taking responsibility. All of a sudden Bruno has instinctively taken care of Steve. He voluntarily goes to the police station, admits that he was the thief. His actions lead at once to his own imprisonment and the release of Steve.

Bruno has resisted holding Jimmy. Neither does he want to see his child, and he does not look at him. He has not named the child. When he asks what he is called, Sonia has said, "Jimmy, as you wanted." She tells him that they will have to go to the town registry and register the birth.

The French term is *reconnaître*: the child in being given a second name must be legally recognized. Bruno must recognize himself as the father. Bruno knows he is the child's father, both biologically, and since he does register the child, he is legally his father too in the eyes of the state. The French term is *officalese*, but it carries the film's full force of a moral recognition. Yet after legally recognizing Jimmy, Bruno denies to the police that the child is his, after he has sold him and returned him as he attempts to escape the rigour of the law. While in hospital after her faint on the river, Sonia has told the police what Bruno has done. Now Bruno denies his paternity, accusing Sonia of cheating on him with other men. Even though Bruno has got Jimmy back, he has no idea what fatherhood means. We might say that he disowns the knowledge of his paternity.

Acknowledgment implies that what is acknowledged is true. And this means that its opposite is not knowledge but rather denial, avoidance. Bruno is avoiding paternity, refusing it. He knows he is Jimmy's father, but he has not taken that on. The language of denial and avoidance indicates that what is being avoided is a truth we can't bear to see.

At the end of the film Bruno and Sonia acknowledge each other in the prison where she visits him for the first time. It is a miracle of film-making and acting. He asks her how Jimmy is. It is the first time he has expressed genuine care or concern for the child, and it is the first time he has named the child, thus recognizing him as worthy to have a name and to bear the name given him by Sonia. The camera has followed her in a long panning shot, taking in the other visitors in the prison. Then it focuses on Bruno's face, then Sonia's. As Bruno puts the coffee cup to his lips, he suddenly starts to cry. As the camera moves between them, we see that Sonia too answers his tears with her own, and for several minutes we watch these two look directly at each other, hold each other's hands over the coffee as their tears spill over their hands. Gently they butt their heads together as if they are now solid creatures for each other again. It is the first time they face each other since the hospital visit. They are tears of lament, of sorrow, perhaps also tears of joy. It is an astonishing moment in the film.

Can we say here that the child is acknowledged as Bruno's when he recognizes his own position in relation to Jimmy, fully, irrevocably, and here, remorsefully? What is involved in recognizing yourself as a father? In seeing your child as yours?

Acknowledgment, then, is shot through our relations with each other. It involves understanding where we stand in relation to others. That Bruno is Jimmy's father is not a matter of biology – though he may try to use biology to deny paternity. Nor is it a matter of the law. To recognize Jimmy in the law is to grant him a name, to register him as a citizen of the polity of the city Liège. To acknowledge him as his child, and to thus take on the position of father in relation to him, not to any child, and not abstractly, is a matter of personal, painful biography. It is clear in this astonishing scene that Bruno has surprised himself with his question about Jimmy. Caring for Steve has made him understand himself as a creature who cares and is bound up in and with the cares of others.

In his stunning book, composed with the photographer, Jean Mohr, about the English country doctor, John Sassall, John Berger writes about how he sees Sassall weep. Observing that the suffering that doctors witness carries a large strain, he suggests that in his dealings with his patients he must come close enough to recognize his patients fully. Berger says,

> A man or a woman who is sobbing reminds one of a child, but in the most disturbing way. This is partly because of the particular social convention which discourages adults (and particularly men) from breaking into tears but permits children to do so. Yet this is by no means the whole explanation. There is a physical resemblance between a sobbing figure and a child. The "bearing" of the adult falls away and his movements are limited to certain very primitive ones. The centre of the body again seems the mouth: as though the mouth were simultaneously the place of pain and the only way by which consolation might be taken in. There is a loss of the control of the hands which again can only clench or paw. The whole body tends towards a foetal position.... Why is the similarity so disturbing? Once more I believe the explanation goes further than our sense of compassion. In some way the similarity, once established, is brutally denied. The sobbing man is not like a child. The child cries to protest. The man cries to himself. It may even be that by crying again like a child he somehow believes that he will regain the ability to recover like a child. Yet that is impossible.[16]

Bruno's hands clench and paw, as do Sonia's. And his mouth opens in pain and cannot hold its shape in its woundedness. But this man is not crying to himself. His tears are involuntary: he cannot help them, and they surprise him, they bring him back into Sonia's world, for he can cry for her and cry for Jimmy, cry for what he has done and left undone, cry for the transcendental loss of Jimmy and for Jimmy's recovery, for the loss of Sonia and for her return to him, a return that happens through their tears. His tears *are* his acknowledgment of her, they are not after the fact of his acknowledgment. In his responsiveness is his responsibility as they come into view for each other through their tears. So Bruno's tears are the tears of a child who is growing up. They are his growing pains.

Cavell's understanding of acknowledgment entails that to recognize himself as the father of Jimmy – to acknowledge it, for he knows he knows it – is to be able to see himself as the man who sold him, it is to recognize *his* relation to Jimmy, his fatherhood.

If the film traces out the very lineaments of this acknowledgment for Bruno, what are we asked to acknowledge?

In closing, I wish to suggest that the concept of acknowledgment can help us envisage the claims made by literary, dramatic, or filmic works on us. This is a film we can learn from and not just about. Derek Gottleib suggests that this might be a first condition of literature or film's educative capacity for us – that we are in a position to learn *from* it.[17] Furthermore such acknowledgment will not emerge from various facts about the film but by virtue of our own response to it as an untranscendable horizon. Literary, filmic, and theatrical art bears on us.

NOTES

1 Ludwig Wittgenstein, *Philosophical Investigations* trans. G.E.M. Anscombe, P.M.S. Hacker, and Joachim Schulte, 4th ed. (Oxford: Wiley-Blackwell, 2009), henceforth PI, Remark 244.

2 Chapters 9 and 10 respectively in Stanley Cavell, *Must We Mean What We Say? A Book of Essays* (Cambridge: Cambridge University Press, 2002).

3 Stanley Cavell, *The Claim of Reason: Wittgenstein, Skepticism, Morality, and Tragedy*, updated ed. (Oxford: Oxford University Press, 2002,), henceforth *CR*.

4 *CR*, 341. Peter Dula is excellent on this topic in *Cavell, Companionship and Theology* (Oxford: Oxford University Press, 2011), 78–9. I treat the private language fantasy at greater length in my book on Shakespearean tragedy currently in progress.

5 *CR*, 343.

6 *CR*, 45.

7 *CR*, 351.

8 *PI* 253, "I have seen a person in a discussion on this subject strike himself on the breast and say: 'But surely another person can't have *this* pain!' And the answer to this is that one does not define a criterion of identity by emphatic stressing of the word 'this.'"

9 Edward Minar, "Living with the Problem of the Other: Wittgenstein, Cavell and Other Minds Scepticism," in *Wittgenstein and Scepticism*, ed. Denis McManus (London: Routledge, 2004), 233.

10 John Gibson, *Fiction and the Weave of Life* (Oxford: Oxford University Press, 2007), 108.

11 See now Toril Moi, *Revolution of the Ordinary: Literary Studies after Wittgenstein, Austin, and Cavell* (Chicago: University of Chicago Press, 2017), especially chapter 9, 196–221.

12 Articulated in "Aesthetic Problems of Modern Philosophy," in *Must We Mean What We Say?*, 73–96.

13 On judgment as predication and proclamation, see *CR*, 35; for the Kantian underpinnings and extensions of Cavell's aesthetic, see "Aesthetic Problems," 88*ff.*

14 On counting, see "Recounting Gains, Showing Losses," in Stanley Cavell, *In Quest of the Ordinary: Lines of Skepticism and Romanticism* (Chicago: University of Chicago Press, 1988), 86.

15 Cavell, *In Quest of the Ordinary*, 86, for "transcendentally lost."

16 John Berger and Jean Mohr, *A Fortunate Man: The Story of a Country Doctor* (London: Vintage International, 1997), 116.

17 Derek Gottlieb, *Skepticism and Belonging in Shakespeare's Comedy* (London: Routledge, 2016), for the concepts of teaching and learning in literature.

chapter four

Judgment

KEVIN CURRAN

Judgment offers a powerful framework for understanding some of the most basic and profound components of theatrical experience, from bodily sensation and the spatio-temporal dynamics of the stage to the strange creative alchemy involved in getting audiences to make collective leaps of imagination. I will explain what I mean by all this in due course, but first we need to understand what exactly judgment is. This is trickier than it may sound. For example, is judgment an act or a process? Is it a concept or an experience? To which cultural or theoretical field does it belong, and to what set of social practices?

As this short list of questions indicates, judgment is a uniquely protean thing. Part of its history is legal, with the courtroom serving as its primary institutional home. Judgment is also a central feature of the Abrahamic religions, lending them moral force and, in the case of Christianity, managing the spiritual and temporal thresholds between prelapsarian and postlapsarian and salvation and damnation. In a variety of Renaissance sources, ranging from sermons to moral interludes, we find divine judgment being contrasted with the inflexible and error-prone judgment of the secular common law courts.[1]

The history of aesthetics is also bound up with conceptions of judgment. In the vernacular literary criticism that developed in England over the course of the sixteenth and seventeenth centuries, programmatic descriptions of good writing and right reading by figures such as Philip Sidney, George Puttenham, Samuel Daniel, and Henry Peacham were heavily invested in judgment, citing it as both the faculty responsible for proper discernment and the attribute that stands to benefit from superior writing and oratory. This link between *inventio* and *scientia iudicandi* (the science of judging) was not strictly literary, however. Deriving from Aristotle and Cicero, it also applied to political "invention," or what we might now call policymaking. Both versions of invention, the literary and the political, involved the principle of *decorum*, a version of judgment in which careful consideration is given to the particulars of circumstance rather than general moral precepts.[2]

Finally, judgment is also a key term in the Renaissance discourse of sociality, in which context it is viewed as a practice that knits the individual's sense of self into a larger community of taste. For example, Stephen Guazzo in *The Civile Conversation* (1581) writes, "The judgment which we have to know ourselves is not ours, but we borrow it of others … the knowledge of ourselves, dependeth of the judgment and conversation of many."[3] Comments like this in Renaissance conduct books intersect with the long philosophical tradition of thinking about how judgment links individuals to larger collectives. This line of thought begins with Aristotle and the Stoics and is taken up with particular rigour in the eighteenth century when writers like the Third Earl of Shaftesbury, Jean-Jacque Rousseau, and especially Immanuel Kant formulated new ideas about the role of judgment in social and political life.[4] Later, in the twentieth century, Hannah Arendt developed the moral and political implications of Kant's arguments in a series of influential essays. At the time of her death in 1975, Arendt was planning a final volume of her seminal work *The Life of the Mind* on "Judgment."[5]

What we can say for sure, then, is that judgment has an assemblage-like structure. It sprawls across the thought-worlds of law, religion, aesthetics, rhetoric, and philosophy and signifies across several semantic fields. In this chapter I will be attentive to all of these intellectual contexts, but my larger aim will be to show something new: judgment, I will argue, is part of the basic DNA of theatricality. Understanding how it works – what it enables and what it structures in theatrical contexts – offers one way to map out how performance constitutes a unique form of embodied philosophical thought.

The chapter will unfold in three parts: "The Feeling of Judgment," which will focus on *Hamlet*; "The Physics of Judgment," which will focus on *Measure for Measure*; and "The Ethics of Judgment," which will focus on *The Tempest*. By the end of the chapter, I hope to have shown not only how judgment helps us understand what happens at plays – emotionally, physically, and ethically – but also how Shakespearean theatre helps us recover a way of thinking about judgment that has largely been left out of the post-Enlightenment liberal tradition; a way of thinking about judgment that is collective, physical, and creative rather than individual, rational, and normative.

1. The Feeling of Judgment

What does it feel like to judge? This probably sounds like an odd question, since we do not typically think of judgment as a sensory experience. Judging is something we do with our mind, not our body. We also do not tend to think of judgment as an emotional experience. Indeed, most would say that sound judgment is exercised when reason overrides the distorting effects of passion. These are the first assumptions I would like to overturn in this chapter, and I will be enlisting *Hamlet* to help me do so. Once we have established an account of judgment that is physical and interactive, we will be ready to consider the physics and ethics of theatrical judgment in the next two sections.

Our scene is Queen Gertrude's bedroom, act 3.4, the "closet scene." Hamlet has impulsively killed a snooping Polonius, and he now confronts his mother about marrying his uncle so soon after his father's death. The scene is structured around a comparison of two pictures, one of Hamlet Senior, the other of Claudius. It is a scene that essentially stages looking, and, more specifically, stages the connection between vision and discernment. Hamlet asks his mother to "Look here upon this picture, and on this, / The counterfeit presentment of two brothers" (3.4.51–2).[6] He starts by presenting his father:

> See what a grace was seated on this brow,
> Hyperion's curls, the front of Jove himself,
> An eye like Mars to threaten and command,
> A station like the herald Mercury
> New-lighted on a heaven-kissing hill,
> A combination and a form indeed
> Where every god did seem to set his seal
> To give the world assurance of a man;
> This was your husband. (3.4.53–61)

Hamlet then presents Claudius:

> Look you now what follows:
> Here is your husband like a mildewed ear
> Blasting his wholesome brother. Have you eyes?

> Could you on this fair mountain leave to feed
> And batten on this moor? Ha, have you eyes? (3.4.61–5)

What is notably missing from this passage is an appeal to reason. Interpretation and moral choice are, instead, securely anchored to the body and its methods of gathering information. Gertrude is impelled to "see" and to "look," for this, according to Hamlet, is how one discerns between "Jove" and "a mildewed ear." Twice he demands of his mother, "Have you eyes?" The connection between sensation and judgment becomes more explicit as the passage progresses:

> what judgment
> Would step from this to this? Sense, sure you have –
> Else could you not have motion. But sure, that sense
> Is apoplexed, for madness would not err
> Nor sense to ecstasy was ne'er so thralled
> But it reserved some quantity of choice
> To serve in such a difference. What devil was't
> That thus hath cozened you at hoodman-blind?
> Eyes without feeling, feeling without sight,
> Ears without hands or eyes, smelling sans all,
> Or but a sickly part of one true sense
> Could not so mope. (3.4.68–79)

It is not a lack of reason or any other higher, disembodied faculty that has led to Gertrude's misjudgment. It is the fact that "*sense* / Is apoplexed" (emphasis added). Nor are we to understand that term *sense* as equivalent to the modern *common sense*, a kind of foundational, self-evident logic. On the contrary, the metaphor of blindfolding – "What devil was't / That hath cozened you at hoodman-blind?" – reinforces the physiological valence of the word. Judgment is a species of spectatorship in Hamlet's speech. Had the queen been able to see, she would have been able to judge. This sort of judgment – good judgment – involves a clear alignment of perception and emotion. Bad judgment, on the other hand – Gertrude's judgment – is associated with the misalignment of these two things: "Eyes without feeling, feeling without sight." The closet scene places moral decision at the crossroads of sensation and emotion. It impels Gertrude, along with all the spectators in the theatre who are gazing on with her, to look hard, not with the inner eye of the soul or the mind, but with the outer eye of the body.

Where does this conception of physiologically based discernment come from? The starting point is the *Nichomachean Ethics*, where Aristotle observes that ethical behaviour "is not easy to determine by reasoning, any more than anything else that is perceived by the senses; such things depend on particular facts, and the decision rests with perception."[7] This observation laid the foundation for a tradition of thought concerned with pre-rational sensate judgment that influenced writers in the Middle Ages and Renaissance, as well eighteenth-century theorists of aesthetics. Within this tradition, judgment was understood to be a faculty that functioned by relating sensible particulars – that is to say, specific things that we see, hear, and feel – to intelligible universals – that is, broadly applicable notions of good and bad, right and wrong. Renaissance faculty psychology inherited two distinct versions of this Aristotelian scheme. In the first version, judgment is described as an expression of reason rather than feeling. In the writings of Thomas Wright, Philippe de Mornay, and, later, John Locke, passion and bodily sensation impede good judgment.[8] In the second version, which is much closer to Aristotle's own writings, judgment is viewed as a collaboration among the senses, which, over time, generate universal principles or what we now might call "standards of judgment." As Aristotle put it in *De Anima*, the animal soul – the site of sensory knowledge and the aspect of our being that we share with other non-human creatures – is not just the faculty that generates movement, it is also the source of our "capacity to judge, which is the function of thought and perception." "Each sense," he writes, "judges the specific differences of its own sensible object.... Sight produces upon white and black, taste upon sweet and bitter, and so with the rest."[9]

In the sixteenth century we find some English scholars rehearing this account of the relationship between judgment and sensation. Abraham Fraunce, for example, writes in *The Lawyers Logike* (1588), "For as Aristotle teacheth in the second of his demonstrations, every sensible creature hath a naturall power and facultie of judging, which is called sence; & this sence (2. Topic) is of him sayde to bee a certayne kinde of judgement: and without doubt, the sence is a most upright judge of suche thinges as are properly under his jurisdiction, as the sight of colours, the hearing of soundes, the smelling of smelles (4. Metap)."[10]

For Fraunce, following Aristotle, judgment is common to "every sensible creature," because sensation constitutes a "certayne kinde of judgment." At the heart of this argument is the idea that how you *feel* bears directly on how you discern and, eventually, on how you act. Taken to its logical conclusion, it is an argument that accommodates the notion of passion leading ultimately to moral action. This is noteworthy because it runs counter to more than one powerful tradition of thought in the Renaissance, including Calvinism, which in general urges the repression of passion, and Stoicism, which generally sees virtue rather than sensation or emotion as the source of moral action. However, as Timothy Hampton has shown, even Montaigne, a writer strongly influenced by Cicero and Seneca, acknowledged in essays like "De l'inconstance de nos actions" and "Apologie de Raymond Sebond" that there were limitations to the Stoic ideal of virtue over passion, that direct bodily experience (being disgusted by something you witness or being aroused by a speech, for example) could impel a kind of *applied* virtue.[11] This, certainly, is what Hamlet has in mind in act 3.4 when he urges his mother to *see* right, to *feel* right, to *judge* right, and finally, therefore, to *act* right: "Confess yourself to heaven, / Repent what's past, avoid what is to come" (3.4.147–8) and "Not this, by no means, that I bid you – / Let the bloat King tempt you again to bed" (3.4.179–80).

Hamlet has often been placed on the path to individuality and interiority, but the closet scene inhabits a different terrain, a place where judgment, responsibility, and action cohabit with sensation, emotion, and collectivity. This path leads, in one direction, to the Aristotelian materialism I have commented on. In the other direction, it leads to eighteenth-century sentimentalism – most notably, the work of David Hume, Adam Smith, Henry McKenzie, and Samuel Richardson. Sentimentalism, as both R.F. Brissenden and Hina Nazar have shown, distinguished itself from other paradigms of Enlightenment liberalism by entwining judgment and feeling. In Nazar's words, "Judgment emerges under sentimentalism as a worldly and contingent process, one that is inextricably tied to feelings and sociability."[12] My aim in pointing out these links is not to make the Enlightenment beholden to the Renaissance, or Hume beholden to Shakespeare, or both beholden to Aristotle. My objective, instead, has been to use the closet scene in *Hamlet* as a starting point for thinking about the history and theory of judgment, not so much as a straight line of development, but rather as an evolving constellation of ideas in which sense and emotion move in and out of view. *Hamlet* helps us see this kaleidoscopic process in action by staging a scene of judgment that point us both backwards and forwards, curating a set of conceptual links between Aristotelian materialism, early modern faculty psychology, and a particular strain of Enlightenment liberalism. What it leaves us with finally is a set of historical and philosophical coordinates than can help us reframe judgment as a form of collective participation in the-world-out-there, a way of feeling with others, and of translating common experience into action.

2. The Physics of Judgment

So far I have suggested that judgment is an embodied process, that it is collective, and that it is participatory. This section will reinforce these claims by showing how theatre sets judgment in motion. Toward this end, I will be focusing on act 5.1 of *Measure for Measure*, a scene in which two faces – Mariana's and Duke Vincento's – are crucial to the play's final scene of condemnation and forgiveness. I am especially interested in how the spatial, object-oriented grammar of the face invites us to think of judgment less as an individual decision or rational cognitive procedure than as a physical, dimensional event that involves orientating oneself in space and time. I will be referring to this as the "physics of judgment."[13]

The theatre provides an especially compelling locale for thinking about the physics of judgment. Indeed, judgment shares with theatre its most basic raw materials: people and things arranged in space and time. The face is crucial to this discussion, because in *Measure for Measure* it stands at the crossroads of theatre and judgment, indexing their shared fields of location and duration and their common orientation toward the future. With this in mind, I will begin this section by mapping out how the physics of judgment works in act 5.1. The scene brings together two deception plots. The first of these involves Duke Vincento who throughout the play dresses as a friar to observe the behaviour of his subjects undetected. The other involves Mariana, a woman who was betrothed to, then abandoned by, Angelo, the hypocritically puritanical deputy filling in for the duke. Mariana, Isabella, and the duke trick Angelo into consummating his marriage to Mariana by sending her to a garden-house where Angelo thinks he is having a tryst with Isabella. The collision of these two plots in the final scene of the play leads to a series of revelations in which the face plays an essential role.

The first of these revelations occurs when, in the wake of Isabella's accusations of sexual blackmail, Mariana is led onstage, supposedly to absolve Angelo of Isabella's charges. Here is the initial part of the scene:

DUKE: Give us some seats.

Two seats are brought in.
Come, cousin Angelo,

In this I'll be impartial: be you judge
Of your own cause.
The Duke and Angelo sit
Enter Friar Peter with Mariana veiled
Is this the witness, friar?
First let her show her face, and after speak.

MARIANA: Pardon, my lord, I will not show my face
Until my husband bid me. (5.1.165–70)[14]

This is clearly a scene of arbitration. A charge has been made and a witness is being brought in to testify. The duke even has some seats set up to make the exchange feel more like a trial with judge and jury presiding. We should also note that Mariana's face is at the centre of this judgment-event. The duke's command, "First let her show her face, and after speak," seems to assume that the forensic and moral evaluation integral to judgment is possible only under certain baseline conditions of collective ethical orientation: the mutual acknowledgment and recognition intrinsic to the face-to-face encounter. But Mariana refuses: "I will not show my face / Until my husband bid me." A little further on, Angelo echoes the duke's request, at which point Mariana finally acquiesces:

ANGELO: This is a strange abuse. Let's see thy face.
MARIANA: My husband bids me, now I will unmask.

She unveils
This is that face, thou cruel Angelo,
Which once thou swor'st was worth the looking on. (5.1.204–7)

Two aspects of this exchange are important for understanding the physics of judgment. To begin with, the component parts of this judgment-event consist predominantly of actions and reactions centred on Mariana's veiled face. This stage business is marked verbally throughout: "give," "come," "show," "not show," "let's see," "*unveils*." That is to say, Mariana's face indexes the way the judgment-event unfolds in space. In addition – and this is the second aspect – Mariana's face indexes the way the judgment-event unfolds through time. All terms pertaining to temporal positioning – what linguists call "time deixis" – are used in reference to Mariana's face: "first," "after," "until," "now."[15] Here is the relevant passage once again, this time with time deixis marked in bold and references to Mariana's face underlined:

Is this the witness, friar?
First let her show her *face*, and **after** speak.

MARIANA: Pardon, my lord, I will not show my *face*
Until my husband bid me. (5.1.165–70)
...

ANGELO: This is a strange abuse. Let's see thy *face*.
MARIANA: My husband bids me, **now** I will unmask.

She unveils (5.1.204–5.1)

Marking the exchange in this way highlights the peculiar theatrical role played by the face in this scene. Though obviously part of the actor's and character's body, the face also functions almost like a prop. It is instrumentalized in a way that exceeds the demands of character in order to advance elements of plot and theme. To this extent, the face muddles some of the standard categories of theatrical semiotics established by scholars such as Patrick Pavis, Erika Fischer-Lichte, and Keir Elam. Consider some basic examples of these categories: linguistic signs, paralinguistic signs, kinesic signs, and proxemic signs. Linguistic signs function both rhetorically and acoustically. They comprise both the meanings of individual words spoken on stage and the tone and pace of delivery. Paralinguistic signs, meanwhile, include such things as props, music, scenery, and lighting. Kinesic signs are self-contained bodily movements, such as gestures. Proxemic signs, on the other hand, are movements of bodies through the space of the stage.[16]

Mariana's face does not fit in a straightforward way into any of these categories. Instead it performs two different kinds of signification simultaneously – kinesic and proxemic – while also challenging received wisdom about how these signifying units are supposed to work. Mariana's face is a kinesic sign in the way that all faces always are on stage, but the fact that it remains veiled for most of the exchange seriously undercuts its ability to do what kinesic signs are supposed to do: express or gesture. Mariana's face is a proxemic sign to the extent that it occasions the scene's primary actions and reactions. Indeed, it is at the centre of the scene's orbit of movement. And yet it does very little in the way of significant movement through space itself. A full semiotic reckoning of Mariana's face would also require the addition of a new sign-category, the "chronemic," which would allow us to isolate the face's time-indexical function in the scene. As a chronemic sign, Mariana's face is consistently pointing to the temporal context in which it appears. It creates a scene of judgment, which does not manifest itself in a flat present of decision, but rather unfolds sequentially through a linear process of action and response: "**First** let her show her face, and **after** speak"; "I will not show my face / **Until** my husband bid me"; "**Now** I will unmask."

The face in *Measure for Measure* bursts the seams of our received systems of theatrical interpretation. It demands a more flexible and expansive set of critical concepts. As the material anchor in the final scene's culminating moments of punishment and forgiveness, it offers a vantage point from which we can observe the physics of judgment at work, the way in which adjudication unfolds through the space and time of a mimetic environment comprising bodies, voices, and objects. From this perspective, judgment takes the form of a collaborative event. It has less to do with individual evaluation than with the collective application of knowledge toward a specific end. And as with all forms of applied knowledge – geometry, mechanics, even rhetoric – the aim of judgment is to make something: in this case, a liveable future, a shared sense of truth, and new conditions of social possibility in Vienna. We see the beginning of this process unfolding gradually during the scene of Mariana's unveiling: collective appraisal of the situation evolves as false knowledge and misperception give way to true knowledge. The revelation of Mariana's face is the hinge on which the former swings toward the latter. Here is the scene with references to knowledge – first false, then true – set in bold:

MARIANA: Why, just, my lord, and that is Angelo,
Who thinks he **knows** that he ne'er **knew** my body,
But **knows**, he thinks, that he **knows** Isabel's.

ANGELO: This is a strange abuse. Let's see thy face.
MARIANA: My husband bids me, now I will unmask.

She unveils

This is that face, thou cruel Angelo,
Which once thou sworest was worth the looking on;
...

DUKE: **Know** you this woman?

...

ANGELO: My lord, I must confess I **know** this woman, (5.1.201–7, 213, 217)

This moment – the first phase of act 5.1's extended judgment-event – marks the beginning of a shared coming-into-knowledge. Mariana's unveiling and the acknowledgement it triggers – "I know this woman" – establishes a new truth about the relations among the characters on stage that will lead eventually to fundamental changes in the social fabric of Shakespeare's Vienna. We may tend to think of judgment as a singular decision or decree, something that ends or resolves things. But the dynamics of the face in *Measure for Measure* shows us something different: a version of judgment that is not only collective, but also creative, and which therefore has as much to do with the future as with the past.

3. The Ethics of Judgment

Judgment, we have seen, is fundamentally theatrical because it is physical, collective, transactional, and creative. But why does this matter? What are the broader ethical implications of theatrical judgment? How might it affect an audience's sense of themselves as moral stakeholders and empowered world-makers? This section addresses this final cluster of questions.[17] The discussion will move between two locales. One is a public amphitheatre in London where around 1611 an old man, a father and a magician, asks his audience for forgiveness and approval. The other is a stuffy courtroom in Jerusalem where in 1961 a philosopher-cum-journalist, a German-Jewish émigré to the United States, was tasked with covering the trial of a Nazi leader.

We start on the London stage, where Shakespeare's play *The Tempest* is drawing to a close. Prospero has released the island castaways and set his servant Ariel free, and says the following to the audience:

Now my charms are all o'erthrown,
And what strength I have's mine own,
Which is most faint. Now 'tis true,
I must be here confined by you,
Or sent to Naples. Let me not,
Since I have my dukedom got,

And pardoned the deceiver, dwell
In this bare island by your spell,
But release me from my bands
With the help of your good hands.
Gentle breath of yours my sails
Must fill, or else my project fails,
Which was to please. Now I want
Spirits to enforce, art to enchant;
And my ending is despair
Unless I be relieved by prayer,
Which pierces so that it assaults
Mercy itself, and frees all faults.
As you from crimes would pardoned be,
Let your indulgence set me free. (5.1.319–38)[18]

Prospero presents his case to the playgoers who are expected to consider two related questions: (1) Was the play good? (2) Has Prospero behaved in an ethical manner? Importantly, though, the playgoers are not simply being prompted to pass judgment. More precisely, they are also being asked to imagine through judgment a future for Prospero, an imaginative addendum to the fiction presented on stage. If the audience disapproves and does not clap, Prospero will remain imprisoned on the island. If they approve and do clap, he will return to Milan. This latter context is important because, as I hope to show, attending to the interplay between judgment and invention helps us understand how the epilogue contributes, in a culturally specific way, to a much larger set of questions about the relationship between freedom and responsibility in the theatre.

Though it may seem arbitrary to us, the idea that judgment and invention are inherently connected would have been familiar to many in Shakespeare's time, including a considerable number of playgoers and playwrights. It finds its source in a long tradition of rhetorical learning that stretches from Aristotle though Cicero and Quintilian and onwards to the Renaissance humanists.[19] Thomas Blundeville's commentary in *The Arte of Logicke* (1599) is fairly standard. He explains that while "invention finds matter," judgment "frameth, disposeth, and reduceth the same into due forme of argument."[20] In other words, invention is the skill of deciding which line of reasoning is most likely to strike a particular audience as especially compelling. Judgment's role is to break that line of reasoning down into component parts and then arrange them in a sequence calculated to achieve maximum persuasiveness. Judgment, that is, turns ideas into arguments by lending them organizational form.

With this in mind, we can begin to see how judgment might be conceived as one crucial point along a continuum of creative endeavour. For those with some training in rhetorical theory, judgment was a form of *making* rather than a form of decision, as we would now tend to view it. The request for judgment in Prospero's epilogue is also an appeal to the audience's capacity for literary invention, specifically their ability to craft an imaginary afterlife for Prospero: "Release me from my bands / With the help of your good hands," he implores; "As you from crimes would pardon'd be, / Let your indulgence set me free." According to the terms set by Prospero, then, clapping is an act both evaluative and generative, a verdict on the past and a vision for the future. This gives theatregoers a different kind of ethical stake in the play they are watching than would otherwise be the case. As fellow makers, rather than just consumers, the audience's collective sense of the good, of what is right and what is wrong, is implicated in the play's imagined conclusion, and all the more so for the moral freight Prospero so insistently attaches to the epilogue. Judgment here develops out of a sense of responsibility to communal norms –which are both moral and aesthetic. Not to judge, accordingly, would be a failure of responsibility.

Taking the link between judgment and responsibility as a cue, I want now to shift our critical gaze from seventeenth-century London to twentieth-century Jerusalem where, in 1961, Hannah Arendt, writing for the *New Yorker*, sits alongside other journalists in a different kind of theatre: the courtroom. This courtroom hosts the trial of the Nazi leader Adolf Eichmann. Arendt is underwhelmed by Eichmann. She thinks he is forgettable, unintelligent, even unfrightening. She is also critical of the trial itself. It seems to her a show trial, one that uses Eichmann as a proxy to condemn and punish anti-Semitism in general. Against this method of retribution, Arendt argued that the Holocaust called for specific and nuanced forms of condemnation, mostly of Nazis, but also of Jewish leaders who cooperated with the Nazis. That this did not happen represented for her a "fundamental problem" common to "all these postwar trials," which had to do with "the nature and function of human judgment." She writes,

> What we have demanded in these trials, where the defendants had committed "legal" crimes, is that human beings be capable of telling right from wrong even when all they have to guide them is their own judgment, which

> moreover happens to be completely at odds with what they must regard as the unanimous opinion of all those around them.... Since the whole of respectable society had in one way or another succumbed to Hitler, the moral maxims which determine social behavior and the religious commandments – "Thou shalt not kill!" – which guide conscience had virtually vanished. Those few who were still able to tell right from wrong went really only by their own judgments, and they did so freely; there were no rules to be abided by, under which the particular cases with which they were confronted could be subsumed. They had to decide each instance as it arose, because no rules existed for the unprecedented.[21]

Judgment for Arendt, in other words, is not an expression of external social or legal norms, but rather an expression of personal responsibility. So long as you are human, there is an expectation that you will be able to tell "right from wrong." What post-war trials like Eichmann's threw into sharp relief for Arendt was the degree to which so many were willing to shirk this responsibility, either by refusing to judge or by issuing a sort of judgment that was so broad and sociological, so resistant to the concrete threshold between right and wrong that it amounted to non-judgment. Arendt understood, of course, the reluctance of both Germans and Jews to examine closely what took place in Europe between 1933 and 1945, to pinpoint definitively the many groups and individuals – Nazi officers and bureaucrats, "Christian churches," members of "the Jewish leadership" – who had a hand in what she calls "the totality of moral collapse." However, she concludes that "this understandable disinclination is insufficient to explain the reluctance evident everywhere to make judgments in terms of individual moral responsibility."[22]

In the years following her coverage of the Eichmann trial, Arendt finally did arrive at an explanation. In an essay called "Personal Responsibility under Dictatorship" she recalls, "I was told that judging itself is wrong: no one can judge who had not been there."[23] At the heart of this fiercely neutral stance, Arendt decided, was deep scepticism about the possibility of human freedom:

> There exists in our society a widespread fear of judging that has nothing whatever to do with the biblical "Judge not, that ye be not judged," ... [f]or behind the unwillingness to judge lurks the suspicion that no one is a free agent, and hence the doubt that anyone is responsible or could be expected to answer for what he has done.... [W]e're all alike, equally bad, and those who try, or pretend that they try, to remain halfway

decent are either saints or hypocrites, and in either case should leave us alone.[24]

What Arendt does brilliantly in her writings on judgment is triangulate between three large, difficult concepts – judgment, responsibility, and freedom – in a way that deepens our understanding of all three. Judgment is an expression of responsibility, and responsibility, in turn, is a condition of being a free agent capable of moral decision and active world-making. Viewed in this way, judgment is a means of manifesting our status as free agents in moral terms – in terms, that is, of a collective obligation to the good that only a free agent could enter into. The refusal to judge is troubling to Arendt because it indicates an unwillingness to be accountable for the world we all must share. It rehearses a vision of politics as something that works upon rather than through human actors and in this way advances precisely the sort of detached acquiescence that forms the necessary conditions for totalitarian disasters like the Third Reich.

Hannah Arendt's work on the Eichmann trial establishes a framework for thinking about judgment that helps us uncover some of the ethical deep-structure of Prospero's epilogue. Specifically, she equips us with a vocabulary and a set of concepts that allow us to think about the audience's evaluative response in *The Tempest* as an expression of responsibility rather than authority, and therefore as something grounded in, and oriented toward, sociality and recognition. This has the effect of re-describing the historical particulars of Prospero's epilogue in terms of the more universal ethical dynamics of participatory politics. It shows us, in other words, that at the heart of Prospero's judgment-invention linkage is an implicit assumption that the playgoers assembled in the theatre are free agents and therefore not just *able* to judge, but also *expected* to judge. For it is through judgment that they shape the moral contours of the future – Prospero's future.

Conclusion

My aim in this chapter has been to guide readers through the feeling, the physics, and the ethics of judgment in Shakespearean contexts – three largely neglected components of the theory and practice of discernment. The point of this exercise has been not only to broaden our conception of what judgment is and how it works, but also, and more specifically, to lay claim to "judgment" as a useful critical keyword for the philosophical study of theatre. Viewed in the broadest terms, judgment is both a methodology for social and material interaction and a systematic form of future-oriented thought. The former is rooted in the sensory experiences, physical choreographies, and temporal rhythms of living. The latter is rooted in the impulse to create new worlds of objective, aesthetic, and/or moral consensus. Accordingly, in the theatre, judgment helps us understand how a play's affective environment and orchestration of time and space generate its capacity for creative and moral empowerment. Indeed, within the arc of its unfolding, judgment bridges the gap between what we feel and do together now – condemn Claudius, forgive Angelo, applaud Prospero – and how we live and believe together later. Theatrical judgment forms communities by translating common physical experience (looking, hearing, moving) into common axes of value (a shared sense of right and wrong, good and bad). To this extent, judgment reminds us that theatre is always both particular and universal; a *specific* constellation of material bodies and artefacts deployed toward a certain narrative end and a *general* system of meaning-making whose component parts foster collective leaps of imagination and speculation.

NOTES

1 See further Lorna Hutson, *The Invention of Suspicion: Law and Mimesis in Shakespeare and Renaissance Drama* (Oxford: Oxford University Press, 2007), 30–7.

2 See further, Michael Moriarty, "Principles of Judgement: Probability, Decorum, Taste, and the *je ne sais quoi*," in *The Renaissance*, vol. 3 of *The Cambridge History of Literary Criticism*, ed. Glyn P. Norton, 522–8 (Cambridge: Cambridge University Press, 1999); Brian Vickers, ed., *English Renaissance Literary Criticism* (Oxford: Oxford University Press, 1999), 44–55; and Kevin Curran, *Shakespeare's Legal Ecologies: Law and Distributed Selfhood* (Evanston, IL: Northwestern University Press, 2017), 107–10.

3 Stephen Guazzo, *The Civile Conversation* (London, 1581), 4–5.

4 See further Vivasvan Soni, ed., "The Crisis of Judgment," special issue of *Eighteenth Century: Theory and Interpretation* 51 (2010); and Hina Nazar, *Enlightened Sentiments: Judgment and Autonomy in the Age of Sensibility* (New York: Fordham University Press, 2012).

5 Much of the raw material for this unfinished volume can be found in "Judging: Excerpts from Lectures on Kant's Political Philosophy," an

appendix to Hannah Arendt, *The Life of the Mind* (San Diego: Harcourt, 1978), 255–72.

6 All quotations are from *Hamlet*, ed. Ann Thompson and Neil Taylor, rev. ed. (London: Bloomsbury, 2016).

7 Aristotle, *Nichomachean Ethics*, trans. H. Rackham (Cambridge, MA: Harvard University Press, 1934), 1109b20.

8 See, for example, Thomas Wright, *The Passions of the Minde in Generall* (London, 1601), 12–14; Philippe de Mornay, *The True Knowledge of a Man's Owne Selfe* (London, 1602), 2; and John Locke, *An Essay Concerning Human Understanding* (London, 1689), book 2.

9 Aristotle, *On the Soul. Parva Naturalia. On Breath*, trans. W.S. Het (Cambridge, MA: Harvard University Press, 1957), 432a15, 426b–c.

10 Abraham Fraunce, *The Lawyers Logike* (London, 1588), 91.

11 Timothy Hampton, "Difficult Engagements: Private Passion and Public Service in Montaigne's *Essais*," in *Politics and the Passions, 1500–1850*, ed. Victoria Kahn, Neil Saccamano, and Daniela Coli, 30–48 (Princeton, NJ: Princeton University Press, 2006).

12 R.F. Brissenden, *Virtue in Distress: Studies in the Novel of Sentiment from Richardson to Sade* (New York: Barnes and Noble, 1974); Nazar, *Enlightened Sentiments*, 2.

13 For a longer version of this argument, see Kevin Curran, "The Face of Judgment in *Measure for Measure*," in *Face-to-Face in Shakespearean Drama: Ethics, Performance, Philosophy*, ed. Matthew J. Smith and Julia R. Lupton, 163–75 (Edinburgh: Edinburgh University Press, 2019).

14 All quotations are from *Measure for Measure*, ed. N.W. Bawcutt (Oxford: Oxford University Press, 1991).

15 There is a great deal written on this topic, but good starting points are John Lyons, "Deixis, Space, and Time," *Semantics* 2 (1977): 636–724; and Geoffrey Nunberg, "Indexality and Deixis," *Linguistics and Philosophy* 19 (1993): 1–43.

16 See further, Keir Elam, *The Semiotics of Theatre and Drama*, 2nd ed. (London: Routledge, 2002); Erika Fischer-Lichte, *The Semiotics of Theater*, trans. Jeremy Gaines and Doris L. Jones (Bloomington: Indiana University Press, 1992); Patrice Pavis, *Languages of the Stage: Essays in the Semiology of the Theatre* (New York: Performing Arts Journal Publications, 1982); and Pavis, "Performance Analysis: Space, Time, Action," trans. Sinéad Rushe, *Gestos* 22 (1996): 11–32.

17 For a fuller discussion of these questions, see Kevin Curran, "Prospero's Plea: Judgment, Invention, and Political Form in *The Tempest*," in *Shakespeare and Judgment*, ed. Kevin Curran, 157–71 (Edinburgh: Edinburgh University Press, 2017).

18 All quotations are from *The Tempest*, ed. Stephen Orgel (Oxford: Oxford University Press, 1987).

19 See further, Peter Mack, *Elizabethan Rhetoric: Theory and Practice* (Cambridge: Cambridge University Press, 2002), 11–47; Jon Hesk, "Types of Oratory," in *The Cambridge Companion to Ancient Rhetoric*, ed. Erik Gunderson (Cambridge: Cambridge University Press, 2009), 150–6; and Quentin Skinner, *Forensic Shakespeare* (Oxford: Oxford University Press, 2015), 11–25.

20 Thomas Blundeville, *The Arte of Logicke* (London, 1599), 1.

21 Hannah Arendt, *Eichmann in Jerusalem: A Report on the Banality of Evil* (London: Penguin, 2006), 294–5.

22 Arendt, *Eichmann in Jerusalem*, 297.

23 Hannah Arendt, "Personal Responsibility under Dictatorship," *Responsibility and Judgment*, ed. Jerome Kohn (New York: Random House, 2003), 18.

24 Arendt, "Personal Responsibility," 19.

chapter five

Entertainment

JEFFREY KNAPP

I'll fit you.

– Thomas Kyd, *The Spanish Tragedy*

The chief aim of Renaissance actors and dramatists, or so they typically said, was to please their audiences – "to entertain this presence with delight," as John Marston declared at the start of his 1600 comedy *Jack Drum's Entertainment.* But Marston's *Entertainment* takes a strangely twisted path to assuring its spectators that it will indeed delight them. The show begins with a warning from a stagehand, the tireman, that the audience may have to disperse, "for he that composed the Book we should present" – the playwright Marston – "hath snatched it from us, upon the very instance of entrance, and with violence keeps the boys from coming on the Stage." "You much mistake his action, Tireman," says a child actor who next appears, having somehow broken through Marston's barricade. The author's "violence proceeds not from a mind / That grudgeth pleasure to this generous presence"; on the contrary, "he was loath, / Wanting a Prologue, & ourselves not perfect, / To rush upon your eyes without respect."[1] According to the child actor, the only reason that Marston stands in the way of entertaining his audience is that he's so committed to entertaining them.

No sooner has the boy finished speaking than *Jack Drum* begins in earnest, which makes its opening turbulence all the more puzzling. Why, at the outset of a play that Marston wishes he could "sweeten" for his spectators with "the music of the spheres," would he cause them even momentary distress? In part, he must want to emphasize for his audience how willingly, as the boy claims, he would "sweat" in order to maximize their “delights.” But the violence that the child actor no less than the stagehand attributes to Marston also highlights an element of aggression in the author’s ostensible devotion to his audience. “If you’ll pardon his defects and ours,” says the boy, “he’ll give us passage, & you pleasing scenes.”[2] What at first appears to be a humble request for the audience’s leniency turns into the author’s threat that he will withhold his entertainment until he and the actors receive their pardon in advance. Several years later, in the first edition of another comedy, his *Parasitaster, or The Fawn*, Marston even more plainly mixed his signals to his audience. After a letter to the reader in which he modestly refers to his plays as his “stage-pleasings,” Marston lards the prologue to *Parasitaster* with the most extravagant praise of his spectators: “For we do know that this most fair-filled room / Is loaden with most Attic judgments, ablest spirits, / Than who there are none more exact, full, strong.” “O you are all the very breath of Phoebus,” the prologue continues effusing: “In your pleas’d gracings all the true life blood / Of our poor author lives; you are his very graces.” But then the final lines of the prologue turn all this servility to affront: if “any” of the playgoers should “wonder why” the author has been “drawn / To such base soothings” of them, then “know his play’s – *The Fawn*.”[3] Now it’s impossible to mistake the object of Marston’s hostility: he resents his audience for expecting him to bow and scrape to them. But by contriving to insult them *through* flattery, Marston also manages to retain the strange double edge of his earlier self-presentation as the author who stops his own entertainment from starting: in the prologue to *The Fawn*, that is, Marston still associates his belligerence with his desire to please.

Other dramatists of the period tempered Marston’s apparent mood swings from obsequiousness to defiance by more moderately asserting their rights to the audience’s respect. “Your silence and attention, worthy friends,” begins the prologue to *The Merry Devil of Edmonton* (ca. 1600), which then invites the audience to share the work of entertainment by asking them to “entertain the subject of our play.” In the prologue to his comedy *If It Be Not Good, the Devil Is in It* (1611), Thomas Dekker declares that he seeks applause “for *Merit*,” not “for *Pity*.” But few if any dramatists maintained that they could command the attention of their audiences without also delighting them. The prologue to *The Merry Devil* requests silence from its spectators so that “your free spirits may with more pleasing sense / Relish the life of this our active scene”; in the prologue to his own *Devil* play, Dekker anticipates that he’ll be “crowned” by the audience only “if he please” them.[4] The best playwrights, Ben

Jonson declares at the start of his 1601 *Poetaster*, address their audiences with neither the "arrogance" of a master nor the "dejection" of a slave. Rather, they choose "a mean 'twixt both," which is to instruct as well as entertain – and ideally, the instruction should itself prove entertaining: in the prologue to his 1611 comedy *The Alchemist*, Jonson hopes that his audience will "be pleased" by the "fair correctives" he offers them.[5] "To the wise," as Jonson's disciple Francis Beaumont argues in the prologue to *The Knight of the Burning Pestle* (1607), it is "as great pleasure to hear counsel mixed with wit, as to the foolish to have sport mingled with rudeness." Although another Jonsonian playwright, Peter Hausted, conceded that the "satire" in his comedy *The Rival Friends* (1632) had so offended his audience that they "cried down" the play, he nevertheless insisted that his entertainment had been "made to please":

> and had the vicious age
> Been good enough, it had not left the stage
> Without its due applause. But since the times
> Now bring forth men enamoured on their crimes,
> And those the greater number, 'twere disease
> To think that anything that bites should please.[6]

In Hausted's view, "good" playgoers should accept a dramatist's violence against them as a form of entertainment – they should love it when he "bites" them.

"I'll fit you," promises a more sinister version of Hausted in one of the foundational triumphs of the commercial Renaissance theatre. Thus far, I've been drawing my evidence about Renaissance theories of entertainment from the comic drama exclusively; it seems reasonable, in plays that end happily, for dramatists to assure their audiences that the action will unfold "as you like it." But the violence and loss in tragedies makes them likelier settings for dramatists to reflect on their own ill will towards their audiences, however self-defeating that hostility may be. So it is that, in Thomas Kyd's *Spanish Tragedy* (ca. 1587), the playwriting knight marshal of Spain, Hieronimo, stages a tragedy that wreaks havoc on all parties to the performance: the author, the actors, and the audience, too. What could be more emphatic a repudiation of the dramatist's obligation to please? And yet when Hieronimo mocks his spectators for assuming that the murdered actors of his play will "revive to please tomorrow's audience," he does not mean that the playgoers he is addressing have been left feeling disgruntled by the performance they have just witnessed. On the contrary, he knows that they have thoroughly enjoyed it: "Old Marshal," the king of Spain had just exclaimed, "this was bravely done!"[7] Contemporary evidence indicates that Kyd's own play was just as successful as Hieronimo's at entertaining its audience, even though it so brazenly expressed a fantasy of harming them. For the rest of this chapter I'll explore the play's surprising account of how it could achieve such perverse appeal. And I'll end by suggesting that the popularity of *The Spanish Tragedy* may have inspired a similar approach to entertainment in many later Renaissance plays, which aimed to please their audiences by encouraging them to see their relationship to author and actors as profoundly conflictual and therefore as itself dramatic.

I

Perhaps the first question to ask about *The Spanish Tragedy* as entertainment is why anyone ever finds tragedies entertaining. "The beholding of troubles and miserable slaughters that are in Tragedies," argued the theatre hater Stephen Gosson in 1582, "drive us to immoderate sorrow, heaviness, womanish weeping and mourning, whereby we become lovers of dumps, and lamentation." The action of *The Spanish Tragedy* begins in the aftermath of a war between Spain and Portugal that has taken the lives of some "three hundred" soldiers on the Spanish side alone. One of these murdered Spaniards, Don Andrea, is now a ghost whom the powers of the underworld have sent back to earth so that he can witness more killing. As his escort Revenge informs him, "Thou shalt see the author of thy death, / Don Balthazar, the Prince of Portingale, / Deprived of life by Bel-imperia."[8] What good, as Gosson asked, can come from all this butchery?

"Victory," declares a "cheerful" Spanish general in the very next scene. "Blest be heaven," replies the Spanish king, who asks the general to augment the king's "pleasure" at such "good news" by going into more detail about the bloodshed. From the general's account of the war, the king is delighted to learn that Hieronimo's son Horatio distinguished himself in combat: "Frolic with thy King," the king joyfully exclaims to his knight marshal. So elated is Spain's monarch by his "war's success" that he shares his high spirits with his enemies, too. Rather than lord it over the captured Portuguese prince Balthazar, he magnanimously decides to feast Balthazar instead as "our friendly guest." "We pleasure more in kindness than in war," the king subsequently informs the Portuguese ambassador; indeed, he asks the ambassador to think of their two countries now as friends, not foes. "Spain is Portugal, / And Portugal is Spain," he insists, and to prove his point, he offers to marry his niece Bel-imperia to his prisoner Balthazar. That's not all: if "the match go forward," the king declares, then "the tribute which you pay shall be released," and if Balthazar and Bel-imperia should eventually "have a son," then "he shall enjoy the kingdom after us." Just as killing has led to frolicking, so, the king believes, it can promote an international accord. "Our peace," he assures the ambassador, "will grow the stronger for these wars."[9]

Such an unexpectedly comic outcome to the hostilities between Portugal and Spain does not please everyone at the Spanish court. It incenses Balthazar's prospective bride, Bel-imperia, who cannot reconcile herself to Balthazar because he killed her lover Andrea in battle. Yet even before Bel-imperia reveals her continuing enmity toward the Portuguese prince, the ghost of Andrea already highlighted the controversial nature of merging friends with foes when, in the first scene of the play, he reported to Revenge how the judges of the underworld take special care to separate the ghosts of dead warriors from the ghosts of dead lovers. "It were not well / With loving souls to place a martialist," one of these judges had cautioned; "either sort" must be "contained within his bounds." Andrea posed a dilemma for the judges, because in life he had been both a lover and a warrior, and that same confusing blend of concord with discord resurfaces in the next scene of the play when the king commands his subjects to "entertain" Andrea's killer Balthazar "with greatest pleasure that our court affords." Not even Balthazar can quite fathom why his Spanish enemies are treating him so remarkably well: "I frolic with the Duke of Castile's son," he marvels to the Portuguese ambassador, "wrapped every hour in pleasures of the court."[10]

By refusing to entertain Balthazar as a lover, Bel-imperia thinks that she is preserving the proper distinction between enmity and amity that the king has subverted, and yet she herself clouds the same issue when she decides to "love Horatio" in order "to spite the Prince." Her very choice of Horatio as lover demonstrates how Bel-imperia herself hopes to convert the horrors of war into the pleasures of peace: it is Horatio's record as a fighter, she tells us, that recommends him to her as her "second love." In her subsequent flirtations with Horatio, Bel-imperia tempts him to believe "that pleasure follows pain, and bliss annoy" – the same counterintuitive logic that the Spanish king had proposed to the Portuguese ambassador. "Let dangers go," she urges Horatio; "thy war shall be with me, / But such a war as breaks no bond of peace." Exceeding the king's own blandishments, Bel-imperia does more than replace war with love; she *equates* the two:

> Speak thou fair words, I'll cross them with fair words;
> Send thou sweet looks, I'll meet them with sweet looks;
> Write loving lines, I'll answer loving lines;
> Give me a kiss, I'll countercheck thy kiss.
> Be this our warring peace, or peaceful war.

Love conquers war, these playful incongruities suggest, through a "loving" likeness that assimilates the hostile actions of crossing and counterchecking to the friendly actions of meeting and answering. In their next scene together, Horatio accepts Bel-imperia's invitation to re-enact his earlier violence as lovemaking. "Then thus begin our wars," he declares as the two embrace: "Put forth thy hand, / That it may combat with my ruder hand." "Set forth thy foot to try the push of mine," an aroused Bel-imperia replies. For the lovers, such erotic reciprocity replaces conflict with imitation. Yet in his earlier account of battle, the Spanish general had already defined war as itself a series of imitations, in which provocation leads to provocation, then to incursions across the shared border that otherwise contains each nation within its bounds, then to a close combat that renders one fighter indistinguishable from his opposite, reducing them to the reflexive aggression of "*pede pes et cuspide cuspis,*" foot-to-foot and pike-to-pike.[11] The unmistakable echo of the general's speech in Bel-imperia and Horatio's foreplay further complicates the underworld's opening distinction between loving likeness and hateful opposition, but not with the effect that Bel-imperia intends: if war generates likeness no less than love does, then how can love claim likeness as its distinctive property?

Bel-imperia and Horatio mistakenly believe that their "mutual amity" has been insulated from the violence it resembles in the same way that Hell keeps lovers separated from martialists – through containment; they think that they are "safe" within the bounds of Hieronimo's "pleasant" arbour. But Bel-imperia has shared the secret of her tryst with her servant Pedringano, and although she assures Horatio that Pedringano "is as trusty as my second self," her confidence turns out to be fatally misplaced: Pedringano betrays the lovers to Balthazar and to Bel-imperia's villainous brother Lorenzo. This act of treachery does not mean that Bel-imperia was wrong to think of Pedringano as her second self: it means that she was wrong to think of a second self as inevitably subservient to the first, when it can just as easily be understood as a self that *exceeds the bounds* of the original. Knowing what Bel-imperia knows, Pedringano is able to conduct Lorenzo and Balthazar inside Hieronimo's pleasance, where they witness the no longer private lovemaking between Bel-imperia and Horatio and grow more incensed and belligerent the more they watch. "Whereon dost thou chiefly meditate?" they overhear Bel-imperia asking Horatio. "On dangers past and pleasures to ensue," he replies. "On pleasures past and dangers to ensue," Balthazar whispers to his co-conspirators. Then Bel-imperia: "What dangers and what pleasures dost thou mean?" "Dangers of war, and pleasures of our love," answers Horatio, to which Lorenzo bitterly responds, "Dangers of death, but pleasures none at all." Unnervingly, Balthazar and Lorenzo express their hostility to the lovers not merely by opposing or negating what the lovers say but also by imitating and echoing them. In effect, the haters become a kind of second self to the lovers, and the next time that Lorenzo and Balthazar spy on them, their very responsiveness to Bel-imperia and Horatio excites a violent reaction that reflects the lovers' own equations of love and war. Watching Bel-imperia say to Horatio, "I dart this kiss at thee," and Horatio reply, "Then I retort the dart thou threw'st at me," Lorenzo can no longer contain himself. Rushing out from cover, he stabs Horatio again and again – taking his cue, as he himself claims, from the erotic provocations of the lovers: "Ay, thus, and thus! These are the fruits of love."[12]

II

Two kinds of borders collapse when Lorenzo kills Horatio. One of them had already been breached when the king of Spain and then the two lovers had overridden the conventional distinction between violence and pleasure. But now Lorenzo transgresses a further boundary by refusing to accept any distance as a spectator from the action he observes, and *The Spanish Tragedy* never allows either line of demarcation to be restored in full. Just as the confines of Hieronimo's pleasant arbour fail to shelter Bel-imperia and Horatio from their enemies, so Lorenzo and Balthazar discover that they cannot keep their killing of Horatio hidden there. Hieronimo overhears "outcries" that rouse him from his bed and lead him to the "murd'rous spectacle" of his son's body hanging in the garden. Revenge is the play's general name for the logic that will shortly transform Hieronimo from a spectator of violence to an enactor of it, but that change begins in this scene with a blurring of Hieronimo's vision, which causes him to perceive Horatio's corpse as both identical and antithetical to his son: "Alas, it is Horatio, my sweet son! / Oh, no, but he that whilom was my son." Soon enough, Hieronimo will speak of his powers of sight in the same self-oppositional terms: "O eyes, no eyes, but fountains fraught with tears!" This famous line epitomizes the dialectical relation between loving likeness and violent opposition that now comes to dominate the play. At the heart of Hieronimo's own outcry is a simple metaphor: "my eyes are fountains." But Hieronimo posits that similitude through negation, as if his eyes could not resemble fountains unless they first stopped being eyes. A recurrent term for likeness in *The Spanish Tragedy* is the "counterfeit": literally something made in opposition as well as imitation, like Bel-imperia's "countercheck" of Horatio's kiss.[13] In a later scene of the play, Hieronimo loses his mind at precisely the moment where he recognizes the counterfeit or "lively portrait" of himself in an old man whose son has also been murdered. Claiming to see his "selfsame sorrow" in the face of this second self, Hieronimo can no longer think of himself as contained within his own bounds – as selfsame.[14]

The lovers imagine themselves to be resolving the problem of broken borders by embracing the likeness between them as a twinning that excites a loving "twining" or merger. In his more lucid moments, Hieronimo takes a somewhat different though still similarly contractual view of likeness. He believes that, in order to contain a malefactor's "outrage," the law must answer "blood with blood"; he is praised for his "pursuit of equity." Yet the increasingly powerful account of likeness in the play is that it amplifies rather than contains, through a redoubling or (to borrow a term from the general's battle speech) a *rebounding* that exceeds the boundaries of the selfsame; thus Hieronimo's grieving wife Isabella likens her own eyes to fountains that "gush out" tears.[15] Revenge in *The Spanish Tragedy* follows the same principle of reciprocity as justice does, only more so. After Lorenzo and Balthazar learn that Pedringano has murdered a servant of Balthazar's (a killing that Lorenzo had secretly arranged), Lorenzo urges Balthazar to reject the hierarchy of imitation that would limit his answering violence to a merely reflexive echo of the original. According to Lorenzo, Balthazar should instead think of revenge as outdoing the crimes it imitates – as exacerbating or in his terms "exasperating" them: "Take the pains / To exasperate and hasten his revenge." Similarly, when the viceroy of Portugal learns that his courtier Villuppo has falsely accused another courtier of murdering Balthazar, the viceroy promises to punish Villuppo not with "so mean a torment as we here / Devised for him, who thou said'st slew our son, / But with the bitterest torments and extremes / That may be yet invented for thine end." Even the magnanimous Spanish king will later threaten Hieronimo with "th'extremest kind of death / that ever yet was invented for a wretch." Increasingly, the play depicts revenge as a rebounding that provokes its actors to entertain the notion of a *boundless* response: an "endless tragedy" is what Revenge himself promises to perform in the final line of the play.[16]

This is not to say that *The Spanish Tragedy* ultimately places likeness on the side of enmity rather than amity, of war rather than love, of exasperation rather than pleasing. On the contrary, likeness defeats such oppositions, and the play represents pleasing as itself a form of transgression. The first of the forty times that a version of the word *pleasing* crops up in *The Spanish Tragedy*, it is associated with a border crossing: Don Andrea recalls how, after arriving at the gates of Hell and "there pleasing Cerberus with honeyed speech," he "passed the perils of the foremost porch." When Balthazar later asks Hieronimo "to entertain" his father the viceroy and the Spanish king with "suchlike pleasing motion" as his earlier "entertainment" of the Portuguese ambassador, Hieronimo agrees to "fit" his royal audience with the art of poetry, which he characterizes as "passing pleasing to the world": *surpassingly* pleasing, that is, pleasing past ordinary bounds. To give an audience a play that fits them is to please them by reflecting their own desires back to them – as they like it – but Hieronimo seizes on his play as an opportunity to harm his audience as well as delight them, through a redoubling of them that breaks the bounds of their own self-sameness. His first step in alienating his audience from themselves is to induce the former onlookers Lorenzo and Balthazar "to play a part" in his show.[17]

From the start of *The Spanish Tragedy*, Kyd had been fitting his own audience for such self-alienation by placing a version of *them* onstage, in the spectating figures of Don Andrea and Revenge. This "audience visible to the audience," as Lukas Erne puts it, is redoubled in turn when Kyd's own spectators go on to watch Don Andrea and Revenge watch Balthazar and Lorenzo as they watch Bel-imperia and Horatio – and then these additional blurrings of the boundary between audience and actors get exacerbated further when Lorenzo leaps from his seat to stab the man he's been watching, just as Hieronimo, in a later echo yet also a reversal of Lorenzo's earlier "trespass," will reach from the stage to stab an audience member. "Haply you think … / That this is fabulously counterfeit," Hieronimo derisively exclaims to his audience after they have applauded him: what they don't yet understand, he believes, is that his entertainment has been *genuinely* counterfeit, insofar as it has countered the audience in the very act of pleasing them.[18]

To judge from the spectating Andrea, this rebounding effect to entertainment does more than appal the viewers: it transforms them, too. At the start of *The Spanish Tragedy*, Andrea says not one word about desiring revenge. The first indication of any bloody thoughts on his part comes after he has witnessed the Spanish king turn from warring with Balthazar to entertaining him: "These pleasant sights," Andrea then protests, "are sorrow to my soul."[19] The more Andrea watches, the more exasperated he grows. Two acts later, his spectatorship has so markedly intensified his bitterness that he denounces Hieronimo's apparently friendly overtures to Lorenzo as blocking his own "passage to revenge." By the end of *The Spanish Tragedy*, when Andrea expresses his delight at having witnessed the deaths of friends and enemies alike, his thirst for violence seems to have passed all bounds:

> Horatio murdered in his father's bower,
> Vile Serberine by Pedringano slain,
> False Pedringano hanged by quaint device,
> Fair Isabella by herself misdone,
> Prince Balthazar by Bel-imperia stabbed,
> The Duke of Castile and his wicked son
> Both done to death by old Hieronimo,
> My Bel-imperia fall'n as Dido fell,
> And good Hieronimo slain by himself –
> Ay, these were spectacles to please my soul.[20]

Seneca, from whom Kyd copied the framing device of Andrea and Revenge, was also the source for Kyd's dramatization of a spectator who finds himself desiring ever more "murd'rous spectacles." In Seneca's tragedy *Thyestes*, for instance, the avenging King Atreus looks on with delight as his brother Thyestes unwittingly eats the flesh of his own children, until the king realizes that *hoc quoque exiguum est mihi*, that even this is too little for him: he now wishes that his brother had been fully conscious of the horror he was committing. The best way for a ruler to demonstrate his power, Atreus had earlier asserted, is to turn his subjects against themselves. *Quod nolunt velint*: what they don't want is what they must want – a principle Atreus puts into action by making Thyestes cannibalize his own children.[21] Hieronimo's entertainment manages to provoke his audience into wanting what they don't want, not only by encouraging them to applaud a violence that is targeted at them but also by exciting a bloodlust in them they might not otherwise have known they possessed. "Fetch forth the tortures!" exclaims the Spanish king at the end of Hieronimo's play, the same king who had earlier tried to convince everyone that his chief pleasure was in kindness.[22] The difference between *Thyestes* and *The Spanish Tragedy* is that Kyd makes outrageously explicit what had merely been implicit in Seneca: he transforms the revenger from a king to a dramatist, who perverts his audience not so much by tyrannizing over them as by entertaining them.[23]

It seems unlikely that *The Spanish Tragedy* could have gone on to become one of the most popular and influential plays of its time in spite of the hostility towards its audience that it so plainly manifests. The play itself suggests instead that its commercial success, and the success of other Renaissance plays like it, depended not only on actors and dramatists who were ambitious to do more than please their audiences but also on audiences who were ambitious to experience more than being pleased – who were, indeed, ready to surrender their spectatorial detachment from actors and playwrights in exchange for a more immersive relation with them, no matter how compromising that collapse of boundaries might prove to be.[24] So powerfully did *The Spanish Tragedy* make its mark on its first audiences that echoes of the play rebound throughout the subsequent drama of the period. These, however, are not exclusively subservient reflections of the original. "When this eternal substance of my soul / Did live imprisoned in my wanton flesh," Andrea solemnly intones at the start of *The Spanish Tragedy*, "I was a courtier in the Spanish court." Later imitators have their characters say, "When this eternal substance of the soul / Did live imprison'd in my wanton flesh, / I was a Tailor in the Court of *Spain*"; "When I was mortal, this my costive corpse / Did lap up figs and raisins in the Strand"; "When this transforméd substance of my carcass / Did live imprison'd in a wanton hogshead," and so on.[25] By perverting its horrors into comedy, Renaissance parodies of *The Spanish Tragedy* pleased their audiences by helping them take *their* revenge on Kyd, their entertainer.

NOTES

1 John Marston, "Introduction," *Jack Drum's Entertainment*, in *The Plays of John Marston*, ed. H. Harvey Wood, vol. 3 (Edinburgh: Oliver and Boyd, 1939).

2 Marston, "Introduction."

3 John Marston, *Parasitaster, or The Fawn*, ed. David A. Blostein (Manchester: Manchester University Press, 1978), 6; "Prologue," 23–35.

4 Thomas Dekker, "Prologue," *The Merry Devil of Edmonton*, ed. William Amos Abrams (Durham, NC: Duke University Press, 1942); Dekker, "Prologue," *If It Be Not Good, the Devil Is in It*, in *The Dramatic Works of Thomas Dekker*, vol. 3, ed. Fredon Bowers (Cambridge: Cambridge University Press, 1953).

5 Ben Jonson, "Prologue," *Poetaster*, in *The Cambridge Edition of the Works of Ben Jonson*, vol. 2 (Cambridge: Cambridge University Press, 2012), lines 74–85; Jonson, "Prologue," *The Alchemist*, in *The Cambridge Edition of the Works of Ben Jonson*, vol. 3 (Cambridge: Cambridge University Press, 2012), line 18. See Thomas Dekker's optimistic claim about his *Whore of Babylon* in the prologue to that play: "What in it is grave, will most delight," in *The Collected Works of Thomas Dekker*, ed. Fredson Bowers, vol. 2 (Cambridge: Cambridge University Press, 1953), line 8.

6 Francis Beaumont, *The Knight of the Burning Pestle*, in *English Renaissance Drama: A Norton Anthology*, ed. David Bevington et al. (New York: Norton, 2002), Prologue, 10–12; Peter Hausted, *The Rival Friends*, ed. Laures J. Mills (Bloomington: Indiana University Press, 1951), A2v.

7 Thomas Kyd, *The Spanish Tragedy*, in *English Renaissance Drama: A Norton Anthology*, ed. David Bevington et al. (New York: Norton, 2002), 4.2.70; 4.4.82 and 68.

8 Stephen Gosson, *Playes Confuted in Five Actions* (London: 1582), C5v–C6r; Kyd, *Spanish Tragedy*, 1.2.108, 1.1.86–9.

9 Kyd, *Spanish Tragedy*, 1.2.7, 4, 10, 18, 85, 96–7, 17, 197; 1.4.118 and 132–3; 2.3.18–21; 1.2.146.

10 Kyd, *Spanish Tragedy*, 1.1.45–6 and 62; 2.3.47–8; 1.4.123–4.

11 Kyd, *Spanish Tragedy*, 1.4.61 and 67–8; 2.2.11 and 32–8; 2.4.36–8; 1.2.55.

12 Kyd, *Spanish Tragedy*, 2.2.42–4; 2.4.9; 2.2.26–31; 2.4.40–1 and 55.

13 Kyd, *Spanish Tragedy*, 2.5.1, 9, 14–15; 3.2.1. "Counterfeit" appears at 1.3.65, 2.4.30, 3.12.116, 4.1.2, and 4.4.77.

14 Kyd, *Spanish Tragedy*, 3.13.85 and 169.

15 Kyd, *Spanish Tragedy*, 2.4.43; 3.6.35; 3.9.1; 3.13.54; 1.2.30; 2.5.43.

16 Kyd, *Spanish Tragedy*, 3.4.30–1; 3.1.98–101; 4.4.198–9; 4.5.48.

17 Kyd, *Spanish Tragedy*, 1.1.30–1; 4.1.60–74 and 83.

18 Lukas Erne, *Beyond* The Spanish Tragedy*: A Study of the Works of Thomas Kyd* (Manchester: Manchester University Press), 97; Kyd, *Spanish Tragedy*, 1.2.138; 4.4.76–7.

19 Kyd, *Spanish Tragedy*, 1.5.3. Gregory Semenza similarly points out that Andrea says nothing about seeking vengeance in his opening speech. In Semenza's view, "Proserpine's 'doom' should not be read as the just satisfaction of Andrea's desire for revenge": instead, "it should be read as a pass to commit an unlawful act, an invitation to moral depravity," in "*The Spanish Tragedy* and Revenge," in *Early Modern English Drama: A Critical*

Companion, ed. Garrett A. Sullivan, Jr. et al. (Oxford: Oxford University Press, 2006), 57.

20 Kyd, *Spanish Tragedy*, 3.15.16 and 4.5.3–12.

21 Seneca, *Thyestes*, in *Seneca: Tragedies II*, trans. John G. Fitch (Cambridge: Harvard University Press), 1053 and 212; for Jasper Heywood's Elizabethan translation of these lines, see his *The Second Tragedie of Seneca Entituled Thyestes* (London, 1560), E1v and A7v. See also this version of the second passage from *Thyestes* in Thomas Hughes's 1588 *The Misfortunes of Arthur*, ed. Brian Jay Corrigan (New York: Garland, 1992): "Then is a Kingdom at a wished stay, / When whatsoever the Sovereign wills, or nills, / Men be compell'd as well to praise, as bear, / And Subjects' wills enforc'd against their wills" (2.2.78–81).

22 Kyd, *Spanish Tragedy*, 4.4.185.

23 Jonathan Bate, among others, stresses that "theatrical self-referentiality is the very essence, not some contingent feature, of the genre of English Renaissance revenge drama," although he does not point out how much more blatant a feature this self-referentiality is in Kyd's "seminal" play than in his "Senecan" sources. Bate, "The Performance of Revenge: *Titus Andronicus* and *The Spanish Tragedy*," in *The Show Within*, ed. François Laroque (Montpellier: Publications de Université Paul-Valery, 1992), 2:268–9.

24 For a different view of Renaissance revenge tragedy as "eliciting guilt-free pleasure from the audience" (26), see Grant Williams, "Being Seen Is Believing: Spectacle, Ethics, and Others of Belief in Elizabethan Revenge Tragedy," in *Theta VIII, Théâtre Tudor* (2009): 253–74. I'm not arguing that a play such as Kyd's *necessarily* had the effect of implicating the audience in the moral disequilibrium they witnessed; my point is that Kyd's making room for this effect broadened the appeal of the play. For the dramatic uses to which Shakespeare put his own resentment toward his audience see my essay "Shakespeare's Pains to Please," in *Forms of Association: Making Publics in Early Modern Europe*, ed. Paul Yachnin and Marlene Eberhart (Amherst: University of Massachusetts Press, 2015), 256–71.

25 Kyd, *Spanish Tragedy*, 1.1.1–4; John Rawlins, *The Rebellion* (London, 1640), I2r; Francis Beaumont, *The Knight of the Burning Pestle*, 5.3.129–30; Thomas Tomkis, *Albumazar*, ed. Hugh G. Dick (Berkeley: University of California Press, 1944), 4.6.1–2. In the "Praeludium" to *Cynthia's Revels* (1600), Jonson combines an attack on both his audience and *The Spanish Tragedy* when he mocks the playgoers who believe "that the old *Hieronimo* ... was the only, best, and judiciously penned play of Europe" in *The Cambridge Edition of the Works of Ben Jonson*, ed. David Bevington, vol. 1 (Cambridge: Cambridge University Press), lines 163–7.

chapter six

Curse

BJÖRN QUIRING

Cursing is given a strange prestige in some of Shakespeare's plays. The intermediate status of the curse, floating between temporalities, between institutions, and between power and subordination, renders it analogous to the theatrical form and interesting to the theatre of the early modern period.[1] Shakespeare first explores its intricacies in *Richard III.* With an extraordinary clarity, this play reflects on the character and significance of the curse, first and foremost its odd, paradoxical status and its intimate relation both to the theatre and to the question of divine law. For the curse is a speech act marked by a strange ambiguity: it can be defined as both an appeal to and a condemnation through a punitive divine judgment.[2] The word *curse* traditionally designates a mythical, exclusionary divine judgment that posits a new law and gives the world a new structure. Both Yahweh's curse upon the serpent, man, and the ground in the Book of Genesis (3.14–19), and Jesus's apocalyptic condemnation of the reprobate (Matthew 25:14) conform to this description. In this context, curses not only determine the future, but also legitimate the past and the present; they serve as explanatory devices. One might say that the mythical curse establishes a mythical guilt a priori. This primordial guilt finds its most pertinent expression in a legal demand that is impossible to meet insofar as its transgression is antecedent to any subject's behaviour. In this respect, the curse functions as the verbalization of a exclusionary "ban"[3] that God as the sovereign has always already imposed upon humankind, either directly or through his representatives. Christian jurisdiction proceeds to institutionalize this collective guilt as the basis of its legal structure.[4]

But the curse is not only a mythical speech act, articulating a primeval guilt; the term also designates the ritual representation of these judgments within the legal order itself, as exemplified by the biblical obligation to repeat every seven years the curses in Deuteronomy that perpetuate the covenant with Yahweh (Deut. 27–8 and 31:10). These curses represent a transcendental world order within the juridical system; and in this respect they do not appear as law-making but as law-preserving.[5] Legitimate, effective cursing therefore tends to insert itself into a chain of pre-existent curses that it extends and cites. Subjects may damn their opponents, but only by quoting and thus re-actualizing the word of God. They may also damn themselves in this fashion: one of the most prominent variations of the curse is the oath as conditional self-execration.[6]

The resultant problem of this speech act is that the curse simultaneously posits and negates the difference between world and divine judgment: in the empirical act of cursing, the creative power of a foundational mythic Word is referenced as a force that from the outset determines the situation in which the curser and the cursed find themselves. This suggests that the curse as an empirical speech act reduces itself to an empty, repetitive gesture: it posits what it already presupposes, forever redundant. The condemnable deeds or the condemnable persons have already brought a pre-existent curse down on themselves to which the execrator merely lends his or her voice in repetition. Yet on the other hand, on many occasions it is obvious that the imprecator aspires to carry out this condemnation personally through the curse, supplementing a universal justice that seems to have failed. Thereby the maledictor insinuates that, at the moment of its utterance, judgment and world do not coincide after all. Since the curse, while denying the divergence of judgment and world, at the same time upholds this difference as its own cause and origin, it subverts itself.

On account of this paradoxical structure, curses cannot have any effect that is univocally demonstrable and determinable by language. Absolute power and complete impotence converge in this speech act. For this reason, it is structurally impossible to disprove or to prove the effectiveness of curses empirically. Insofar as it affirms the course of the world and at the same time denies it, the curse touches upon the problem of representation in general: it aims to create a reality by referring to it as pre-existent. Seen from this perspective, the curse per se can be seen as an eminently theatrical speech act, positioned at the boundary between fantasy and fact and mediating between them.

Over the centuries, this self-suspending, theatrical dimension of the curse has always been an issue in the polemical struggle of competing parties for power over this performative act. Nevertheless, the curse has remained a mark of spiritual authority for a long time. For example, the superior political position of the medieval popes vis-à-vis the secular rulers is based in part on their power to curse, i.e., to excommunicate – as can be demonstrated by the circumstance that the dispute over lay investiture in the eleventh century was solved temporarily when Pope Gregory VII excommunicated the Holy Roman Emperor Henry IV.[7] The ecclesiastical discourse about this topic (e.g., in the writings of Gregory the Great) regularly contrasts curses that are to be rejected for their lowly personal motivations with the Christian curse that is necessary as an instrument of eternal justice.[8] The church therefore considered extra-ecclesiastical cursing as pagan and prohibited it to the laity by decree.[9]

At the beginning of the early modern age, the rite of excommunication constituted the most visible institutionalized act of condemnation by divine judgment. The ceremony marks the expulsion of a parishioner from the congregation of the faithful by the clergy. It is part of the liturgy; its announcement (which is subject to major local differences of formula and frequency) is incorporated into the church service.[10] Excommunication formulas are not freely invented by the clergy but consist almost entirely of reworked, rearranged, and refunctionalized biblical and patristic quotes. In addition to these extensive formulas, the ritual of the major excommunication involves the representational use of sacred objects. This is what the traditional phrase "bell, book and candle" refers to, evoking three forms of symbolically expulsing and murdering the accursed. Firstly, during the excommunication ceremony, the clergy frequently extinguish candles that represent the anathematized person's light of life.[11] Secondly, the ceremony includes the ringing of bells "in churches throughout the city," some legends suggesting that they imitate funereal knells.[12] Thirdly, the ritual of excommunication involves the forceful closing of a holy book, generally a Bible or a Book of Psalms.[13] This is associated with a blotting out from the "book of life" (*liber vitae*), i.e., from the roll of the blessed that God keeps.[14]

The evident theatricality of this ritual emphasizes the close relation between curse and drama. Indeed, theatre itself has evolved to a considerable degree through an engagement with the problem of the curse, its derivatives like the oath and other forms of binding speech. It has repeatedly been pointed out that theatrical performances have developed out of religious rituals all over the world. In the case of England, these were mainly church rituals – first those of the Easter ceremonies, then those of the Corpus Christi festivities, which developed into Mystery plays.[15] These stagings included representations of exclusionary ceremonies, such as the cursing of Judas during the Last Supper.[16] English theatre has evolved to a high degree through an engagement with the ceremonies of church and state; it has imitated them, but also deviated from them. It is an institution that must arrange and embed itself in very specific ways within persistent social rituals if it wants to survive and to perpetuate itself.

Elizabethan England around 1600 was a society whose use of rituals had thoroughly changed in the course of the Reformation. A lot of church ceremonies had been removed from the liturgy, among them the ritual of excommunication. The English Reformation had suspended the papal power to exclude Christians from the congregation, not least because Henry VIII (in 1533) and Elizabeth I (in 1570) were excommunicated by the pope and for a long time ruled England under a ban. Thus, under Henry VIII, the pope's power to excommunicate was declared null and void,[17] but the ritual curse did not disappear after this abolition. Rather, it was appropriated and transformed by the state and continued to play an important role in new customs and institutions. Especially during the sixteenth century – in part even before the Reformation – secular power took over the rhetoric of execration. In 1521, for example, the mayor of Lincoln published "a formal curse on those who had improperly removed the records and books of the Common Council."[18] And the oath ceremonies of self-execration became even more important than they had been in medieval times; indeed, they became an essential component of the English Reformation itself. In 1534 the Act of Supremacy demanded that all officials and the clergy to swear an oath of loyalty to the king as the head of the English church.[19] Thomas More is the most prominent victim of the resultant conflict and the subsequent consolidation of Anglicanism.

The Anglican Church, however, was not successful in its attempts to establish a curse monopoly. Several competitors claimed the malediction for themselves: besides the Church of England, these rivals included the pope (represented by those Catholics who remained in England), but also the leaders of more or less radical Protestant groups. Puritans and other sects used excommunication ceremonies in their congregations as an instrument of power, while making no effort to codify the causes and forms of cursing. Some Puritan preachers, for example, tended to execrate unruly members of their community;[20] Quaker leaders imprecated their enemies and collected legends about the subsequent divine judgments.[21] In English theologico-political literature of the sixteenth and early seventeenth centuries, there was a proliferation of texts containing curses or pertaining to curses, while at the same time questioning their efficacy and intensifying attempts to control them.[22]

Curses in early modern England functioned as remainders that, after the abolition of the rites into which they were firmly integrated, became apparently placeless and redundant, but continued to play an important role in their marginalized position. At this time splinters of excommunication ceremonies found their way into the secular theatre. The theatrical curse was ideally suited to unfolding and questioning the aporetic, crypto-theatrical structures of a jurisdiction supported by political theology. Thus, theatre engaged in an analytical "work on myth"[23] that linked it to the project of philosophy.[24] However, this semi-philosophical work was not so much motivated by an upwelling of enlightened zeal as by the theatre's own self-interest. One can generally observe that the Elizabethan drama established itself by appropriating conventions and ceremonies and by reshaping them in accordance with its own goals and those of its controlling organizations.[25] The role commercial theatre played in the struggle for power over the curse was related to the fact that the English government tried to use drama as a propaganda instrument, for theatre was heavily regulated by a state apparatus that tried to consolidate its own authority. The Queen's Men, for example, were from the very beginning conceived as a troupe of propagandists who were supposed to spread royalist enthusiasm.[26] This general task occasionally also included the appropriation of the excommunication and of other rites, a process in which these adoptions often assumed the form of parody. The theatre often ridiculed excommunication as a stupid, malicious act full of empty pathos, and as an illegitimate meddling of the "pope's playhouse" in British affairs.[27] For example, conflating excommunication and exorcism, Christopher Marlowe ridicules both of them in *Doctor Faustus* (3.1.73–87)[28]; and when James I came to Cambridge in 1615, the university likewise staged "a play containing an episode mocking the whole procedure of exorcism."[29] Within the diegetic action of these plays, ritual acts are performed in a way that the hollow fetishism underlying them is exposed; they are marked as inherently unsuccessful and as dependent on deceptive staging. In these appropriations of the curse, an untimely ceremony is, on the one hand, exposed as an empty, outdated, "undead" ritual; but on the other hand, its tenacious forms and formulas are perpetuated and given a new home, which keeps them both problematizable and profitable.

Shakespeare's intervention in this situation adds a new twist to the general development: the curse appears in Shakespearean drama as a thoroughly theatrical speech act, even within the diegetic framework. The insufficient binding power of this theatrical performative is represented by his plays in such a way that the distinction between reality and theatrical "misplay" appears to have been shifted into the interior of the representation. But their emptiness notwithstanding, many of these Shakespearean curses appear to be opportune and necessary; they turn out to fulfil an important function despite, or even precisely because of, their ineffectuality. This transposed form of performative effectivity is related to the importance Shakespeare accords to the stage as a space in which social roles can be both analysed and renegotiated.[30]

All this is pertinent to the Yorkist tetralogy, first and foremost to *Richard III.* The ambivalence of excommunication and its problematic efficacy is frequently demonstrated in this play. In this context, it needs to be pointed out that the history play *Richard III* has all the trappings of a propaganda play, designed to legitimate the reign of the Tudors. The Tudors relied on this kind of propaganda, because the dynastic legitimacy of the first Tudor, Henry VII, was dubious. In order to conceal this questionable state of affairs, the court disseminated the myth that Henry VII had been installed as the King of England because he was favoured by God and therefore destined for that role.[31] For this reason, Henry's predecessor, Richard III, had to be represented as evil incarnate, so that his deposition and murder, no matter by whom, could be represented as justified and that the goodness of Henry VII could shine all the more brightly against this dark background. A substantial number of the characteristics and misdeeds that were ascribed to Richard at that time have turned out to be inventions.[32]

When Shakespeare uses these propaganda topics, he brackets them to a certain degree by blending the legitimacy crisis of the Wars of the Roses with the legitimacy crises his contemporaries experienced, for the massive crisis of legitimacy that is represented in *Richard III* in many aspects resembles that of the sixteenth century more than that of the actual fifteenth century: feudal, liturgical, and other obligations perpetuate themselves in Shakespeare's play, despite their obvious obsolescence or mutual incompatibility. In the course of the three parts of *Henry VI,* references to religious and secular authorities have already been subverted, because these references have been too flagrantly employed in the service of self-interest. Within the action of play, ritual acts are thus performed in such a way that their underlying hollowness is exposed. Oath ceremonies are one prominent example: they have become altogether powerless, although everybody still insists on them. This strange state of affairs unfolds above all in the first scene of the second act when the dying king, Richard's brother Edward, tries to regulate the intrigues at his unruly court by instituting an oath ceremony that is obligatory for all parties:

EDWARD: Rivers and Hastings, take each other's hand;
Dissemble not your hatred: swear your love....
Take heed you dally not before your King,
Lest He that is the supreme King of kings
Confound your hidden falsehood, and award
Either of you to be the other's end....
Wife, love Lord Hastings, let him kiss your hand:
And what you do, do it unfeignedly....
Dorset, embrace him; Hastings, love lord Marquess.

(2.1.7–8/12–15/21–2/25)[33]

The problem with this sacred invocation of oath-based universal reconciliation is that the political career of the Yorkists has been defined by perjuries. The decisive battle for the victory of their party was won after York had broken his holy oath of loyalty against Henry VI at the insistent urging of both Edward and Richard. Edward himself had in this context proclaimed:

EDWARD: But for a kingdom any oath may be broken.
I would break a thousand oaths to reign one year.

(*3 Henry VI*, 1.2.16–17)

That is the fetishism of the society in which Richard lives: it believes in the eternal validity of divine rituals and at the same time manipulates them in the pursuit of personal interests. For this reason, all statements invoking the godhead and the higher decrees of morality appear to be empty and theatrical in this play. For example, in the discussion between Richard's brother Clarence and his murderers, the two sides become entrapped in the contradictions of their position; when the murderers try to legitimate the killing and when Clarence tries to convince them that it is unlawful, their exchange becomes ever more circular, since nobody can point to an authority that has not been subverted (1.4.171–201). Under these auspices, political theology itself turns out to be a theatrical affair.

At this point Richard, who doesn't seem to share the fetishism of his environment, enters the scene. He turns the empty ritual into a mere farce he can manipulate, as if he were its director. Richard's behaviour and his utterances hint at the fact that rituals for him are just empty representations that he may turn to his own advantage by making ironical use of floating curses, oaths, and portentous prophecies (see, e.g., 1.1.36–40, 1.2.68–9, and 2.1.54–60). With his skill at manipulating remnants of sacredness and at the same time ironically subverting them by taking on various roles, he brings about what Elizabethan drama does in the public arena, and in this respect he appears on stage as an allegory of theatre. A.P. Rossiter and others have discussed how in Richard the public persona of the Elizabethan actor and stage director seems to have been reproduced within drama itself.[34] Just as the drama of Shakespeare's time tends to appropriate outdated, obsolete rituals, above all those of the church, for its own purposes, Richard, as a born actor, does the same thing within the diegetic reality of the play. Richard's success derives from his exploitation of the fetishistic belief of his antagonists in the world's religiously mediated intelligibility, a belief he himself does not want to share. From his advanced perspective, he can control the other characters, because he controls the signs and symbols by which they make sense of the world.

In that sense, Richard III is a modernizer; and that is why the traditionalist ex-Queen Margaret is his great opponent in the field of ritual. Margaret, the widow of Henry VI, is, without doubt, the most prominent execrator in *Richard III*. As a monument to outmoded power relations, she pronounces, in her two scenes on stage, almost nothing but curses and laments; even her "gentle counsel" assumes the form of a ban that she articulates in order to polarize the court (1.3.289–94). Quoting snippets of excommunication formulas and their biblical precedents, Margaret directs her curses above all against the Yorkists. She does not perform a complete excommunication ceremony, but there are many fragmentary quotes from execration formulas among her numerous curses. They reach their most prominent and richly allusive fury in 1.3, during her major execration of the entire attendant court:

MARGARET: Though not by war, by surfeit die your King,
As ours by murder, to make him a king.
Edward thy son, that now is Prince of Wales,

For Edward my son, that was Prince of Wales,
Die in his youth, by like untimely violence.
Thyself, a queen, for me that was a queen,
Outlive thy glory like my wretched self:
Long may'st thou live to wail thy children's death,
And see another, as I see thee now,
Deck'd in thy rights, as thou art stall'd in mine;
Long die thy happy days before thy death,
And, after many lenghten'd hours of grief,
Die neither mother, wife, nor England's Queen.
Rivers and Dorset, you were standers-by,
And so wast thou, Lord Hastings, when my son
Was stabb'd with bloody daggers. God, I pray Him,
That none of you may live his natural age,
But by some unlook'd accident cut off. (1.3.197–214)

This speech is structured by the imitation of traditional patterns: allusions on the level of form as well as content evoke the great curse of the Covenant in Deuteronomy 28 that is a favoured source of excommunication formulas even in the Anglican Church. The threat, for example, that the execrated ones will survive their children and die in loneliness, is reminiscent of Deut. 28:32*ff.*; the proclamation that they will be forced to relinquish their position to a usurper, of Deut. 28:43*ff.* An influence of the Psalms is also discernible.[35] These curses and laments that Margaret as well as the other former queens (i.e., the Duchess of York and Elizabeth) pronounce subvert the dialogic situation and dissolve it into conventional ceremonies of mourning and cursing. Their speakers are exponents not only of outdated power relations, but also of outmoded forms of representation. What is notable about Margaret's maledictions, however, is the fact that both the curser and the cursed are being defined by terms of deprivation: loss of position, loss of social connections, and loss of perlocutionary power. In her representations, the curse appears as a congregation created by violent degradations in which the position of the excommunicate largely coincides with that of the excommunicator: curses are received and passed on in concatenated series in which the execrators are at the same time the execrated. Margaret is not the first link in this chain of curses, as Richard is the first to point out: he refers to the curse that his father pronounced against Margaret before she executed him:

RICHARD: The curse my noble father laid on thee
When thou didst crown his warlike brows with paper,
And with thy scorns drew'st rivers from his eyes,
And then to dry them, gav'st the Duke a clout
Steep'd in the faultless blood of pretty Rutland –
His curses then, from bitterness of soul
Denounc'd against thee, are all fall'n upon thee,
And God, not we, hath plagu'd thy bloody deed. (1.3.174–81)

Richard thus points out that Margaret's deeds in the three parts of *Henry VI*, when she was still in power, were not godlier than those of Richard, even though she now constantly invokes God's name. Once again, the sanctifying performatives of all parties are subverted by an inherent irony. Margaret's curses appear superior only by virtue of the fact that she subordinates herself explicitly and entirely to the fatal dynamics and the aporetic structure of this speech act. The horizon of this unfolding *lex talionis* is total destruction since the pure logic of vengeance can find no other end. Margaret herself recognizes this constitutive excess of her maledictory inventory:

MARGARET: Think that thy babes were sweeter than they were,
And he that slew them fouler than he is:
Bettering thy loss makes the bad-causer worse.
Revolving this will teach thee how to curse. (4.4.120–3)

But even this inherent excess is shadowed by an inherent redundancy: it is the problem of all cursing queens and ex-queens that Richard, whom they curse, is already cursed by his deeds, which makes their work seem tautological. In Anne's words, they "curse [the] cursed self" (1.2.80). All this makes it seem not too farfetched to understand Margaret and her outmoded and undead rituals as an allegory of English Catholicism in its decline. But that would overly simplify the dramatic constellation: like all of Shakespeare's characters, Margaret represents a theatrical potential that can at best be overdetermined by political parables. Representations of diverse social tendencies coalesce in this placeless personification of a past that is marked as a simulacrum.

Nevertheless, Richard at times displays almost timid reactions to Margaret, such as his oddly childish interruption of her cursing tirade

(1.3.234). He seems to be in awe of her liturgical curses against him and apparently wants to prevent their propagation (see also *3 Henry VI*, 5.5.43, and *Richard III*, 4.4.149–51), for Richard wants a new distribution of curses in the social field, that is freely manipulable and functionalized in the interest of dramatic power.

But the curse cannot be subdued so easily; it soon becomes apparent that it escapes Richard, and the latter cannot altogether keep it under control, not least because Richard the universal impersonator and cynic is still a believer in one thing: he believes in the sacredness of the crown. He considers it the unmoved centre of history (the earthly Paradise, "Elysium," *3, Henry VI*, 1.2.30) and the king's name "a tower of strength" (5.3.12). The crown functions as Richard's one fetishistic object, around which his deceptive reality structures itself, but which is itself not deceptive. More than his amorality, it is this perverse faith in a fixed point in the universe that proves his undoing. When he finally achieves the crown, he attempts to further legitimize his position by either murdering or marrying all other legitimate pretenders to the crown; but he goes about this project with so much political clumsiness that he increasingly comes to resemble his predecessor. Like Edward IV, he involuntarily establishes double binds (e.g., in 4.2.442–55), and begins to harken after "drunken prophecies" (4.2.94–105). In the process he neglects the realm of politics as if it had grown irrelevant in the new "dark monarchy" (1.4.51). When he hears of the attack by the new pretender to the throne, Richmond, who lacks real dynastic legitimacy, he seems genuinely confused (4.4.469–73).

His final downfall begins at the night before the Battle of Bosworth Field, with the entrance of the cursing dead (5.3.118–77). The ghost scene almost seems redundant in a play that swarms with characters who count themselves among the living dead (see, e.g., 4.3.26–7) and whose series of executions resembles the procession of a danse macabre. But this episode is as necessary as *The Mousetrap* is for *Hamlet*: as a mirror image of the drama, it opens the play onto a meta-theatrical level, for the dead perform an abridged version of the play: their entrances are chronologically arranged according to the point in time at which they were killed, and their accusations repeat the plot development of *Richard III*. Ghostly apparitions often introduce this meta-theatrical dimension in Shakespeare's dramas; they are not only histrionic themselves, but also direct the spectator's attention to the theatrical character of reality by pointing towards a different scene, "*ein anderer Schauplatz*."[36] However, the entrance of the dead in 5.3 is more ceremonious than was customary in the Elizabethan theatre.[37] The ghosts dialogue neither with each other nor with the living; instead, they recite formulas. The stereotypical and only superficially varied exhortation "Despair and die!" in all ten cases is combined with a "Think on ..." formula that is a reminder of the speaker's murder. Often, but not consistently, two other locutions occur: "Let me sit heavy on your soul" and "Let fall thy sword." The formulaic character of these utterances again suggests liturgical performatives; the scene of the ghosts mixes elements of the sacrificial mass with ecclesiastical excommunication ceremonies. Together with the dead, a dead ceremony returns. But in contrast to the mass, the revenant dead do not testify to anything beyond themselves in the theatre. They demand neither their own deliverance nor Richard's eternal damnation nor other interventions of divine powers. All they insist on is commemoration and the defeat of Richard, resulting from his awareness of former guilt. The ghosts are, as it were, "enlightened" ghosts who already take into consideration their own possibly phantasmatic status as personified pangs of conscience:

RIVERS, GREY, VAUGHAN: Our wrongs in Richard's bosom
Will conquer him. (5.3.145–6)

However, this wish involves a slight paradox: the dead insistently demand commemoration even though the dream in which they appear must itself be understood as a form of this commemoration. The princes make this dilemma explicit by cursing Richard with a bad dream in which they themselves appear:

PRINCES: Dream on thy cousins, smother'd in the Tower. (5.3.152)

Since Richard is experiencing this very dream at the very same moment, the curse wishes for something that is already happening, emphasizing its redundant nature. The political claims of the cursing ghosts, however, remain unreconciled behind the facade of a ritual univocity; their curse is less a communal than a serial act. (According to the stage directions of the Folio, never more than three ghosts have to be on stage at the same time.) Contrary to Tillyard's dictum,[38] this scene, then, does not signal the inception of a new epoch of theologico-political unity, but represents incompatible and obsolete claims on symbolic positions of power. The revenants do indeed echo each other but without actually speaking in harmony: polyphonic notes tending toward dissonance are softly audible in their chorus. They continue to speak as Yorkists and Lancastrians, and it is precisely the residual claims to legitimacy on the two competing sides that lend performative strength to their curses. The dead do not articulate a law but an abundance of mutually exclusive obligations. Consequently, the curse pronounced on Richard remains overdetermined, and Richard's subsequent defeat remains a matter of interpretation: it can be ideologically appropriated, but it has no indisputable meaning beyond itself.

It is all the more necessary that the curse perpetuate itself after Richard's downfall and death. His successor, the future Henry VII, does not suspend but actually affirms the logic of theatrical execration that has kept the mechanism of the drama in motion until that point. His blessing of England and her monarch is supplemented by a prospective curse on their traitors that ends the drama:

RICHMOND: Abate the edge of traitors, gracious Lord,
That would reduce these bloody days again,
And make poor England weep in streams of blood.
Let them not live to taste this land's increase,
That would with treason wound this fair land's peace. (5.5.35–9)

Their use of metaphors as well as their content and their symmetrical positioning establish connections between Richard's opening monologue and the concluding speech of Richmond.[39] The similarity of their names and the symmetry of the scenes in which they share the stage brings them closer together and thereby puts an ironic twist on their statements. As is true of other Shakespearean dramas, the ending of this play is a pseudo-ending inasmuch as the curses pronounced by and over Richard III apparently continue to be in effect in the kingdom of the Tudors. In the final analysis, Richmond is a shadow of Richard; he imitates him. Richard has prepared the ground on which his successor can justify his usurpation. At the end, the curse that has unfolded in the social field is not dissolved, but passes from one constellation to the next; the problem of its persistence in spite of its secularization remains unresolved.

However, by appropriating and analysing the curse, Shakespeare has successfully represented the theatre as the better, more enlightened church. After all, it is the theatre that makes it possible to compare and judge Richard and Richmond in this way. So the theatre with all its ironies has shown itself as the medium in which the social structures and conflicts of the recent past can be given their adequate representation. Theatre is allied with deception, but on stage this deception is marked as a deception and can be problematized, discussed, and perhaps even renegotiated and transformed. But while theatre turns out to be a better representation of the relevant forces constituting early modern English society, its effectiveness is still associated with the persistence of ancient rituals. The form of the ban that it delineates and turns into an object of political thought and critique also lends it some latent force of legitimacy. *Richard III* opens a space for philosophical reflection on the mythical curse, but the curse nonetheless persists within the theatre and cannot be overcome because the social effectivity of Shakespeare's drama still relies on it. The curse as a destructive source of social cohesion remains a factor inherent within theatrical representation; theatre has given it a new home, but its reflexivity has not been able to unravel the knot of ritual exclusion and thus save the spectators from its destructive potential.

NOTES

1 Björn Quiring's essay "Curse" is based on his book, *Shakespeare's Curse: The Aporias of Ritual Exclusion in Early Modern Drama*, trans. Michael Winkler and Björn Quiring (London: Routledge, 2014), and is reprinted with the permission of Routledge through PLSclear.

2 See John S. Kselman, "Curse and Blessing," in *Harper's Bible Dictionary*, ed. Paul J. Achtermeier (San Francisco: Harper & Row, 1985), 198.

3 In Giorgio Agamben's sense. See Giorgio Agamben, *Homo Sacer*, trans. Daniel Heller-Roazen (Stanford, CA: Stanford University Press, 1998), 28–9.

4 Agamben, *Homo Sacer*, 27.

5 On these concepts see Walter Benjamin, "Critique of Violence," in *Selected Writings*, ed. Michael Jennings, trans. Edmund Jephcott (Cambridge, MA: Harvard University Press, 1996–2003), 1:238–52.

6 See, e.g., Andreas Holzem, "Eid und Eidschwörer. Wahrheitssuche und Loyalitätsverpflichtung im frühneuzeitlichen Sendgericht," in *Eid und Wahrheitssuche. Studien zu rechtlichen Befragungspraktiken in Mittelalter und früher Neuzeit*, ed. Stefan Esders and Thomas Scharff (Frankfurt a. M.: Peter Lang, 1999), 230.

7 See, e.g., Wilfried Hartmann, *Der Investiturstreit* (Munich: R. Oldenbourg, 2007).

8 Gregory I, *Morals in the Book of Job* (Oxford: J.H. Parker, 1844), 185–6, quoted in Lester K. Little, *Benedictine Maledictions: Liturgical Cursing in Romanesque France* (Ithaca, NY: Cornell University Press, 1993), 98.

9 Little, *Benedictine Maledictions,* 89, 91.

10 Little, *Benedictine Maledictions,* 188.

11 Regino of Prüm, *Libri duo de synodalibus causis et disciplinis ecclesiasticis* (Leipzig: Engelmann, 1840), 371–2. See Little, *Benedictine* Maledictions, 38.

12 Little, *Benedictine Maledictions,* 43, 139. Even until the early modern age an analogous practice is widespread (though officially illegal), namely that of "Mortbeten," i.e., of reading funeral masses for living persons. A presumably Franciscan treatise from fifteenth-century England polemicizes, for example, against those "that … do sing mass of requiem for them that be alive, in hope that they should fare the worse." Keith Thomas, *Religion and the Decline of Magic: Studies in Popular Beliefs in Sixteenth- and Seventeenth-Century England* (London: Penguin, 1991), 37–8.

13 *Dictionary of Christianity,* ed. Jean C. Cooper (Chicago: Fitzroy Dearborn, 1996), *s.v.* "Bell, book and candle."

14 See, e.g., the annotations by Paul Hammond and David Hopkins in John Dryden, *The Poems of John Dryden,* ed. Paul Hammond and David Hopkins (Harlow, UK: Pearson/Longman, 2005), 5:561.

15 See, e.g., Sarah Beckwith, *Signifying God: Social Relation and Symbolic Act in the York Corpus Christi Plays* (Chicago: University of Chicago Press, 2003), 76*ff.*

16 Rosemary Woolf, *The English Mystery Plays* (Berkeley: University of California Press, 1980), 243.

17 David Gordon Newcombe, *Henry VIII and the English Reformation* (London: Routledge, 2003), 50–1.

18 Thomas, *Religion and the Decline of Magic,* 600.

19 Thomas, *Religion and the Decline of Magic,* 600.

20 On the relation of Puritans to excommunication, see also Edmund Sears Morgan, *Visible Saints: The History of a Puritan Idea* (Ithaca, NY: Cornell University Press, 1963), 10, 47–52.

21 Thomas, *Religion and the Decline of Magic,* 601–2.

22 See Ashley Montagu, *The Anatomy of Swearing* (Philadelphia: University of Pennsylvania Press, 2001), 159–61: "The printed works against swearing published between 1601 and 1650, from broadsides to books, numbered many hundreds."

23 On the concept of "work on myth," see Hans Blumenberg, *Work on Myth,* trans. Robert M. Wallace (Cambridge, MA: MIT Press, 1985).

24 On this complicity between theatre and philosophy, see also Walter Benjamin, *The Origin of the German Mourning Play,* trans. John Osborne (London: Verso, 1998), 113–18.

25 Walter Cohen, *Drama of a Nation: Public Theatre in Renaissance England and Spain* (Ithaca, NY: Cornell University Press, 1985), 73 and passim.

26 Scott McMillin and Sally-Beth MacLean, *The Queen's Men and Their Plays* (Cambridge: Cambridge University Press), 1998. See also Stephen Greenblatt, *Will in the World* (New York: Norton, 2004), 162.

27 Samuel Harsnett, *A Discovery of the Fraudulent Practises of John Darrel* (London: John Wolfe, 1599), A3r, quoted in Stephen Greenblatt, *Shakespearean Negotiations* (Berkeley: University of California Press, 1988), 113.

28 Christopher Marlowe, *Doctor Faustus*, in *English Renaissance Drama: A Norton Anthology*, ed. David Bevington, Lars Engle, Katharine Eisaman Maus, and Eric Rasmussen (New York: Norton, 2002), 270.

29 Thomas, *Religion and the Decline of Magic*, 579.

30 Greenblatt, *Shakespearean Negotiations*, passim.

31 E.M.W. Tillyard, *Shakespeare's History Plays* (London: Chatto & Windus, 1959).

32 See, e.g., David Horspool, *Richard III: A Ruler and His Reputation* (London: Bloomsbury, 2015).

33 All citations from *Richard III* according to William Shakespeare, *King Richard III*, ed. Anthony Hammond (London: Arden/Thomson, 2002).

34 A.P. Rossiter, *Angel with Horns and Other Shakespeare Lectures* (London: Longmans, 1961), 16.

35 See also Quiring, *Shakespeare's Curse*, 51–2.

36 Greenblatt, *Shakespearean Negotiations*, 200. See also Sigmund Freud, *Die Traumdeutung* (Frankfurt a. M.: Fischer, 1991), 64.

37 Wolfgang Clemen, *Kommentar zu Shakespeares Richard III: Interpretation eines Dramas* (Göttingen: Vandenhoeck & Ruprecht, 1969), 301.

38 Tillyard, *Shakespeare's History Plays*, 208.

39 Compare 1.1.1–9 and 5.5.29–41.

chapter seven

Way of Life

JAMES KUZNER

Over the last several years, I have been thinking about literature in general, and Shakespeare in particular, as offering a way of life.[1] My inspiration here, at least in part, came not from work in literary studies but from work in philosophy, especially that of Pierre Hadot. Hadot believes that ancient philosophy's offer was not so much an aporia-free system of doctrine as a robust way of living, of confronting problems that were as everyday as they were ontological.[2] Philosophers across classical schools aimed as much to form as to inform, and so Hadot places *askesis* at philosophy's core. Philosophy once was and ought to be not just about identifying what is true and good but also about attending to problems of life and living. In *Shakespeare as a Way of Life*, likewise, I wrote as much about how Shakespeare's plays offer a way of life as about how those plays offer, or are subject to, ideological critique.[3]

Many of Shakespeare's plays, I argued, might sensibly be read as urging *askesis* in some of Hadot's senses: for instance, in prompting an "existential choice" intended to transform the self and in showing far more concern with the kind of life one lives than with elaborating a coherent system of belief. Reading Shakespeare as a sceptical thinker, I tried to highlight his concern with how doubt might allow us to relate to our minds and bodies, to be free, and to love. In the present chapter, I would like to think further about how Shakespeare offers a way of life – and in particular, an art of love – in *A Midsummer Night's Dream*. For Hadot, philosophy is realized through its performance, through becoming a way of life; in Shakespeare's comedy, similarly, love is realized not simply through performance, but through the performance of doubt.

From its first scene, characters in *A Midsummer Night's Dream* conceive of love in terms of violence, war, and conquest. Theseus has wooed

Hippolyta by doing her injuries, Demetrius wants to slay Lysander and feels as if Hermia has slain him, and Helena for her part seems happy to be beaten. Indeed, one of the play's solutions to the violence that structures love involves its own kind of violence: Oberon and Puck forcing homicidal characters into sleep and then drugging them. Conjoining love and violence so often, Shakespeare's play can make "love is war" seem like the only apt metaphor for romance.[4]

All the same, the play also offers alternative, non-violent versions of love.[5] We might look, as some readers do, to two moments when characters conceive of love in terms of union: when violence between lover and beloved seems not possible because there isn't much of a "between" separating lovers at all. Specifically, we might look to Helena's portrayal of what her relationship with Hermia once was, when they felt "as if our hands, our sides, voices and minds, / Had been incorporate" – when these friends, "like to a double cherry," had "two seeming bodies, but one heart" (3.2.200–12).[6] If we take what Lysander says seriously, we might also look to one of his declarations of love for Hermia, when he says that their love might comprise "one heart, one bed, two bosoms, and one troth" (2.2.41). Helena and Lysander may well use the rhetoric of unity in order to manipulate Hermia, but they both at least portray love as gentle, mutual, and reciprocal,[7] so much so that their portrayals are sometimes said to accord with Aristophanes's famous account of love in Plato's *Symposium*, in which the search for love is the search for a lost unity.[8] Here the story of love becomes not a story of conquest but a story of self-completion, of the self's move from lack to wholeness, from restlessness to peace.

But Shakespeare conjoins peace and love in other ways as well. When love in the play is not a story of conquest, it is not always a story of completion. In at least one moment, love and peace come together when love involves what we often think that it ought to overcome – serious, thoroughgoing doubt – and when the story of love, the end toward which it moves, cannot be discerned.

The moment I have in mind occurs in act 4, when Theseus and Egeus awaken the central quartet of lovers after the chaos in the wood. The lovers all seem changed. They may have changed in many ways, but the change most obvious to me is in how tentative they are, how unsure of themselves and their love. When Lysander attempts to account for himself, and for how these four reached a "gentle concord" after so much discord, he seems not to know what to say. "I shall reply amazedly," he says, "Half sleep, half waking; but as yet, I swear, / I cannot truly say how I came here" (4.1.145–7). Lysander eventually remembers how they entered the wood, but not how they entered their present state of peace. He certainly doesn't conceive of that state as one he has deserved, earned, or achieved, and that seems important. More important, perhaps, is the fact that Lysander's inability to account for himself, to "truly say" what has happened to him, arises here for the first time, when he is less combative than he has ever been.

Demetrius, for his part, can recall how he got to the wood: with Helena's help. But he cannot recall how he ended up loving her again:

> I wot not by what power –
> But by some power it is – my love to Hermia,
> Melted as the snow, seems to me now
> As the remembrance of an idle gaud
> Which in my childhood I did dote upon,
> And all the faith, the virtue of my heart,
> The object and the pleasure of mine eye,
> Is only Helena. (4.1.163–70)

Demetrius, too, abandons the wilful, headstrong behaviour that defined his earlier encounters with nearly everyone. He realizes that he is subject to a power greater than him, so much greater, in fact, that he cannot give it a name. This pleases Theseus, who arranges for the couples to be wed. The duke and those with him then exit, leaving the lovers to themselves, and now we see that their self-doubt is deep-seated, not merely performed so as to satisfy authority. Their lingering uncertainty is interesting enough – to me, anyway – to dwell on the next six lines. They speak enigmatically:

> DEMETRIUS: These things seem small and undistinguishable,
> Like far-off mountains turned into clouds.
>
> HERMIA: Methinks I see these things with parted eye,
> When everything seems double.
>
> HELENA: So methinks:
> And I have found Demetrius like a jewel,
> Mine own, and not mine own. (4.1.186–91)

Bewilderment abounds. Given that, we might wonder whether these lovers have learned anything about love. I think that they have, and that they've actually learned something pretty important. (Even if, arguably, they forget what they've learned by the time of the rude mechanicals' performance in the play's final act.) To explain what they've learned, I'll examine three of the lovers in turn.

Let me begin with Demetrius, simply because he comes first. When he says, "These things seem small and undistinguishable," "these things" could refer to many things: to the wood outside Athens, to the interaction they've just had with Theseus and Egeus, to the circumstances of their awakening. At the least, "these things" would seem to refer to what has happened in the wood and to the resolution. Demetrius has just professed certainty as to how he now loves Helena and only Helena. At the same time, he also clearly acknowledges limits to clear perception, and to how far his certainty extends. He's admitting that he can't see what's in the distance. Whatever it is, is "small and undistinguishable."

The simile in the second line I find especially telling. Some readers, with reason, see the "far off mountains turned into clouds" as Shakespeare drawing our attention to love's metamorphic quality, its power to transform us for good and for ill.[9] Still, I think the simile draws our attention as much to the sheer murkiness of love as it does to its metamorphoses. Demetrius hopes, perhaps, that the future to which he tends with Helena has a mountain's solidity. But it could be no more substantial than a cloud; and right now, after whatever has happened in the wood, clouds are what the horizon seems to hold. Maybe the future, when they reach it, will impress them with its dimensions and its splendour, will implant in them the wish to reach love's summit. Or maybe they will not meet anything so solid, and whatever substance love has had, or could have, has already been eroded and soon will evaporate altogether. Whatever the case, Demetrius's hesitancy, uncertainty, and doubt about his own powers seem to me far superior to the aggressive resolve characteristic of him hitherto, and far more auspicious when it comes to love.

Hermia, too, sees "these things," these changes in their lives, with incertitude. When she entered the wood, she saw all through the lens of a single-minded, uncomplicated love for Lysander, viewing him as her other half so adamantly that when he leaves her side, she imagines that the only options left to her are to find him or die, as though her heart could not beat without his: "I well perceive you are not nigh. / Either death or you I'll find immediately" (2.2.154–5). Now, though, she lays claim to double vision and a complicated, ambivalent love. Perhaps Hermia, deflated a bit, dimly recalls Lysander's vitriol, his spurning of her not long ago. Perhaps she realizes, as Nancy Cass does in *Silas Marner*, that nothing, not even love, is as good as it seems at first.[10] Perhaps

Hermia realizes, as Nancy's husband Godfrey fails to realize, that no life can be thoroughly joyous.

Whatever Hermia realizes, she at least realizes that love for her is no longer a simple story by which two become one, the story that Lysander tells her in the wood and that I referred to earlier. When "everything seems double," as it does for Hermia, love cannot make one of two. Love is a story in which two remain two, or even a story in which one becomes two. Once Hermia saw herself and her love simplistically, marked by Cupid's "best arrow with the golden head" and by "the simplicity of Venus's doves" (1.1.170–1). Now she sees all with a parted eye. Lysander lodges no objection, so perhaps he has learned something similar. I hope that he has.

Early in the play, Hermia and Lysander famously lament that the course of true love never does run smooth, for reasons that even they view as rather hackneyed. Lovers are either too distant in rank or years, or too reliant on the advice of friends. That, or war, sickness, or death gets in the way. In this view, we might say, the course of true love runs crooked because of obstacles that appear on love's path and that force lovers to stray from a course that, in itself, runs clear and straight.

Were Hermia and Lysander to have this exchange again in act 4, they would need to alter their view. Love's course won't run smooth, not because of obstacles that arise on the path but because there are two paths, because – when you see all with a parted eye – it becomes hard to answer the question of which path is right. Seeing double, how could Hermia know which path to take? How could she know whether to pledge fidelity to Lysander absolutely, or whether, instead, to commit to him with only half a heart? How could she know that both paths won't lead to the same place? Whatever answers a reader might offer, I leave the scene thinking that never again can love, or her sense of Lysander, be simple.

Hermia's double vision has received considerable comment, but the reading perhaps most germane to this chapter – and collection – comes from David Marshall.[11] Marshall argues that we must understand Hermia in terms of performance, of a certain theatrical self-consciousness that she possesses at different moments in the play, and perhaps never more acutely than here: "Hermia's double vision of these things, her parted eye, comes from her parted I: the doubling and dividing of her 'I' into two parts – Hermia and not Hermia, the part and the actor before us."[12] While I might use different terms, I certainly agree that Shakespeare has in mind a paradox having to do with love and its performance. On the one hand, love is not love unless it is performed, inventively and artfully.

For Shakespeare, how could it be otherwise? On the other hand, the performance of love can call love into question, as we see, for instance, when Demetrius and Lysander profess their love for Helena while drugged in the wood. Just as Hermia does not know which path of love to take – the one in which she commits to Lysander whole or half-heartedly – so she cannot know just how to interpret Lysander's own expressions of devotion. Should she respond with conviction, with uncertainty, or with conviction of uncertainty?

Helena, equally perplexed, elaborates her own double vision. She explores what such vision entails not for the path of love, but for possession of the one that she loves. Helena *does* say that she has happened upon Demetrius as one would happen upon a jewel, and this might set off alarms for those looking to practise an art of love, especially since much of the play has been about who, in love, has a right to whom, about who gets to possess whom: about whether Demetrius or Lysander has a right to Hermia, and then Helena; about whether Oberon or Titania has a right to the changeling boy; about whether Helena has a right to Hermia as a friend. Conflicts over possession have made love more like war.

That Helena refers to Demetrius as a jewel is not encouraging. Yet even though Helena conceives of subjects as being like objects, she leaves the wood having accepted that she might not have any unassailable right to Demetrius. The beloved is only ever, at best, one's own and also not one's own.[13] The dream of total, and totally secure, possession can never be realized. (And that dream, the play has shown, was always a nightmare to begin with.) Demetrius being Helena's own but not her own also means that love can't complete Helena in the way that her relationship with Hermia once did. If Demetrius does and does not belong to her, he can never be Helena's other half in any straightforward way. Whatever love they now have will need to be more complex than that.

In thinking of Demetrius as a jewel, Helena falls short of a certain standard: of the "non-will to possess" that, according to Roland Barthes, might define the art of love. We are, Barthes writes, "to let come (from the other) what comes, to let pass (from the other) what goes; to possess nothing, to repel nothing; to receive, not to keep."[14] Helena cannot keep from wanting to keep Demetrius. But if she still dreams of possession, perhaps she has managed to rid her love of the possessiveness – the desire to make Demetrius indisputably, certainly hers – that makes violence more likely.

There may even be another sense in which Helena's comparison of Demetrius to a jewel is not solely discouraging. If we understand the jewel not only as a possession but also as a cut stone, it refracts light and bends lines. If we see Helena as not only looking *at* Demetrius as a jewel, but also as looking *through* him as a jewel, we can see how he might change, colour, and double her perspective without quite determining it. Just as she does and does not possess him, then, so he does and does not possess her or her way of seeing. How far this is from the moment when the drugged Lysander wakes and sees "Transparent Helena!," when all seemed so clear (2.2.102).[15]

One common technique that sceptics use in order to achieve tranquillity, and that I explored in *Shakespeare as a Way of Life*, is the holding of opposed visions in an equipollence.[16] At least as early as Sextus Empiricus, balancing views against each other, being double-minded in that sense, allows us not to be so single-minded about pursuing our passions. In the scene I've been discussing, the quartet of lovers practise something like this. Helena views Demetrius as hers and as not hers; Hermia sees an attractive path of love and a less attractive one; Demetrius sees a future of solid mountains and of insubstantial clouds. These double visions of love, I think, account for the *ataraxia* that these lovers seem to have achieved. In this, Shakespeare's play suggests that one way to counter overpowering passion – whether of love or hate – is to entertain opposed notions. Think that someone belongs to you absolutely? Entertain the idea that no one belongs to anyone. Convinced that your future is rock solid? Imagine that it might dissolve into nothing. Sure that your lover embodies all the best ideals? Consider that they could be just awful. Perhaps, Shakespeare suggests, such a practice could help settle your heart.

The reading that I have offered so far may seem to make too much of too little. After all, Demetrius now questions whether they are even awake or still sleep. We can, if we want, interpret his bewilderment as Shakespeare's way of suggesting that there's little of substance to be taken from what has come before. The fogginess of it all – the emphasis on the small, indistinguishable, and doubled – could be Shakespeare's way of suggesting that there isn't much to be learned about why, who, and how we love. It could be Shakespeare's way of preparing us for the apology that comes in the play's epilogue.

I don't think that this is quite how the scene's uncertainty works. I think that uncertainty in love *is* what the characters have learned, and what the audience is meant to learn.[17] We must remember that until Oberon and Puck separate the four lovers so that they do not kill each other, they have been nothing if not certain. Hermia and Lysander start out certain that their love is true love, and that they must run away. Demetrius is certain that he must run after Hermia, so certain that he feels his pursuit of this singular, irreplaceable person gives him every right to kill Lysander. Helena is adamant that any relationship with Demetrius is better than nothing, that any place in his life is a place of high privilege.

After love-in-idleness adds to the confusion in the wood, certainty ratchets up – as do threats of violence. Lysander insists that he would run through fire for Helena, and Demetrius that Helena is a goddess; each man vows to slay the other. Helena is convinced that both mock her and that Hermia mocks her too, while Hermia becomes convinced that her former best friend has betrayed her and deserves to die.

Act 4 does away with all this. Sure about their futures in the sense that they know whom they will marry, the lovers are unsure about nearly everything else. They are unsure about what their married futures hold, whether they are as solid as mountain ranges or as insubstantial as clouds. Until act 4, Oberon had offered the only way to pry love and violence apart, a way that involves an incapacitating violence of its own. Then uncertainty and humility arrive, with Lysander and Demetrius so unsure of themselves that threats of violence seem inconceivable, and Helena and Hermia so unsure of love that desire is not the violent perturbation that it once was. Uncertainty quells the violence of desire and desire that leads to violence.

In *A Midsummer Night's Dream* uncertain love brings peace. Marshall reads the play as asking whether it would be possible to have a powerful theatrical vision without imposing it on someone else, and Laura Levine answers that question in the negative. According to this play, in her view, theatre is always a kind of violence, even a kind of rape.[18] Anytime someone has a vision of love, one seeks to force that vision on someone else. This is true at some points in the play, to be sure, but not this one. Openness, not imposition, defines the doubt that these lovers perform, and the visions that they have, at the wood's edge.

What might all this imply about the art of love? Here are some of the more basic implications. Just as these lovers cannot account for how they have ended up as they have, so we ought not to assume that we understand why our own hearts are the way they are, or that our hearts are only one way. Just as Demetrius both is and is not Helena's, so we ought to assume that the beloved is at best ours and not ours, and only so for a time. Just as Demetrius knows that he cannot say what the future of his love might hold, so we ought to take little for granted about our own horizons, to admit that those horizons are open.[19]

Accepting such a clouded vision might seem opposed to the art of love. In *The Art of Loving*, for instance, Erich Fromm writes that in love we must aim for clarity, must strive to move from narcissism to objectivity. To practise the art of love we must develop "the faculty to see people as *they are*, objectively, and to be able to separate this *objective* picture from a picture which is formed by one's desires and fears."[20] *A Midsummer Night's Dream*, by contrast, suggests not only that objectivity is impossible, but also that striving for it may be undesirable. I say this not, or at least not only, because love in this play needs fantasy – because characters "as *they are*" need to be gilded by imagination in order to even appear lovable (because, to cite just two examples, Lysander may well be weak of faith and Demetrius almost certainly a monster). Objectivity may not be worth striving for, the play suggests, not so much because love depends upon fantasy but because striving to see someone objectively assumes an overly confident view of our capacity to see clearly.[21] Love in Shakespeare's play demands acknowledging not our capacity for this but our incapacity; it demands more that we see the limits of our powers of perception than that we sharpen those powers.[22]

In this, Shakespeare's play exists at some distance not just from Fromm but even from Alain Badiou's more nuanced sense of how love should change our way of seeing. For Badiou, love is not an essentially inward experience but an outward looking one, a construction made not "from the perspective of One but from the perspective of Two."[23] Whereas Fromm believes that love involves developing as objective a view of the beloved as possible, Badiou believes that love involves incorporating the beloved's perspective into one's own and seeing the world accordingly. Love demands fidelity to this new perspective, to seeing through the prism of difference and to constructing a truth, moment by moment and day by day. Badiou advocates fidelity to a perspective that is, in some way, doubled by the beloved's; he advocates, in this sense if not Hermia's, seeing the world with a parted eye. But Shakespeare suggests that anyone who has loved for very long – who has been through that wood – will know that we cannot quite construct a truth together. Our vision is too feeble and fragmented for that.

Such a kind of love, based more in incapacity than capacity, in some ways may be dull and disappointing. In fact, for all its fancy, *A Midsummer Night's Dream* compresses the trajectory of many relationships. When love begins, we're often full of confidence – as Stendhal has it, we endow the beloved with a thousand perfections, and we imagine that the beloved might perfect us.[24] The beloved seems divine and seems to inspire a certain divinity in us. Robert Solomon, in fact, opines that the only reason for loving is that the beloved will bring out the best in us, will help us to become our best selves.[25] (To cite just one example from the play, desire for Hermia leads Lysander to think that he has power to thwart authority, until his newfound desire for Helena makes him think himself flame-retardant, able to thwart the natural order [2.2.102].)

Then time passes. Those we love start to seem less perfect. We're less sure of their flawlessness, and we're less sure of ourselves. If the play suggests that this can be a good thing and that love can make us better – if it can do anything apart from make us more deluded, and more likely to murder – it would do so not by making us more perfect or more powerful. Instead, love would make us better by making us more aware of our own inability. Love would make us better by making us humbler. We would learn to live with the uncertainty that comes from the certainty of imperfection and of imperfect perception, and we would acknowledge the hazy future that this promises. Then, and only then, love might last.

Enduring love has a hard time finding its way onto the stage. Badiou writes that literature in general, and theatre in particular, "contains very little in terms of the experience of its [love's] endurance over time."[26] Indeed, Badiou goes so far as to say, "If you watch plays that show the struggles of young lovers against the despotism of the family universe – a classic theme – you could give them all as sub-title Marivaux's *The Triumph of Love*.... It's the triumph of love, but not its duration" (81–2). If Badiou is right, *A Midsummer Night's Dream* would be rather unusual. The play ends uncomfortably, and, as many readers have pointed out, Shakespeare might not show us love's triumph.[27] But in the way that he compresses a long course of love, Shakespeare does show us how we might make for love's duration.

Shakespeare gives us licence, if we want, to pass over the lines I've treated as ones spoken by impaired characters who remain in an altered state. But if we do, I think we miss out on one important way that love can avoid tragedy: when lovers admit how much they don't know. Admitting this, they are changed, bettered not by being made more powerful, or more adept, or more perfect, but by being made to see the limits of their powers and their perfections. When their certainty becomes uncertainty, the war of love becomes peace. The art of love, in this play, is an art of doubt.

NOTES

1 See, for instance, *Shakespeare as a Way of Life* (New York: Fordham University Press, 2016).

2 For Hadot's most straightforward articulation of this position, see *Philosophy as a Way of Life,* ed. Arnold I. Davidson (Malden, MA: Blackwell, 1995).

3 For a book-length account of the virtues and vices of the critique of ideology, see Rita Felski, *The Limits of Critique* (Chicago: University of Chicago Press, 2015).

4 For a few of the many readings of the play that focus on connections between desire and violence, oftentimes to reinforce patriarchal and misogynist stereotypes, see, for instance, Louis Adrian Montrose, "'Shaping Fantasies': Figurations of Gender and Power in Elizabethan Culture," *Representations* 2 (1983): 61–94; Laura Levine, "Rape, Repetition, and the Politics of Closure in *A Midsummer Night's Dream*," *Feminist Readings of Early Modern Culture: Emerging Subjects,* ed. Valerie Traub, M. Lindsay Kaplan, and Dympna Callaghan, 210–28 (New York: Cambridge University Press, 1996); Bruce Boehrer, "Economies of Desire in *A Midsummer Night's Dream*," *Shakespeare Studies* 32 (2004): 97–117; and Gabriel Rieger, "'I woo'd thee with my sword, / And won thy love doing thee injuries': The Erotic Economies of *A Midsummer Night's Dream*," *Upstart Crow* 28 (2009): 70–87.

5 I agree, then, with Hugh Grady's sense that *A Midsummer Night's Dream* explores "one of the fundamental possibilities of aesthetic representation: to distantiate us from the familiar human world, to lead us into imagining other modes of living and loving, to look critically into received ideologies of love and marriage." Grady, "Shakespeare and Impure Aesthetics: The Case of *A Midsummer Night's Dream*," *Shakespeare Quarterly* 59, no. 3 (2008): 274–302, esp. 290.

6 All references to the play are to *A Midsummer Night's Dream,* ed. Harold F. Brooks (New York: Bloomsbury, 2015).

7 For one account that upholds Lysander and Hermia as a kind of relationship ideal, see Maurice Hunt, "Individuation in *A Midsummer Night's Dream*," *South Central Review* 3, no. 2 (1986): 1–13, esp. 8.

8 For an account that reads the play as Neoplatonist in a thoroughgoing sense, see Jane K. Brown, "*Discordia Concors*: On the Order of *A Midsummer Night's Dream*," *Modern Language Quarterly* 48, no. 1 (1987): 20–41.

9 C.L. Barber, in a mostly positive vein, writes, "The teeming metamorphoses which we encounter are placed, in this way, in a medium and in a moment when the perceived structure of the outer world breaks down, where the body and its environment interpenetrate in unaccustomed ways, so that the seeming separateness and stability of identity is lost." *Shakespeare's Festive Comedy: A Study of Dramatic Form and Its Relation to Social Custom* (Princeton, NJ: Princeton University Press, 2012), 153. Maurice Hunt, by contrast, argues that while Demetrius's lines have "captured the metamorphic

quality of the most popular of Shakespeare's early comedies," aspects of Shakespeare's play nonetheless "confirm the importance of individuation for Shakespeare's design" and for love. "Individuation in *A Midsummer Night's Dream*," esp. 1.

10 George Eliot, *Silas Marner* (New York: Alfred A. Knopf, 1993), 186.

11 For two interesting glosses here, see Jeffrey Shulman, "Bottom Is Up: The Role of Illusion in *A Midsummer Night's Dream*," *Essays in Arts and Sciences* 16 (1987): 9–21, esp. 9, and James Calderwood, "*A Midsummer Night's Dream*: The Illusion of Drama," *MLQ* 26, no. 4 (1965): 506–22, esp. 522. Shulman argues that we need to approach the play with a parted eye or "double focus" – with love on the one hand, and art on the other (9). Calderwood, for his part, finds "an unmistakable doubleness" in the play, one by which reality and fantasy "fuse and yet separate" (522). As C.L. Barber puts it, this is a play marked by "conscious double vision" (*Shakespeare's Festive Comedy*, 163).

12 David Marshall, "Exchanging Visions: Reading *A Midsummer Night's Dream*," *ELH* 49, no. 3 (1982): 543–75, esp. 563–4.

13 Marshall reads Helena's bewilderment as evidence of her ambivalence about Demetrius (as opposed to Hermia) as a partner. While Helena "perhaps regards newly affectionate Demetrius with a look of dazed recognition, as if he were both familiar and strange, both a part of herself and not herself ... it is hard to imagine that such a union would adequately repair what has been sundered or restore what has been lost" ("Exchanging Visions," 562).

14 Roland Barthes, *A Lover's Discourse*, trans. Richard Howard (New York: Farrar, Straus, and Giroux, 1978), 233–4.

15 Here I am grateful to Julia R. Lupton, who suggested this thought to me.

16 See especially chapter 5, "Looking Two Ways at Once in *Timon of Athens*." The reading I offer in the present chapter is more (or at least differently) optimistic about the potential of looking two ways at once.

17 For a somewhat more positive reading of what the quartet of lovers feel here, see Ronald F. Miller, "*A Midsummer Night's Dream*: The Fairies, Bottom, and the Mystery of Things," *Shakespeare Quarterly* 26, no. 3 (1975): 254–68. Miller writes, "There is something profoundly suggestive in the reverent mix of wonder and joy the lovers convey when they wake to find themselves blessed with an end to their tribulations. They are not unlike Milton's Adam, waking to find his dream was real" (259). Miller, along with other readers, also turns to Bottom to explore how mystery operates in the play. For another example, see Frank Kermode, *Shakespeare, Spenser, Donne: Renaissance Essays* (London: Routledge, 2005), esp. 208–9.

18 Marshall, "Exchanging Visions," 546; and Levine, "Rape, Repetition, and the Politics of Closure," 216.

19 For another, ecocritical perspective on how the play highlights our deficits in self-knowledge, see Robert N. Watson, "The Ecology of Self in *Midsummer Night's Dream*," in *Ecocritical Shakespeares*, ed. Lynne Dickson Bruckner, 33–56 (Burlington, VT: Ashgate, 2011).

20 Erich Fromm, *The Art of Loving* (New York: Open Road Media, 2013), 109.

21 For an essay that shows how the overall pattern of the play can be hard to perceive, see Andrew D. Weiner, "'Multiformitie Uniforme': *A Midsummer Night's Dream*," *ELH* 38, no. 3 (1971): 329–49.

22 As R.W. Dent puts it in a classic essay, the love of the central quartet remains "in its essence as inexplicable as ever." R.W Dent, "Imagination in *A Midsummer Night's Dream*," *Shakespeare Quarterly* 15, no. 2 (1964): 115–29, esp. 117. Another way of putting this would be as Marjorie Garber does, that "*A Midsummer Night's Dream* is throughout a celebration of the irrationality of love, not a criticism of the failure of reason." Garber, *Dream in Shakespeare: From Metaphor to Metamorphosis* (New Haven, CT: Yale University Press, 1974), 84.

23 Alain Badiou, *In Praise of Love*, trans. Peter Bush (London: Serpent's Tail, 2012), 29.

24 Stendhal, *Love*, trans. Gilbert and Suzanne Sale (New York: Penguin, 2004), 45.

25 Robert C. Solomon, *About Love: Reinventing Romance for Our Times* (Indianapolis: Hackett, 2006), 155.

26 Badiou, *In Praise of Love*, 81.

27 For a recent essay about problems of equity that lists dark aspects involved in the play's "resolution," see Peter C. Herman, "Equity and the Problem of Theseus in *A Midsummer Night's Dream*: Or, the Ancient Constitution in Ancient Athens," *Journal for Early Modern Cultural Studies* 14, no. 1 (2014): 4–31, esp. 24.

chapter eight

Care

SHEIBA KIAN KAUFMAN

King Lear's anxiety to unburden himself of the "cares" of kingship so that he can "crawl toward death," innocent, free, and detached from the oppressive concerns of this earthly plane, dominates the opening scene of Shakespeare's tragedy:

Meantime we will express our darker purpose.
Give me the map there. Know that we have divided
In three our kingdom, and 'tis our fast intent
To shake all cares and business from our age,
Conferring them on younger strengths.[1]

As derived from the old English term for grief and suffering (*caru, cearu*), care is a force to eschew for the aging monarch.[2] As if the physical passing on of the crown could "shake" the "cares and business" of a long reign, Lear's emotional and psychological divestiture is naively conceived as a simple passing of the baton, a mock reading of a final testament that is rendered into the absurd. Cares, however, are obstinate and heavy, clinging tenaciously to Lear's aging soul. In Richard II's description, the crown and cares are immortal partners, inseparable by time and syntax:

Your cares set up do not pluck my cares down.
My care is loss of care, by old care done;
Your care is gain of care, by new care won.
The cares I give I have, though given away;
They tend the crown, yet still with me they stay.[3]

The early modern personification of Care as worry in the realm of worldly ambitions and desires draws upon the classical tradition, as in

Horace's Ode 3.1: "But fear and threats climb up to the same spot as the master; and she withdraws not from the bronze galley, and she even sits behind the horseman – black, gloomy Care."[4] Personified frequently as a masculine figure, Care appears in Edmund Spenser's *Faerie Queene* as the toiling blacksmith:

> Rude was his garment, and to rags all rent,
> Ne better had he, ne for better cared:
> With blistred hands emongst the cinders brent,
> And fingers filthie, with long nayles vnpared,
> Right fit to rend the food, on which he fared.
> His name was *Care*; a blacksmith by his trade,
> That neither day nor night from working spared,
> But to small purpose yron wedges made;
> Those be vnquiet thoughts, that carefull minds inuade.[5]

Care is an intruder in Friar Lawrence's counsel to a perturbed Romeo – "Care keeps his watch in every old man's eye, / And where care lodges, sleep will never lie"[6] – and a fraying force, unravelling man's physical adornments as a reflection of his internal state in *Macbeth*: "Sleep that knits up the raveled sleeve of care."[7] It is the detachment from these "unquiet thoughts" that tantalizes Lear as he approaches retirement and aspires for a rather different form of care – the "kind nursery" he expects from Cordelia as his caregiver in old age.[8]

While detachment from oppressive cares is an envious state of being, the movement from noun to verb, from cares to caring, transforms the burdens of one's ego to concern for others. The dynamics of this semantic movement coexists in *King Lear* and in early modern usage as an active potentiality that transforms individual concern into collaborative possibility, releasing an ego crippled by concern and self-obsession into the emancipatory space of the abode of service to others. The latter state develops individual capacity in empowering others while the former robs the self from attaining a state of self-knowledge that is possible only through an outward-looking orientation. The Latin use of the term *cura* as concept and creation myth, found in the writings of first-century Roman grammarian Hyginus, captures the nature of the keyword *care* as that of both mental oppression *and* the conscientious attention to others that increases one's capacity to empathize with and serve a friend, a family member, a stranger.[9] This chapter draws upon classical conceptions of the multifaceted concept of care and contemporary philosophy engaging with the ethics of care to examine how care as a state of *being* and *doing* develops in Shakespeare's plays.

"Care Is No Cure"[10]

In his *Fabulae* no. 220, Hyginus relates an origin story with a feminine core:

> When Cura was crossing a certain river, she saw some clayey mud. She took it up thoughtfully and began to fashion a man. While she was pondering on what she had done, Jove came up; Cura asked him to give the image life, and Jove readily grant this. When Cura wanted to give it her name, Jove forbade, and said that his name should be given it. But while they were disputing about the name, Tellus arose and said that it should have her name, since she had given her own body. They took Saturn for judge; he seems to have decided for them: Jove, since you gave him life [take his soul after death; since Tellus offered her body] let her receive his body; since Cura first fashioned him, let her possess him as long as he lives, but since there is controversy about his name, let him be called *homo,* since he seems to be made from *humus.*[11]

The origins of man's inevitable life of "care" in both the sense of individual worry and collective concern appears in Robert's Burton's *Anatomy of Melancholy* as a significant contributor to the development of one's melancholic disposition. As Stephanie Shirilan explains, in the *Anatomy,* Burton is "profoundly concerned with the relationship between care as fear or worry and care as *caritas* or charity. His promotion of melancholy rests precisely on the idea that the excess cares and supposedly groundless fears suffered by the melancholic attest to a generosity of spirit evidenced in his or her sensitivity to the suffering of others."[12] Burton "valorizes care (as in worry or fear) as the root of compassionate feeling";[13] Burton, in other words, reads Hyginus's feminine fable in terms of its Old English associations with one's state of being, as in Shakespeare and Spenser's references to the masculine personification of insomnia inducing Care. This dual conceptualization of care is captured, for instance, in Thomas Elyot's Latin-English dictionary, where *Cura* is defined as "care, thought, study, diligence, warke or labour, also loue."[14] Although the Old English etymology of care as worry and grief is distinct from the Latin *cura,* care as verb – to care for – rather than care as a state of being is in use by the thirteenth century. The English derivative of *cura,* cure, circulates in the fourteenth century, leaving a rich linguistic heritage of association with spiritual and medicinal healing called upon in the work of Shakespeare and his contemporaries.[15]

The frequent early modern use of a personified Care departs from its Roman hermeneutic in Hyginus's myth as that speaking to the ethics of caring for others, a concept found in the Stoic writing of Seneca where human perfection is attained through care. As Warren Thomas Reich, drawing upon Konrad Burdach's early twentieth-century work, explains in his seminal essay on the historical evolution of the idea of care, "In this Stoic view, care was the key to the process of becoming truly human. For Seneca, the word care meant *solicitude*; it also had connotations of attentiveness, conscientiousness, and devotion."[16] Martin Heidegger elaborates on this duality or the "ambiguity of the terms 'cura'" in *Being and Time* in terms of Seneca's perfection, claiming that "the *perfectio* of human being – becoming what one can be in being free for one's ownmost possibilities (project) – is an 'accomplishment' of 'care.'"[17] For Heidegger, "being-in-the-word is essentially care."[18]

Warren T. Reich's affirmative reading of the Cura myth has profound implications for the well-known clash of civilizations thesis, a reading of human relationships that maintains an inevitable battle of differences rather than collaborative unity in diversity: "The Myth of Care offers a subversively different image of human society, with very different implications for ethics in general and bioethics in particular."[19] As Reich explains, care is the "glue," the binding source, the aspirational material for human society, the means to perfection of universal virtues from within diverse cultures and religions. Writing from a personalist philosophy, Milton Mayeroff's 1971 *On Caring* explicates the nature of this dynamic state of being in the world that emphasizes the "primacy of process," which often forms through the struggle of "overcoming obstacles and difficulties."[20] Caring is intricately linked with familial relationships and by extension with others in one's community; it is a means of being in the world with oneself and with others that is focused on capacity building: "To help another person to grow is at least to help him to care for something or someone apart from himself."[21] As in the Cura Myth, caring in Mayeroff's estimation concerns the foundation of being in the world: "We are 'in place' in the world through having our lives ordered by inclusive caring."[22]

While caring is not limited to familial responsibilities or simply for vulnerable populations, it is noteworthy to read Shakespeare's engagement with an ethics of care found in *King Lear* alongside *The Tempest*. Both plays depict the needs of two particularly vulnerable populations: the elderly and the poor in *Lear* and an orphaned and disfigured Caliban in *The Tempest*.[23] Through these prominent depictions of poverty and oppression, Shakespeare adumbrates the hard and thorny path to developing virtues in not only Lear and Prospero, but also in Edgar, the future king, and in Caliban, an independent sovereign reigning his reclaimed island by the conclusion of the play. Mayeroff's contribution to the discourse on care includes an inventory of virtues or "major ingredients" that comprise caring: knowing, alternating rhythms, patience, honesty, trust, humility, hope, and courage. In *King Lear*, the limitation of "ethical possibilities," in James Kearney's terms, leaves us with a state of knowledge that is hindered from more than minor acts of caring, the "small ethical moments" that brighten the darkness of the play.[24] In *The Tempest*, Shakespeare takes us to the fringes of care in the guardian–ward relationship between Prospero and Caliban, exploring the challenges and potentials of patience and trust.

Caring on the Heath

Lear's aspirational desire to detach from the cares of kingship depends on his attachment to Cordelia, the daughter who will succour him through her "kind nursery" (1.1.122), an anticipated time of ongoing care that never comes to fruition in the fullness of his expectations at the beginning of the play.[25] Ethical possibility, often hinging on a form of care through hospitality and solidarity with others, is muted, lost, or forgotten in Shakespeare's tragedies, dramaturgically relegated to narration rather than dramatization, and temporally distant from the chaotic tragic actions on stage. In Othello, caring as a form of hospitality is part of Othello's defence of his prior relationships with Brabantio and his daughter as he proclaims in front of the duke, "Her father loved me, oft invited me."[26] He gestures toward a past temporality of hospitality and reciprocity between Othello and Desdemona's family that seems hopelessly lost in the face of Brabantio's accusations toward his new son-in-law.

While the continual care of Cordelia's kind nursery is a desirable state unattainable in Lear's lifetime, Lear's understanding of the work needed to achieve such kindness evolves in his interactions with Edgar as Poor Tom on the heath, an "ethical catalyst in the play"[27] who brings Lear to account through his extreme representation of poverty. Edgar as Poor Tom manifests the characteristics of both the inhabitants of Bedlam Hospital and an assumed con artist, a well-known "social stereotype" as William Carroll describes.[28] In the sixteenth century, various acts, such as the Poor Relief Act of 1601, were considered and passed attempting to distinguish the social situation of the "true" poor or "approved beggars" that could be assisted and those to be physically punished in some form, bringing greater attention to the needs of those marginalized while firmly upholding certain biases, prejudices, and fears of those outside the social constraints of the greater society.[29] Poor Tom, like Caliban, stands as a figure on the fringes of society by mirroring in his entertainment of insanity the breakdown of the kingdom and the family nucleus in the play. In this sense, as scholars have noted, poverty is not only a physical state reflecting the plight of unfortunate citizens of the day, but also a spiritual state, the "nothingness" at the heart of Lear's unexamined life. When Lear spontaneously reflects on his duties towards the destitute in his kingdom, he expresses regret for his neglect:

> Poor naked wretches, whereso'er you are,
> That bide the pelting of this pitiless storm,
> How shall your houseless heads and unfed sides,
> Your looped and windowed raggedness, defend you
> From seasons such as these? *O, I have ta'en*
> *Too little care of this!* Take physic, pomp,
> Expose thyself to feel what wretches feel,
> That thou mayst shake the superflux to them,
> And show the heavens more just. (3.4.28–36; emphasis added)[30]

At this moment before Edgar's entrance, Lear's reflective prayer on the state of the poor is the gateway to the knowledge of those whom he has neglected. As if in answer to his desire to "feel what wretches feel," Edgar's suffering being appears as a test assaying the fledgling virtue of care sprouting in Lear's heart. As Mayeroff writes, to care for others is to saturate oneself in a deep understanding of another person:

> To care for another person, I must be able to understand him and his world as if I were inside it. I must be able to see, as it were, with his eyes what his world is like to him and how he sees himself. Instead of merely looking at him in a detached way from outside, as if he were a specimen, I must be able to be with him in his world, "going" into his world in order to sense from "inside" what life is like for him, what he is striving to be, and what he requires to grow.[31]

As with the progressive development of a newly acquired virtue, such as care, compassion, and even justice, the framework of understanding hinges on the self in its infantile state and as such, Lear responds to Edgar's physical manifestation of poverty as a reflection of his own psychological and spiritual state: "Has his daughters brought him to this pass?" (3.4.60). In his reading of this revealing scene, with patterns reflecting recognition scenes from romances, Kearney suggests that Lear has not cultivated the capacity to fully recognize the alterity of Edgar as distinct from his own being and as such is unable to empathize with him.[32] In this vein, Edgar's appearance as Poor Tom tests the practice of the virtue of caring that Lear summons in his prayer for the poor. The general "wretches" appearing in the particular figure of Poor Tom invoke a range of responses that revolve around Lear's needs rather than a shivering Tom. Thus, while harm may seem to be the opposite of care, the more accurate antonym is the paralyzing force of apathy, a crucible of selfishness and estrangement from others that deteriorates social bonds, leaving individuals alienated, despairing, and insecure.

Although Poor Tom necessitates care, he is also the indirect caregiver serving primarily as one of Lear's interlocutors. More than just a listening ear, the protean Edgar is the obliging child humouring an aged father figure, taking on the mask Lear wants him to assume as the "good Athenian" (3.4.168), the "learned Theban" (3.4.145), the "noble philosopher" (3.4.160). Here Shakespeare's turn to philosophy is performative, a parading of philosophers from antiquity uniting in their emphasis on virtue as a product of philosophical engagement and care for the self.[33] When Edgar assists Lear by turning away three imagined barking dogs and thereby accommodating his distressed state, Lear acknowledges Edgar's service in this instance of solidarity between two abject souls, proclaiming, "You, sir, I entertain you for one of my hundred, only I do not like the fashion of your garments. You will say they are Persian; but let them be changed" (3.6.77–9). Considering Edgar's rags are far from any sartorial symbols of Eastern elegance, riches, and pomp, the image Lear claims to see is ironic and puzzling. At the same time, Lear's lament on Edgar's clothing informs us of the presence of another persona for Edgar, an invisible Persian figure or Englishman dressed as a Persian, possibly a soldier or an ambassador, graciously aiding Lear in his confrontation with the rancorous dogs populating his suffering mind. Thus, Lear does not accept *Edgar as Poor Tom* into his dissolving retinue in his attempt to salvage his dignity and control over his lost fortunes, but rather as an unknown figure with Persian adornments who succours him much like his Greek philosophers and the wise judge – all figures of aid the forsaken king beseeches in his time of need.

Lear's prayerful reflection reveals the fundamental incoherence of his life, that it was impossible to be a devoted father of his daughters if he was not a devoted servant to his realm. Lear's prayer narrates the movement of the cares of the head to caring in the heart, which becomes, in Seneca's terms, a solicitous attitude toward others. In this sense, his epiphany speaks to Mayeroff's description of the potential conflicts of caring: "My carings must be compatible, in some kind of harmony with one another, if they are to be inclusive enough to enable me to be in-place. My life cannot be harmoniously ordered if, for example, there is a basic incompatibility between caring in my work and caring for my family."[34] Lear achieves Mayeroff's state of knowledge on the journey to develop the virtue of caring: "To care for someone, I must know many things. I must know, for example, who the other is, what his powers and limitations are, what his needs are, and what is conducive to his growth."[35] Lear's tardy arrival to the state of knowledge necessary for caring in the world prevents him from moving beyond theory into practice, but he does arrive at the threshold of appreciating the order of values with caring at its core.[36]

While Lear may not have the time or even the capacity to go beyond a theoretical and limited state of empathy for the poor, Edgar's performance leaves open the possibility for greater understanding of social diversity to permeate his capacity as future king. While theatricality separates Edgar from the true oppression of the state he assumes and later dismantles, nevertheless the physicality of his suffering and the initial familial displacement he undergoes offer him opportunities to develop virtues of sympathy and compassion. Through his dramatic experiment as Poor Tom, Edgar can access a glimmering of suffering otherwise distanced from him and those around him. Perhaps this part does in fact affect his capacities, leading him to claim a portion of lost sympathy in the play, to "*speak* what we feel" (5.3.326; emphasis added), if not the desire for sustained empathy with the poor, "to *feel* what wretches feel," as Lear advocates. There is hope, perhaps, that the future reign of Edgar will be informed by his performance of poverty, in some measure.

Tempering Human Care

Despite his staged ramblings and reflections, Poor Tom speaks an indisputable truth: "Tom's a-cold" (3.4.161). Tom's need, however, is overlooked because of Lear's desire to "feel what wretches feel," to experience the "creaturely existence of the human animal stripped of all prosthetic and pretension."[37] Like Tom's physical suffering, Caliban's enchanted pain inflicted by a wrathful Prospero is the only truth both parties acknowledge:

PROSPERO: If though neglect'st or dost unwillingly
What I command, I'll rack thee with old cramps,
Fill all they bones with aches, make thee roar,
That beasts shall tremble at thy din.

CALIBAN: No, pray thee.
[*Aside*] I must obey. His art is of such power,
It would control my dam's god, Setebos,
And make a vassal of him.[38]

Caliban's pain and Tom's cold are parallel physical ailments manifesting the powerful interior suffering of a displaced orphan and an undermined, soon-to-be-orphaned son. Both require care from the father figures in the plays, yet both are consistently denied such care or, worse, are the victims of abuse. While Lear's encounter with Poor Tom reveals how the "realm of ethical possibility" is "beneath" or "behind the world of Lear," how the ethics of care is manifest in small gestures rather than systematic action, Prospero's care, estrangement, and acknowledgement of Caliban speak to the action of caring that Lear never fully achieves.

While acknowledging the significance of seemingly conflicting power structures defining Caliban's being and doing, namely readings that see Caliban as a victim of colonization and those that see Miranda as the victim of attempted rape, with Caliban as the perpetrator of an even greater abuse of brute power, the question of the efficacy of early modern education and servitude as enacted in Prospero's cell, aptly analysed by Tom Lindsay, aligns with the discourse on care I am elaborating.[39] As Lindsay explains, the play is a "drama about the workings of Prospero's household and schoolroom, his 'cell'" that unsuccessfully hosts a training that emphasizes a "set of capacities for political action – submissiveness and assertiveness in particular."[40] While Miranda successfully absorbs this education from the patriarch, well known in the period's educational manuals and procedures, her ultimate outlet for political action is inherent in her nobility, whereas Caliban is unable to channel his learning in action, either through household tasks that are bereft of "edifying" skills or through a greater social reality, that is the goal of such education.[41] Thus, this failure in educational advancement and empowerment is in part because of the limited focus on behaviour and powers of expression.

According to Lindsay, Caliban's frustrations and "disillusionment" lead him to enact his own forms of political agency that attempt to harm the personhood of Miranda, and ultimately Prospero.[42] Perhaps, in both the case of Caliban's oppression and his attempt at sexual and political domination, it is the fundamental loss of the capacity to care or the inability to care appropriately by knowing the needs of the new resident within the cell or household that leads to such abuses of power.

Caliban's counter-narrative to Prospero's claim of kindly guardianship affirms rather than dismisses the care Prospero alleges to have bestowed on an orphaned Caliban on the enchanted island in *The Tempest*:

CALIBAN: When thou cam'st first,
Thou strok'st me and made much of me; wouldst give me
Water with berries in't; and teach me how
To name the bigger light, and how the less,
That burn by day and night. And then I loved thee
And showed thee all the qualities o' th' isle,
The fresh springs, brine pits, barren place and fertile.
Cursed be I that did so!

PROSPERO: Thou most lying slave,
Whom stripes may move, not kindness. I have used thee
(Filth as thou art) with humane care, and lodged thee
In mine own cell till thou didst seek to violate
The honor of my child. (1.2.332–48)

The verbs of care incorporate associations of physical touch ("strok'st"), generosity ("give"), and dedication to capacity building ("teach me"), which lead Caliban to "love" in this seemingly joyful family affair which is never staged and only left to the audience to imagine. This prior time, like Othello's former hospitable welcome and Lear's future dream of kind nursery, remains bracketed, accessible only through narration and shared memory. This off-stage, hidden moment of hospitable care involved taking Caliban into a smaller, more intimate, and familial dwelling within the island, similar to an au pair in Julia Reinhard Lupton's reading of Caliban's minority status. Lupton's powerful characterization of Caliban identifies his various states first as an orphaned child on the island after the loss of his mother, Sycorax, and then as an adopted child in the care of Prospero and Miranda, an erring youth and quasi-peer who is then outcast, shunned, imprisoned, and convicted as an adult for his assault on Miranda.[43] The tragedy of the failure of an ethics of care in the backstory of their relationship is manifest in Prospero's claim to have treated Caliban with "humane care" despite the doubt of the capacities of his "vile race" (1.2.357) that Miranda voices in the opening act. Thus, in his claim of an initial attempt toward some sort of equality, it is evident that "'humane' characterizes both Prospero's moral bearing toward Caliban (he acted humanely) and his expectations for Caliban's moral aptitude (he treated Caliban as a human, capable of personhood)."[44] While Prospero's intentions with the young Caliban may never be fully revealed, his early acts of care for Caliban take him to the fringes of care in his ability to go beyond the state of knowledge into the realm of doing that Lear never arrives at. In Mayeroff's estimation, Prospero's initial welcome of Caliban calls upon a degree of courage to go into the "unknown" in his caring for Caliban and his willingness to "trust in the other to grow."[45]

However, and unfortunately, the tragic denial of "humane care," the loss of trust brought about when Caliban tests the limits of care in his household, reveals the inadequacy of his education to his growing needs as an adolescent, physically and existentially. Following his punishment for his assault on Miranda, rather than apathy, the relationship between Prospero and Caliban turns into one of puerile revenge, of attachment to the anger of being wronged that plagues Prospero in his dealings with all except Miranda and Ariel, although in both the former and the latter he is not above reminding Miranda of her educational and life-preserving debts to him and to chastising Ariel for his forgetfulness of his time of arboreal imprisonment. As Melissa Sanchez explains, while Caliban refers to himself as a "subject," Prospero's designation of him (and Ariel) as "slave" speaks to the play's linguistic conflation of the terms in the realm of servitude, a "philosophical indeterminacy" highlighting "the difficulty of finding a precise account of the origins and extent of authority, whether political, domestic, or erotic. Instead, the play registers the possibility that authority can be defined only insofar as it is resisted."[46]

Prospero's counter-assault on Caliban expresses an ongoing grudge, a psychological state that transforms the verbs of care turn into verbs of torture in the tempus or time of the play:

CALIBAN: All the infections that the sun sucks up
From bogs, fens, flats, on Prosper fall and make him
By inch-meal a disease! ...
His spirits hear me,
And yet I needs must curse. But they'll nor pinch,

Fright me with urchin-shows, pitch me i' the mire,
Nor lead me, like a firebrand, in the dark
Out of my way, unless he bid 'em. But
For every trifle are they set upon me;
Sometime like apes that mow and chatter at me,
And after bite me; then like hedgehogs which
Lie tumbling in my barefoot way and mount
Their pricks at my footfall; sometime am I
All wound with adders, who with cloven tongues
Do hiss me into madness. (2.2.1–14)

While Caliban is in his tortuous exile, feeling the "pinch," "mow and chatter" of Prospero's will upon his body and soul, his attempt at sovereignty through his partnership with Trinculo and Stephano leads to experimenting with his own political will. When all is revealed at the conclusion of the play, Prospero's acknowledgment of Caliban, "This thing of darkness I / Acknowledge mine," is followed with a reintegration, albeit temporary, of the household: "Go, sirrah, to my cell; / Take with you your companions. As you look / To have my pardon, trim it handsomely" (5.1.275–6, 294–7). As both Prospero and Caliban have grown in their understanding of social reality, Prospero's understanding and development of the virtue of forgiveness enables him to attempt a return to the caring stance he failed to maintain at the onset of his relationship with Caliban. His acknowledgment here is, in part, an affirmation of the pain released through his earlier banishment of Caliban, even as it is "painfully partial" in its insistence on the "darkness" of Prospero's claims of Caliban.[47] As Sarah Beckwith writes in this volume, the relationship between acknowledgment and care is contingent on "where we stand in relation to others" and calls for an acceptance that aims to transcend the pain brought about through the tragic denial and avoidance of others.[48] Similarly, Prospero's acknowledgment of Caliban speaks to Mayeroff's claim that care calls upon the virtues of hope and courage, a hope that is not only future-oriented but also "an expression of the plenitude of the present, a present alive with a sense of the possible."[49]

Caliban's experience and subsequent reintegration before Prospero's departure not only chastens him but also inspires him to be "wise" in his return to solitary sovereignty on the island. As in the case of Edgar's learning in action, his dramatic trial as Poor Tom, Caliban's impending sovereignty is similarly informed and chastened by experience and perhaps also tempered with more wisdom than was accessible to him before his state of extreme servitude and poverty. Caliban's desire to rule with wisdom exhibits hope and courage by caring for himself as he embarks on the next phase of his development. Mayeroff's description of the interplay between courage, trust, and hope speaks to both Caliban's enlightened state at the conclusion of the play and Shakespeare's portrayal of the primacy of enabling individual virtue in *The Tempest*: "This is the courage of the artist who leaves the fashions of the day to go his own way, and in so doing comes to find himself and be himself. Such courage is not blind: it is informed by insight from past experiences, and it is open and sensitive to the present."[50]

From Dame Cura to Carers

> If you plant a seed in the ground, a tree will become manifest from that seed. The seed sacrifices itself to the tree that will come from it. The seed is outwardly lost, destroyed; but the same seed which is sacrificed will be absorbed and embodied in the tree, its blossoms, fruit and branches.
>
> – 'Abdu'l-Bahá, 1912

While Cordelia manifests the feminine care Lear hopes will cradle him in his old age, the crisis of care he both experiences and creates results from an individual and collective lack of virtue buttressing the structures of his kingdom. Such a dual moral concern speaks to our modern conceptualization of the work of care.[51] Dame Cura's contemporary avatars include nannies, nurses, and caregivers for the elderly, forms of affective labour that are monetized, marginalized, and minimized in social and economic value. Perhaps one of the most intriguing fictional figures of care is Kathy H., the "carer" in Kazuo Ishiguro's dystopian novel *Never Let Me Go*, which opens with biographical lines that mimic an ad for employment: "My name is Kathy H. I'm thirty-one years old, and I've been a carer now for over eleven years."[52] Destined to be a caretaker of her fellow clones who must go through a series of organ donations until the euphemistic "completion" of their lives, Kathy's humanity is ironically evident in her superior skills as a caregiver despite her status as a clone: "I've developed a kind of instinct around donors. I know when to hang around and comfort them, when to leave them to themselves; when to listen to everything they have to say, and when just to shrug and tell them to snap out of it."[53] If care is what shapes and moulds humans, then it is the capacity to care and empathize that distinguishes Kathy H.

and furthers the tragic lack of acknowledgment of the humanity of the genetically modified youth in Ishiguro's novel. Care is intricately bound up with sacrifice and obligation for Kathy H. as well as the other carers and donors and becomes the binding force that enables the system to continue. As in the myth of Cura, as John Hamilton explains, "Cura's primary task is to unify. With muddied hands she brings together the dual aspects, spirituality and materiality, that define the human condition." As Hamilton observes, in Hyginus' fable, the "donors" are the gods who endow humans with "a form, a body, a spirit, and a name," only to return the donations after death when man is secure from a life of care.[54]

The question of sacrificial obligations haunts our understanding of care. In one sense, Ishiguro's clones are the epitome of sacrificial care, donating parts of themselves until death for the well-being of others. Yet it is the joy of sacrifice, indirectly associated with Kathy H.'s "boasting" of her ability to care for donors, that is perhaps the most admirable and mysterious part of the human condition. From the streaming tears of a birthing mother to the chance heroic encounter of an altruistic Good Samaritan, the joy of sacrifice provides us with glimmerings of our highest nature, noble, virtuous, and caring. What is clear is that mortality and care are bound together in profoundly significant ways, revealing how, in its essence, caring tests one's virtues through the arena of sacrificial service that can be completed or exercised only in one's lifetime. It is the sacrifice of the self that enables the growth of another; it marks the end of estrangement and the beginning of human solidarity. It is the catalyst for a powerful transformation of the self and others. Lear's contemplation on care as he faces his own mortality, a mortality that saturates *Never Let Me Go,* reminds us that the cultivation of humankind's sublime virtues is contingent on the work one completes or ignores in this world.

NOTES

1 William Shakespeare, *King Lear,* ed. Grace Ioppolo (New York; W.W. Norton, 2008), 1.1.34–8. Subsequent references will be to this edition and cited in text.

2 *Oxford English Dictionary Online,* s.v. "care, n.1."

3 William Shakespeare, *The Tragedy of King Richard the Second,* in *The Complete Pelican Shakespeare,* ed. Frances Dolan, general editors Stephen Orgel and A.R. Braunmuller (New York: Penguin, 2002), 4.1.195–9.

4 John T. Hamilton, *Security: Politics, Humanity, and the Philology of Care* (Princeton, NJ: Princeton University Press, 2013), 130.

5 Edmund Spenser, *The Faerie Queene*, ed. Thomas P. Roche (New York: Penguin, 1987), 5.4.35. For a discussion of care as both burden and potential "holy virtue" in Spenser see Benjamin Parris, "'Watching to banish Care': Sleep and Insomnia in Book 1 of *The Faerie Queene*," *Modern Philology* 113, no. 2 (2015): 151–77, esp. 155.

6 William Shakespeare, *Romeo and Juliet*, in *The Pelican Shakespeare*, ed. Peter Holland, general editors Stephen Orgel and A.R. Braunmuller (New York: Penguin, 2002), 2.3.35–6.

7 William Shakespeare, *Macbeth*, in *The Pelican Shakespeare*, ed. Stephen Orgel, general editors Stephen Orgel and A.R. Braunmuller (New York: Penguin, 2002), 2.2.40–1.

8 Janet Adelman writes of Lear placing himself in a "position of infantile need" as he hoped to make Cordelia's "nursery his final resting place" in *Suffocating Mothers: Fantasies of Maternal Origin in Shakespeare's Plays, from Hamlet to the Tempest* (New York: Routledge, 1992), 116.

9 For a discussion on the distinctly Roman aspects of the Cura myth, see K.F.B. Fletcher, "Towards a Roman Mythography: Hyginus' *Fabulae*," in *Writing Myth: Mythography in the Ancient World*, ed. R.S. Smith and S. Trzaskoma, 133–64 (Walpole, MA: Peeters, 2013).

10 William Shakespeare, *The First Part of Henry VI*, in *The Pelican Shakespeare*, ed. William Montgomery, general editors Stephen Orgel and A.R. Braunmuller (New York: Penguin, 2002), 3.7.3.

11 Hyginus, *Fabulae* 220, cited in *The Literary Genres in the Flavian Age Canons, Transformations, Reception*, ed. Federica Bessone and Marco Fucecchi (Boston: De Gruyter, 2017), 76.

12 Stephanie Shirilan, *Robert Burton and the Transformative Powers of Melancholy* (London: Routledge, 2016), 29.

13 Shirilan, *Robert Burton*, 32.

14 Thomas Elyot, *The Dictionary of Syr Thomas Eliot Knyght* (London, 1538).

15 *Oxford English Dictionary Online*, s.v. "cure, n.1."

16 Warren Thomas Reich, "History of the Notion of Care," *Encyclopedia of Bioethics*, rev. ed. (New York: Simon & Schuster Macmillan, 1995), 319–31. Reich notes the tension of the "positive side of care" alongside the tension between earthly concerns and divine aspiration but emphasizes that "the primordial role of Care is to hold the human together in wholeness while cherishing it." See also Konrad Burdach, "Faust und die Sorge," *Deutsche Vierteljahrsschrift für Literaturwissenschaft und Geistesgeschichte*, 1, no. 160 (1923): 1–60.

17 Martin Heidegger, *Being and Time*, trans. Joan Stambaugh (New York: SUNY Press, 1996), 185.

18 Heidegger, *Being and Time*, 180.

19 Reich, "History of the Notion of Care"; for a discussion of adversarial paradigms of human relationships and subsequent responses to the thesis, see Samuel P. Huntington, *The Clash of Civilizations and the Remaking of World Order* (New York: Simon & Schuster, 1996); David Cannadine, *The Undivided Past: Humanity beyond Our Differences* (New York: Alfred A. Knopf, 2013); and Michael R. Karlberg, *Beyond the Culture of Contest: From Adversarialism to Mutualism in an Age of Interdependence* (Oxford: George Ronald, 2004).

20 Milton Mayeroff, *On Caring*, World Perspectives Series, general editor Ruth Nanda Anshen (New York: Harper and Row, 1971), 43:22, 5.

21 Mayeroff, *On Caring*, 7.

22 Mayeroff, *On Caring*, 39.

23 As Debra K. Shuger notes, many of Shakespeare's lower-class characters are comic rather than suffering, with Poor Tom as an anomaly. In reading Poor Tom and Caliban alongside each other, I would add that Caliban is an additional exception in the canon. See Shuger, "Subversive Fathers and Suffering Subjects: Shakespeare and Christianity," in *Religion, Literature, and Politics in Post-Reformation England, 1540–1688*, ed. Donna B. Hamilton and Richard Strier (Cambridge: Cambridge University Press, 1996), 46.

24 James Kearney, "'This Is Above All Strangeness': *King Lear*, Ethics, and the Phenomenology of Recognition," *Criticism* 54, no. 3, Shakespeare and Phenomenology (Summer 2012): 466. Kearney identifies "small ethical acts" in the "everyday exchanges and bodily interactions" of characters such as hand-holding between Edgar and Gloucester on their way to Dover, 466.

25 The reunion scene offers Cordelia a brief but poignant opportunity to care for a "child-changed" Lear following her invocation to the gods to "cure this great breach in his abused nature" (4.7.15).

26 William Shakespeare, *Othello, The Moor of Venice*, ed. Michael Neill (Oxford: Oxford University Press, 2006), 1.3.1.

27 Kearney, "'This Is Above All Strangeness,'" 455.

28 William C. Carroll, *Fat King, Lean Beggar: Representations of Poverty in the Age of Shakespeare* (Ithaca, NY: Cornell University Press, 1996), 191.

29 Carroll, *Fat King, Lean Beggar*, 42.

30 Shuger identifies Lear's invocation as a prayer for the poor: "Superflux is a Shakespearean coinage, a translation of a technical term from medieval canon law referring to the percentage of a person's income or goods that is owed to the poor.... In this painful epiphany, the pagan king for a moment grasps the nature of Christian *caritas*." "Subversive Fathers and Suffering Subjects," 53.

31 Mayeroff, *On Caring*, 30.

32 Kearney, "'This Is Above All Strangeness,'" 457–8.

33 On ancient philosophy as care for the self, see Pierre Hadot, *What Is Ancient Philosophy?* trans. Michael Chase (Cambridge, MA: Harvard University

Press, 2002); and Michel Foucault, *The Care of the Self,* vol. 3 of *The History of Sexuality,* trans. Robert Hurley (New York: Vintage, 1988).

34 Mayeroff, *On Caring,* 42.

35 Mayeroff, *On Caring,* 9.

36 Mayeroff writes that caring provides a "center" that promotes harmony and coherence in life. *On Caring,* 37.

37 Kearney, "'This Is Above All Strangeness,'" 458.

38 William Shakespeare, *The Tempest,* ed. Peter Hulme and William H. Sherman (New York: W.W. Norton, 2004), 1.2.367–73. All subsequent references will be to this edition and cited in text.

39 Tom Lindsay, "'Which First Was Mine Own King': Caliban and the Politics of Service and Education in *The Tempest,*" *Studies in Philology* 113, no. 2 (March 2016): 400.

40 Lindsay, "'Which First Was Mine Own King,'" 400.

41 Lindsay, "'Which First Was Mine Own King,'" 411.

42 Lindsay, "'Which First Was Mine Own King,'" 410.

43 Julia Reinhard Lupton, *Thinking with Shakespeare: Essays on Politics and Life* (Chicago: University of Chicago Press, 2011), 218.

44 Lupton, *Thinking with Shakespeare,* 204. Lupton further distinguishes Prospero's role as upholding his duties as a "curator" (from the Latin *cura* and in reference to Roman law) from Miranda's role as "tutor" who teaches Caliban to speak, 204.

45 Mayeroff, *On Caring,* 20.

46 Melissa E. Sanchez, "Seduction and Service in *The Tempest,*" *Studies in Philology* 105, no. 1 (2008): 63. Sanchez notes that "the early English translations for the Latin word for slave (*servus*) suggests, the terms 'servant' and 'slave' were often used interchangeably in Renaissance England," 62.

47 Lupton, *Thinking with Shakespeare,* 210.

48 Sarah Beckwith, "'Acknowledgment'" (in this volume).

49 Mayeroff, *On Caring,* 19.

50 Mayeroff, *On Caring,* 20.

51 On affective and emotional labour, see, for example, Arlie Russel Hochshild's classic study, *The Managed Heart: The Commercialization of Human Feeling* (Berkeley: University of California Press, 1983). On affective labour in Shakespeare, see Julia Reinhard Lupton, *Shakespeare Dwelling: Designs for the Theater of Life* (Chicago: University of Chicago Press, 2018), 51–68.

52 Kazuo Ishiguro, *Never Let Me Go* (New York: Vintage, 2005), 3.

53 Ishiguro, *Never Let Me Go* 3.

54 Hamilton, *Security,* 4.

SECTION II

EXTENDED ENCOUNTERS

chapter nine

Shakespeare's Now: Atemporal Presentness in *King Lear* and *The Winter's Tale*

SANFORD BUDICK

Concerning *The Winter's Tale*, Frank Kermode remarked that "we value it not for some hidden truth, but for its power to realize experience."[1] I believe the same judgment applies with equal force to *King Lear*, the play to which *The Winter's Tale* is intimately related. Yet even if we feel intuitively that this is the case, we must still ask what it means, concretely, to realize experience in these plays. My goal is to recreate and explain a particular experience, the experience of an *atemporal presentness*, that is realized in both *King Lear* and *The Winter's Tale* and, most remarkably, in the interchanges between these two plays. Shakespeare's carefully framed term for this atemporal presentness is simply *now*. Although I will not press the point here, it may be that, for Shakespeare, realizing the experience of the now is the condition for realizing all other forms of experience, that is, not only for becoming aware of experience ex post facto but for having it in the first place. My focus on this occasion is restrictively on how Shakespeare's language of theatricalization creates the experience of the now, not only for given protagonists within these plays but for the spectator and, indeed, for Shakespeare as well. I will leave for discussion in the appendix the important views of presentness in *King Lear* that have been offered by Stanley Cavell and Christoph Menke, but I note here that both of their views ultimately relate to presentness in a linear temporality within the worlds of the play, whereas the now that concerns me is an interruption of that temporality. Separately and together, *King Lear* and *The Winter's Tale* enable stepping outside time into an experience of the now.

I begin with the closing lines of *King Lear*, which in the Folio are assigned to Edgar:

> The oldest hath borne most; we that are young
> Shall never see so much, nor live so long. (5.3.299–300)

Emily Sun has suggested that Edgar is repeatedly positioned in the play as spectator and that these final words issue to the spectators of the play "the challenge of succeeding *King Lear* in a way that gestures toward the possibility of a future beyond the disaster it dramatizes."[2] The succession of spectatorship that Sun envisions is for "an aesthetics and politics of plurality." It is certainly reasonable to suppose that Shakespeare is here thinking of a politics characterized by an ethical commitment born of the sense of one's own immediate involvement in a community of diverse commitments. Yet I suggest that the more immediately realized succession that he has in mind is something more elemental: this is a continual inward striving for the dynamics of spectatorship that realizes the now itself. We will see that Edgar the spectator exemplifies that realized now in which an ungraspable extent of seeing (so much) and enduring (of living so long) are concentrated.

The Now of the Spectator or Onlooker

I propose that the dynamics of spectatorship in *King Lear* are greatly illuminated by a model of meditative experience that has been available in modern thought, in various forms, roughly from Shakespeare's era. According to the broad outlines of this model the meditating mind goes from (1) achieved suspension of consciousness of the external world, to (2) a residual consciousness of a self in an atemporal now that is independent of the world, to (3) reclaiming intentional consciousness of the external world and its temporality.[3] The best-known expounders of principal elements of this model are the Descartes of the *Meditations*, with his bringing to bear of a systematic scepticism or hyperbolic doubt, and the Husserl of the *Cartesian Meditations*, with his application of a "bracketing," "reduction," or "*epoché* [literally a withholding]" that produces the "now" of the "onlooker."[4] Going further than Descartes, Husserl explained how consciousness of an internal actuality can be disclosed in a transformed "now" by "bracketing" the "natural attitude" toward spatial and temporal reality. In other words, the momentary bracketing of external reality transforms our sense of time into an internal, atemporal "now" or "presence" and suspends us in a sense of "*Wunder*." In that state of wonder the onlooker grasps the "coexistence" of being. Such presence and wonder, as well as a grasp of coexistence, are located outside the temporal and spatial continuity in which we are usually embedded. For Husserl the atemporal now of the *epoché* coincides with the unrepresentable point that is produced by bracketing. For Shakespeare the now characteristically emerges, after bracketing of his own kind, in the unrepresentable point of the "nothing" – which can at times seem to resemble the "*Nichts*" and the "*Néant*" that other modern philosophers have derived within the Husserlian line.

Important bridging elements were available between Descartes's and Husserl's models of this kind and, in the wake of Husserl's *epoché* and now, other prominent models of a transformed temporality were vividly proposed. Such are Heidegger's elaborations of what he grasps as the *"Zeit"* of *"Sein"* or Walter Benjamin's *"Jetztzeit,"* or, lately, Giorgio Agamben's use of Benjamin's model, all of which significantly derive, directly or indirectly, from Husserl's elaboration of "presence."[5] Although Husserl avoided acknowledging it, his own debt to Kant in these matters is particularly great. This debt has a special relevance to my present subject. Husserl's "reduction" in the *epoché* can be seen as a version of Kant's "deduction" in the sublime, Husserl's atemporality as a version of Kant's assertion that the experience of the sublime cancels the time dimension, and Husserl's "wonder" in the *epoché* as a version of what Kant says we may feel in the experience of the sublime.[6] Husserl, however, goes further than Kant in making clear a deliberate meditative work of the *epoché* that is even a chosen ordeal.[7] In Husserl's view, only by bracketing the "natural attitude" in the *epoché* and momentarily breaking with the world in the now, only by achieving what he accordingly calls the *transcendental* status of the *onlooker*, do we attain to awareness and intentionality in the natural attitude itself. Only then are we empowered, in Husserl's phrase, for "accomplishing life."[8]

Yet curiously enough Husserl has little to say about how bracketing or the *epoché* are to be achieved in practice, while Kant, in his parallel account of the "deduction" in the sublime, supplies point-by-point instruction about how we enter not only into the sublime in experience of nature but of art as well.[9] Kant explains that this deduction is achieved when imagination and reason clash in the mind's attempt to follow an infinite progression of items while experiencing the impossibility of grasping the totality of such a progression. The result is a "check to the vital forces" in which (as noted) the time dimension is momentarily cancelled. For

Husserl the realized experience of that atemporal moment is the now of the onlooker.

I take the strenuousness of Derrida's denial – contra Kant and especially contra Husserl – of a "metaphysics of presence" as an indication that in fact many have imagined that they have experienced a transcendental now. Derrida devoted a large part of his writings to drawing as close as possible and then just avoiding the experience of such presence. Quite late in his career he remarked, "For me Husserl's work, and precisely the notion of *epoché*, has been and still is a major indispensable gesture. In everything I try to say and write *epoché* is implied."[10] Rather than address the theoretical framework of Derrida's critique of a "metaphysics of presence," I will proceed somewhat like Dr. Johnson freely kicking his stone to rebut the claim of determinism, that is, in the present case, by materially recreating what I understand to be Shakespeare's realization of the experience of an atemporal now. Shakespeare achieves this, I propose, in his capacity as onlooker.

Shakespeare and the Spectator as Onlookers

In the scene of *Troilus and Cressida* (5.2) in which Thersites watches Ulysses who watches Troilus who watches Cressida with Diomedes, Shakespeare shows the voyeuristic potential of one kind of onlooking. Yet in *King Lear* and *The Winter's Tale* he represents a very different potential in onlooking of another kind. Side-by-side with the plots of both of these plays, Shakespeare projects his authorial presence as onlooker. Right from the beginning his represented foreknowledge in or about these plays is in a completely different order from what we call "dramatic irony." Dramatic irony pertains to knowledge that an audience possesses that is greater than that of the protagonists, yet it is knowledge of the fiction that is gleaned from being witness to scenes of the play in which some of the characters are absent. The suggestion may seem prima facie outrageous, but I propose that although Shakespeare's omniscient authorial knowledge has no signified place or time – no presence – within the temporality of these plays, we (as spectators) nevertheless simultaneously experience it as present in an atemporality outside, looking in on, these plays. To take in the status of Shakespeare's atemporal omniscient knowledge, the spectator must be capable of achieving not a willing suspension of disbelief but – even while watching these plays – a willed suspension of belief in the theatricalized representation itself. Paradoxically, that is, the spectator then becomes capable of seeing that Shakespeare's kind of omniscient knowledge is not merely or principally of the fictionalized action that seems to take place in worldly time. Rather, that knowledge has been made available to Shakespeare *ab extra* in an atemporal now where he looks out upon the counter-forces of being. These counter-forces can be endlessly fictionalized in endless numbers of ways.

Shakespeare's claim to possession of this knowledge is not arbitrary. The validity of his knowledge in his now has been earned as realized experience – as it will be earned by the spectator – by an activity that precedes or is outside the performance of the plays and that can produce the condition of the onlooker. This is the meditative activity – the serial acts of consciousness – that Shakespeare has already experienced as playwright, as script writer, and that he then makes available, as experience, to the spectator. Fragmentarily, this experience is also represented for some of the protagonists of these plays in their own partial equivalents of this meditative activity, thus beginning to create for them something of the same condition as onlookers. Within the plays themselves we thus find protagonists (such as Edgar or Perdita) who approximate the condition of onlookers. The full effect of this detached meditative activity, however, is attained only outside the fiction, outside theatricalization, by the author and spectator.

To be sure, the omniscience of a playwright may be taken to be a given in more or less any theory of composition. What is of interest here (and no doubt in some other plays of Shakespeare) is that the unbodied presence of the author – accompanying but not in the plays – is by the spectator felt as a unique quantity. This feeling of the spectator is correlative with the effect of ominous, undefined pregnancy of meanings, excesses of signification and/or of systematicity that can be assigned only to the author. I submit that for the spectator a perturbation of this extra-theatrical kind is inevitable (even if difficult to bring to the surface of consciousness) as at least one part of our response to these plays, in retrospect, virtually from their beginnings. For example, in *King Lear*, Cordelia's expression of her radically underdetermined "Nothing" stands in total disproportion (by any worldly measure available to the spectator) to her father's question; just so, Gloucester's "Let's see. Come, if it be nothing, I shall not need spectacles" (1.2.34–5) is infinitely too light in a scene that is already headed for extreme danger; and, in *The Winter's Tale*, Camillo's opening reminiscences of Leontes's and Polixenes's childhoods are strained with abstraction of causations that must have their own iron will in a collective futurity, of which Camillo has not the slightest inkling. We do not need to be super-sophisticated spectators to sense that Camillo's words project the author's knowledge of a patterning that subsumes the predictable surprises of thearicalization. Yet it is only when we, too, as spectators, begin to access the atemporal now that we begin to share Shakespeare's now and his knowledge outside theatricalization. As I have begun to suggest, this access is produced by a meditative activity of a special kind.

My claim for a bifurcation between knowledge of theatricalized fiction and a knowledge that is beyond all theatricalization may seem to denature the idea and experience of theatre itself. Yet for a thinker and writer as committed to trying to see reality to the best of human abilities, as was Shakespeare, it was, after all, inevitable and necessary to take into account and to try to overcome the deflections from seeing reality created by theatre and representation, even by the theatre and representation that are at work in thinking itself.

Throughout *King Lear* Shakespeare the onlooker plots Lear's development towards – but never fully reaching – the status of onlooker. After being ejected from Regan's and Goneril's houses, Lear begins to see, from outside, "houseless poverty" and "houseless heads" (3.4.26, 30). His growth as onlooker is expressed in his wish merely to abide in prison with Cordelia as "God's spies" (5.3.17). In his final injunction to "Look on" dead Cordelia's lips – the rounded lips that form, once more, the zero, the nothing of fullness, that he finally begins to comprehend – he stands on the threshold of his own transcendental nothing, born of the knowledge that nothing worldly is further at stake for him. Standing *now* on the boundary line of mortality, he, too, is for an atemporal instant a transcendental onlooker – God's lonely spy – to the coexistence of death and life. We need to understand the something in his experience, the something that is reflected or created in his language, that has given him, for that instant, a place to stand as onlooker.

How the Now of the Onlooker Is Achieved

In *King Lear* and *The Winter's Tale* Shakespeare employs a language of spectatorship that works through and exceeds the theatricalizing oscillations of the human imagination. These oscillations are seen in the back-and-forth movements between *role-playing consciousness* and what can be called, awkwardly, *a would-be non-role-playing consciousness* that is itself never free of role playing. In Shakespeare's language of theatricalization the rhetorical figure that repeatedly represents these cross-purposes is chiasmus. In modern philosophy chiasmus has often been explicated as a key figure in the production of human consciousness.[11] My contention is that in Shakespeare's hands a series of such chiasmata runs through the length of each play and will even be seen to occur between these two plays. The products of these progressions of chiasmata, added on to an element of dynamic progression that inheres in each chiasmus, are a sublime bracketing of the world and the opening of the now that is the onlookers' grasp of the coexistence of being.

Joel Fineman drew close attention to the centrality of Shakespeare's use of chiasmus in the sonnets. Yet Fineman's identification of this usage of chiasmus with thematized contents (such as sexual and bisexual desire) ignores the unrepresentable and atemporal space of negativity that is primary in the experience of chiasmus.[12] Building on Fineman's analysis of the centrality of chiasmus in Shakespeare's sonnets, Lisa Freinkel has noted how the elements of each chiasmus necessarily form an effectively infinite progression: "Repetition becomes inversion and inversion takes us back to where we started," so that chiasmus initiates "an exchange that seems to have no beginning and no end."[13] Thus, she notes, chiasmus "precludes a *present*.... The *now* itself ... is lost," leaving, she says, an "odd temporality."[14] I believe that these observations are correct and important. Yet what Freinkel has seen here pertains to the precluded *present* or lost *now* of worldly temporality, not to the onlooker's inward now that is disclosed in an unrepresentable negativity – such as, indeed, Kant explains in the deduction of the sublime. This Kantian deduction of an atemporality takes place in the mind's attempt to follow an infinite progression of items while experiencing the impossibility of grasping the totality of such a progression. In effect, Shakespeare employs the instrumentality of theatricalized chiasmus to produce this Kantian deduction, which is also (as I have suggested) the Husserlian *epoché*.

I propose that Shakespeare's turning, in his plays, to the use of a chiasmus of theatricalization coincided with the dramaturgical breakthrough that Stephen Greenblatt has located in *Hamlet*. Greenblatt has suggested that in *Hamlet* Shakespeare "made a discovery by means of which he relaunched his entire career.... The crucial breakthrough," he says, "had to do ... with an intense representation of inwardness by a new technique of radical excision," by which Greenblatt means (among other things) "writing about a character suspended" in a "strange interim."[15] I propose that in *Hamlet* the time of the strange interim is not created solely in the construction of plot and character. Instead or in addition, it is a temporality within language that is created by a dynamic of excision and suspension within Hamlet's language of theatricalization. I have recently offered a reading of *Hamlet* along these lines.[16] I will here very briefly extract some elements of that reading, since the core of my argument in the present chapter is that Shakespeare made a further breakthrough by adopting for himself and by perfecting, as playwright, the onlooker condition broached by Hamlet's chiasmus of theatricalization and of the now. To be sure, for Shakespeare this was a radical, almost unthinkable step, for it meant stepping outside his own plays even within the process of conceiving them.

In Hamlet's hands chiasmus is a compact, portable engine of infinite progression and of experiencing the impossibility of grasping the totality of such a progression. Judging by the intensity of Hamlet's recurring to chiasmus we may well conclude that he knows, or at least senses, that the momentary failure it entails can somehow leave him with the residual consciousness of a self in an inward now – a "that within which passes show" (1.2.85). He knows, or senses as well, that paradoxically, the use of this instrument of momentary suspension can ultimately furnish the grounds for his experience and intentional action in the world, for accomplishing life. Here we begin to obtain a fresh understanding of one of the key paradoxes in Hamlet's monumental thinking, namely, his resolute purposiveness or intentionality within apparent vacillation.[17]

Hamlet's most significant use of the chiasmus of theatricalization – serving virtually as a template for all his other employments of this figure – is his self-accusatory question concerning the player's capacity to feel and to express emotion. After asking about that emotion whether it is only "all for nothing – For Hecuba?," he asks further:

> What's *[A]* Hecuba to *[B]* him, or *[B]* he to *[A]* her,
> That he should weep for her? (2.2.492–4)[18]

In the following way the abstracted configuration of the Hecuba chiasmus encompasses the mind's, the imagination's, interminable interchange between kinds of role playing in the quest for authenticity:

> *Play-acting* (experiencing Hecuba in the fiction) to *would-be non- play-acting* ("him," the live actor, in real existence) // *would-be non-play-acting* ("he" the live actor) to *play-acting* ("her" in the fiction).

The interminability of this interchange, and the mind's inability to grasp it whole, produces the *epoché.* With the *epoché* comes the space of the "nothing" and the time of the atemporal now. Hamlet's pronouncement that art must hold the mirror up to nature therefore finds a deeper meaning in his meditative employment – his productive thinking – of chiasmus, right to left and left to right, *AB:BA*, ad infinitum.

The full emergence of Hamlet's inward now takes place as he prepares for being fully present, fully ready, for the close of his journey. His readiness can no longer be altered by changes in worldly time. *Now,* indeed, he can *let* the world (including his fated participation in the world) simply *be*:

> We defy augury. There is special providence in the fall of a sparrow. *[A]* If it **be** *now*, 'tis not to come. *[B]* If it **be** not to come, it will **be** *now*. *[B]* If it **be** not *now*, yet it will come. *The readiness is all....* *[A]* Let **be.**
> (5.2.198–202; emphases added)[19]

Hamlet's employment of chiasmus is a record, or an immediate chiastic enactment, of a partially mute transformative event in his perception of being. The products of such an event are a sublime bracketing of the world and the opening of the now in the onlooker's grasp of the coexistence of multiple "be"-ing.

Such chiastic events also constitute the core of *King Lear* and *The Winter's Tale*. The Fool shows Lear to be in the grip of a lacerating theatricalized oscillation that Lear's imagination has created but which he completely fails to understand:

> *[A]* now thou art an O *[B]* without a figure.
> *[B]* I am better than *[A]* thou art now. (1.4.152–3)[20]

The experience of the chiastic event in this figure belongs to the Fool, not Lear. In the point of intersection of the unrepresentable, of negativity, the Fool opens the now of his "I am" while Lear is located in a nothing of banality, beside the point – the midpoint – of the chiasmus. Here as everywhere in these plays Shakespeare sustains two mutually challenging meanings of the word *nothing*: one is the negativity that opens the now; the other is mere meaninglessness. This play's most spectacular instantiation of that duality is in Shakespeare's takeover of Lear's pronouncement that "Nothing will come of nothing." Lear the martinet has applied emptily to the archetypical chiasm, *Ex nihilo nihil fit.* Shakespeare, not Lear, knows and experiences the chiastic event that is reflected in, or takes place, in these words. Lear is left in the lurch of the meaningless nothing. Here or before the play even commences, Shakespeare has earned the midpoint of the nothing that is the now.

The so-called Gloucester subplot functions in *King Lear* as a massive standpoint of *ab extra* spectatorship if only because the insights it provides into Lear's fate are too perfect to be anything but the made-to-order invention of the all-knowing author. Standing almost shoulder to shoulder with Shakespeare in that standpoint, the principal articulator of the theatricalized oscillations of a tormented human imagination is Edgar. No one else within the tragedy has greater power to trace these oscillations, even about his imagining of his own self. After taking on his disguise as "Poor Tom" he yokes his awareness of this oscillation to a contorted language that is almost unreadable: "Edgar I nothing am" (2.3.21). The outer terms of this chiasmus are "Edgar" and "am." The inner terms are "I" and "nothing." Within this welter of pain Edgar abides in his now of onlooking where he is a recipient of a further dimension of the now, that of a blessing that is independent of any material outcome. In the chiasmata of theatricalization of *King Lear* and *The Winter's Tale*, the blessing of the now emerges as an unforeseen disclosure precisely when there are apparently no possible effects of blessing in sight.

Nothing and Blessing in *King Lear* and *The Winter's Tale*

Gloucester's words, just before he leaps from what he thinks is the cliff at Dover, point, unknowingly, to the blessing of Edgar in his *now*:

If *[A] Edgar live, bless [B]* him.
Now, [B] fellow, fare [A] thee well. (4.5.41–2; emphasis added)

As spectators, we and the audience know that the "Edgar" and "thee," like the "him" and "fellow" of Gloucester's words, are exact chiastic equivalents that unknowingly identify Edgar's onlooker now with blessing, as if signalling that blessing can be accomplished by a formalism of mere language even when the protagonists, who are not God, cannot bring about any material blessing. I will yet return to this triad of the now, the nothing, and blessing in Shakespeare's language of spectatorship. Yet it is worth establishing already that this formal pattern is somehow of climactic importance in *King Lear*. In act 4, after Cordelia begins to bring Lear back from his fevered state and Lear says, "Would I were assured / Of my condition," Cordelia responds,

> *[A]* O look upon me, *[B]* sir,
> And *[B]* hold your hand in benediction *[A]* o'er me. (4.6.54–5)

The Cordelia, the "me," who asks to be looked upon, to be recognized not as stranger but as the undyingly faithful daughter whom Lear has loved, and the "me" who would receive Lear's blessing, are the same; and they oscillate with the "sir" who hardly knows who he is or has been, though his "hand" is a metonymy of that fatherly "sir." Here, too, benediction that is powerless to change fate yet is for all that somehow real blessing, is by Shakespeare imagined as the channelled product of the imagination's oscillations. In act 5 Lear closely mirrors that pattern and that potentiality of blessing in language's formalisms exactly at the nadir of any power to deliver material blessing:

> *[A]* When thou dost ask me blessing *[B]* [*imagining that Cordelia kneels as she did at 4.6.54–6*], *[B]* I'll kneel down *[A]* And ask of thee forgiveness. (5.3.10–11)

Here we have a "forgiveness" that is construed as the equivalent of blessing, together with Cordelia's kneeling and Lear's kneeling. The chiastic oscillations continue and bring us ever closer to an as yet unexplained quantity that can somehow be blessing itself.

The interrelations between *King Lear* and *The Winter's Tale* have a special function in realizing experience of the now. To be sure, what John Pitcher has recently called "the visible flow between the two plays" has been noted frequently. We see it in such things, Pitcher observes, as the "reference in *King Lear* to being caught between a bear and a raging sea (3.4.9–11) [that] is made real in *The Winter's Tale.*" And we feel it "in the harrowing final lines in *King Lear*" when a delirious Lear "believes that Cordelia's lips have life in them. In the final scenes of *The Winter's Tale,*" Pitcher adds, "when Leontes faces what he thinks is the inanimate statue of his dead wife" and believes "that 'the very life seems warm upon her lip' ... as sweet as 'any cordial comfort,' he thinks Hermione is breathing and tries to kiss her" (5.3.66, 76–7). Pitcher notes the remarkable "half-hidden, bitter-sweet pun passing from 'Cordelia' to 'cordial.'"[21] To this we must add the massive parallel in the very openings of these plays, when, in a fit of madness, a king banishes the person he most loves and even, in both cases, brings about the death, or apparent death, of his daughter. I will yet return to this last parallel.

The adhesion of *King Lear* and *The Winter's Tale* to the now, nothing, blessing, and wonder of chiasmus is powerfully exemplified by the figure of Perdita who, as Time the interrupter of *The Winter's Tale* says, is "now grown in grace / Equal with wond'ring" (4.1.24–5). Perdita is the spectator in *The Winter's Tale* who most closely succeeds to the Edgar of *King Lear.* Perdita, the lost one, stands *ab extra* throughout. Polixenes bears unimpeachable witness to her status of this kind: "Nothing she does or seems / But smacks of something greater than herself, / Too noble for this place" (4.4.157–9). She herself views the scene around her as if she continues to be a spectator: "I see the play so lies / That I must bear a part" (4.4.626–7). When the curtain is drawn on Hermione as statue, Perdita explicitly names herself as onlooker: "So long could I / Stand by a looker-on" (5.3.84–5). Shakespeare goes further than giving a name to this onlooker status. He probes it for its structural creation of the place of nothing, its strange or wondrous interim. The "nothing ... but" that Polixenes mentions, which means everything, is by Florizel given its inner meaning of wondrous interval, of still-ness, of a sustained, atemporal present. "When you do dance," he says to Perdita, "*[A]* I wish you / A wave o' the sea, *[B]* that you might even do / Nothing but that: *[B]* move still, *[A]* still so" (4.4.140–3). The power of this country maid to disclose an atemporal interval is startlingly shown in her invocation of timeless Ovidian mythology, all in perfect chiasmus centred in the "now":

> *[A]* O Proserpina,
> For *[B]* the flowers now, *[B]* that, frighted, thou letst fall
> *[A]* From Dis's wagon! (4.4.116–18)

Perdita's inner time fixes the detached inner time that is bracketed within (or outside) the play as a whole. This is already the strong time or *kairos* that Paulina will announce in her exclamation, "'Tis time" (5.3.99). We encounter the same time of the now in the chiasmus that Leontes and Paulina share in one verse that thematizes the *now* of *epoché.* When, Leontes observes, "as she *[A]* lived *[B] now,*" Paulina responds, "As *[B] now* she might have *[A]* lived" (5.3.32; emphases added).

In act 5 Perdita, facing the statue, says,

> *[A]* do not say 'tis superstition, that
> *[B]* I kneel and *[B]* implore *[A]* her blessing. (5.3.43–4)

Paulina provides the iteration for both of the parent participants in the pattern of blessing by interposing Perdita – the Perdita of motionless motion and of an atemporal interval, the *Perdita* of *lost-ness* – both between herself and her mother and between Leontes and Hermione, saying,

> Please you to interpose, fair madam; kneel
> And pray your mother's blessing. (5.3.119–20)

Paulina no doubt here provides the stage director with a kind of blocking cue. More significantly, she has transformed blocking into bracketing and the now.

In *Hamlet* Shakespeare drew the spectator's *ab extra* attention to the gravity of his use of the form of chiasmus by having foolish Polonius call chiasmus "a foolish figure" ("'tis true 'tis pity, / And pity 'tis 'tis true": 2.2.98–9). In *The Winter's Tale* Shakespeare draws a similar *ab extra* attention to chiasmus by echoing Puttenham's term for chiasmus, the "cross-couple," when Leontes chiastically says to Perdita and Florizel,

> *[A]* I lost a couple that twixt heaven and earth
> *[B]* Might thus have stood, *[B]* begetting **wonder**, as
> *[A]* You, gracious couple, do. (5.1.131–3; emphasis added)

Only Shakespeare and the spectator as onlookers can see the chiastic correspondences that couple these couples as well as their standing and doing. For Shakespeare and the spectator or reader of Shakespeare's plays the depth of onlooking is here dizzying indeed. The standing and doing of this couple are as actors who are play-acting the roles of Florizel and Perdita who are play-acting the roles of having been "sent" by Polixenes. Repeating this vision, Leontes formulates it as the heart of his desire for renewed life:

> *[A]* Might I a son and daughter *[B]* **now** *[B]* have looked on,
> *[A]* Such goodly things as you! (5.1.176–7; emphasis added)

The disclosed items at the dead centres of these closely equivalent chiasmata are "wonder" and the "now," precisely the products of the Husserlian reduction that Shakespeare performs in his own way, indeed, well beyond Husserl's resources of language and meditation. Leontes stands in the temporality of the now that can renew life. In the last lines of the play Leontes, addressing the Paulina who has stage managed all this theatre, speaks the chiastic language that exits the play and opens upon the spectator's realized experience of the now:

> *[A]* Lead us from hence, where we may leisurely
> *[B]* Each one demand and answer to his part
> Performed in this wide gap of time *[B]* since first
> We were dissevered. *[A]* Hastily lead away. (5.3.152–5)

The atemporal urgency of the now in the wide gap of time, as well as the unrepresented place of "away," are experienced by the spectator both "leisurely" and "hastily." We reach this strange interim when, as spectators, we follow the "interchange" of the chiasmus that leaves us in the now.

Doubling the Chiasmus of Theatricalization

The dénouement of *The Winter's Tale* – and of *The Winter's Tale* and *King Lear* together – is realized in the double chiasmata and their *epochés* that are made possible by "heavens directing" or "the heavens" continuing "their loves," which is to say, continuing their loves not only from the aborted first half of *The Winter's Tale* but from the tragic interdiction at the close of *King Lear.* The matrix of such doubling of chiasmata is set out within *The Winter's Tale* by Perdita after Florizel has crowned her "queen" of the sheep-shearing festival:

> PERDITA: Sir, my gracious lord,
> To chide at your extremes it not becomes me –
> O pardon that I name them! Your high self,
> The gracious mark o'th'land, you have obscured
> With a swain's wearing, and me, poor lowly maid,
> Most goddess-like pranked up. But that our feasts
> In every mess have folly, and the feeders
> Digest it with a custom, I should blush
> To see you so attired – sworn, I think,
> To show myself a glass. (4.4.5–14)

Where Hamlet saw that art must hold up a chiastic "mirror" to nature – as in his Hecuba chiasmus of theatricalization – Perdita's role in the sheep-shearing festival shows a doubly chiastic "glass" that (she does not yet know) doubles the chiasmus of theatricalization. Hamlet employs the chiastic "mirror" and its *epoché* to disclose his self or subjectivity. Beyond Perdita's immediate knowledge, her "glass" traces a double mirroring that yields the possibility of an intersubjectivity.

The mirror of Perdita's outer chiasmus of Self and Other shows the "extremes" of "queen"-Perdita/"swain"-Florizel // Florizel "so attired"/Perdita "myself." Within these outward terms abides another chiasmus, also of Self and Other, that is a mirror of the other mirror: *Perdita princess of Sicilia/Florizel prince of Bohemia // Florizel prince of Bohemia/Perdita princess of Sicilia.* Perdita, the closest thing to a fully achieved onlooker in these plays, indeed points us to this matrix of a chiastically achieved intersubjectivity. Just such a possibility of achieving intersubjectivity by means of a double mirroring and a double *epoché* has been envisioned by Husserl's inheritors in their effort to achieve the goal of an intersubjectivity that eluded Husserl himself throughout his philosophical career. In the words of Eugen Fink, cited approvingly by Alfred Schütz,

> The experience of the Other involves a reciprocal relationship: in experiencing the Other concurrently I experience the Other's experiencing of me. But this reciprocal relationship is, taken strictly, not only a simple running back and forth from myself to the Other and from the Other to me. This reciprocal relationship allows, potentially, indefinite reiteration. I can therefore say that I so experience the Other as the Other is experiencing me, and that the Other so experiences me as I am experiencing the Other.... We have here an indefinite [i.e., infinite] reciprocal reflectibility somewhat like two mirrors placed one opposite the other reflecting into each other in indefinite reiteration.[22]

Yet the matrix of intersubjectivity that Perdita forms can be fulfilled only in the full detachment of an onlooking, *at* the plays from *outside* the plays. This is effected in reflection on *The Winter's Tale* and *King Lear* together. That chiastic *object of reflection* is constituted by the chiasmata and *epochés* that these plays form with each other.[23]

It is time to observe the experience of the now that is realized between these plays. This is disclosed by the immense chiasmus that the two plays perform jointly. Whereas the trials of the earlier play are set in motion by the repeated utterance of the word "Nothing" by a beloved daughter (1.1.182, 184), which causes a king's maddened outburst on the word "nothing" and the banishment (and ultimate death) of his daughter, the tribulations of the later play are set in motion by a king who himself first lingers madly on the word "nothing" –

Is this nothing?
Why then the world and all that's in't is nothing,
The covering sky is nothing, Bohemia nothing,
My wife's nothing, nor nothing have these nothings,
If this be nothing. (1.2.289–93)

This in turn generates the murderous court trial of his beloved wife together with his order of banishment/execution of his daughter. In near perfect chiastic inversion of the pattern in *King Lear*, in *The Winter's Tale* the king's daughter even utters the word "nothing" in counterfactual counterpoint to Cordelia's earlier counterfactual "nothing." Cordelia's silent point, after all, is that she has everything to say about love for her father. "I cannot speak / So well, nothing so well," speaks Perdita (4.4.360–1) in the very same vein. The effect of this cross-conversation is to create another bracketing of a strange interim, another moment of the now, for Shakespeare and the spectator of these plays. All this is remarkably managed by the onlooker author who thus begins to create an extra-theatrical object of reflection between these plays. Yet the most remarkable expedient for creating this extra-theatrical effect, between these plays, still remains to be described.

Grafting, Nothing, and Blessing

Only Shakespeare and the spectator (on a second viewing) can see that throughout *The Winter's Tale* the disclosure of a "great difference" within chiastic form is redoubled in multiple, reciprocal mirrorings of chiasmus. The opening exchange between Archidamus and Camillo already sets out one such doubling in laying out the reciprocal visitations that will structure the entire plot of the play. Together, Archidamus and Camillo unknowingly present the chiastic schematism of the "great difference" between Bohemia and Sicilia/Sicilia and Bohemia:

ARCHIDAMUS: If *you* [*A – i.e., Sicilia*] shall chance, Camillo, to visit *[B] Bohemia* on the like occasion whereon my services are now on foot, you shall see, as I have said, *great difference betwixt* our [*B*] *Bohemia* and your [*A*] *Sicilia.*

Camillo mirrors and enters into this reciprocity of visitations from where Archidamus left off:

CAMILLO: I think this coming summer the [*A*] *King of Sicilia* means to pay [*B* the *King of*] *Bohemia* the visitation which he justly owes him. (emphases added)

This is only the beginning of the vast network of chiastic relation that will rule in this play and that will ultimately determine its relation to *King Lear*.

I propose that it is central to *The Winter's Tale* that at this opening moment, directly after the chiastic relation of Bohemia/Sicilia // Sicilia/ Bohemia has been presented, Camillo extracts a chiastic pattern of natural grafting from Sicilia's and Bohemia's apparently everyday actions of "separation" and "interchange" (22–3). Camillo cannot know, much less prevent, the "great difference" that is about to erupt between Leontes and Polixenes. Yet in the opening rehearsal of the history of their friendship he proceeds to a meaning that overleaps the material causes of that "great difference" and he locates (blindly) the operations of the far greater transformative "vast" that this play, and its relation to *King Lear*, will ultimately reveal. In *The Winter's Tale* this "interchange" will be achieved in the natural grafting of roots that will (after painful interruption) be duplicated in a natural grafting of branches that is endowed with transcendental and scriptural meanings.

To begin to understand the meanings that Shakespeare attaches to grafting in *The Winter's Tale* we must take in the setting that the play provides to highlight its significance. Polixenes's account of an *artificial grafting* is one of the most often cited and – as far as Shakespeare is concerned – most seriously misunderstood touchstones in the history of aesthetics, that is, in the theory of the relation of "art" to "nature." Polixenes's artificial, hierarchical model of grafting serves as the anti-model that highlights the natural grafting, which is the pivotal trope of the play as a whole. Here is Polixenes:

You see, sweet maid, we marry
A gentler scion to the wildest stock,
And make conceive a bark of baser kind
By bud of nobler race. This is an art
Which does mend nature – changes it rather – but
The art itself is nature. (4.4.92–7)

Shakespeare directly subverts the application that Polixenes claims for such grafting. Polixenes's account presumes to enlighten a supposedly ignorant, low-born Perdita, yet his words fly against him. This "sweet maid" is neither of "wildest stock" nor of "baser kind." The apparently "gentler scion" of apparently "nobler race" – Polixenes's boast for himself and his family line – is no whit gentler or nobler than Perdita. Of course, Polixenes cannot be blamed for not knowing who Perdita actually is, yet his puffed up condescension, as well as the trap that Shakespeare has laid for his ignorance, cast doubt, for us, on the relevance of everything he says about the relation of art to nature – at least, concerning the relation of art to nature in this play.

Shakespeare is indeed pursuing a profound analogy between grafting and art, yet the artificial grafting that Polixenes describes is in *The Winter's Tale* distinctly one of two models of grafting, one artificial, hierarchical,

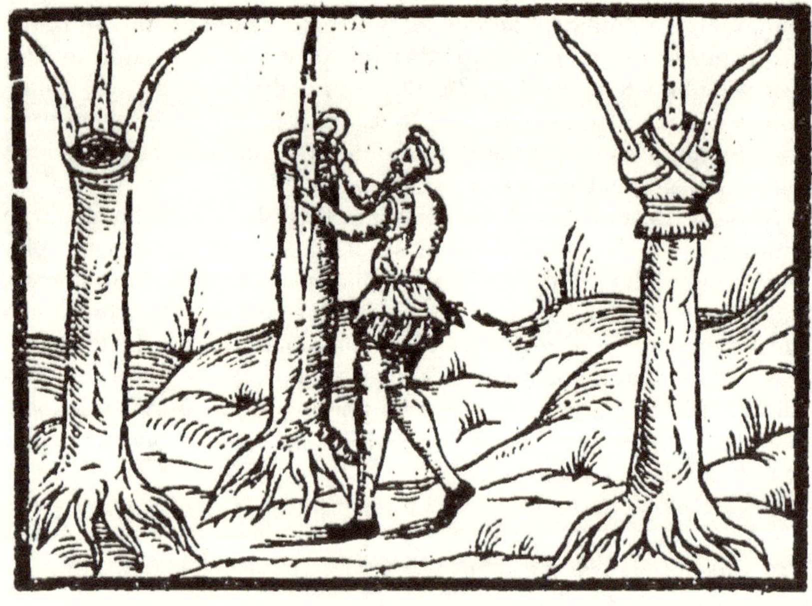

1 Leonard Mascall, *A booke of the arte and maner how to plant and graffe all sortes of trees,* (London: John Wright, 1590), 58. Reprinted courtesy of the University of Cambridge.

2 Mascall, *A booke of the arte and maner how to plant and graffe all sortes of trees*, 74. Reprinted courtesy of the University of Cambridge.

and imposed, the other natural, equal, and spontaneous. In the model of artificial grafting a dominating, vividly phallic "scion" is inserted into the incised cleft of the receiving "stock." Figure 1 is an image of artificial grafting from the title page of Leonard Mascall's manual, *A booke of the arte and maner, howe to plant and graffe all sortes of trees* (1590), reprinted no fewer than ten times in Shakespeare's lifetime. In his right hand the well-dressed gentleman holds the cutting instrument with which he has made the deep cleft in the stock.

Polixenes's wrongheaded invocation and application of this artificial grafting serves only to place in bold relief the play's alternative, pervasive application of a model of natural grafting that is reciprocal and chiastic. In natural grafting, tree roots and/or branches of the same species spontaneously graft when they make physical contact with each other, such that the bark of the roots or branches is stripped away, thereby exposing the vascular cambium and allowing the roots or branches to graft together. In figure 2, also from Mascall's manual,[24] we see the chiastic conditions and chiastic effects of natural grafting, in roots as well as in branches. Seen here graphically is what, we will see in a moment, Camillo will unknowingly prophesy about Leontes and Polixenes and their progeny: "There rooted between them then such an affection which cannot choose branch now." I have drawn a rectangle upon the rooting together that has produced this tree and circles upon three of the branchings-together of the branches that emerge from cross-matchings and generate, as well, their own branchings, each as part of a chiasm around a centre point that cannot be shown.

By a chiastic art that is closely analogous to this natural grafting, the protagonists of *The Winter's Tale*, acting in equality and reciprocity, naturally redeem their consciousness of "nature" through art. This pattern of natural grafting not only configures the whole of the play's plot (including, despite himself, Polixenes's own place within that plot) but already sets out the goal of an intersubjective consciousness, built on chiastic reciprocity, that can be humanity's greatest blessing. Here, as so often elsewhere, for Shakespeare chiastic form expresses both the interchanging flux of sameness and difference in physical reality as well as the meditative reasoning that can be applied to that interchange. In *The Winter's Tale* the art of chiasmus thus configures grafting as an intersection at a point of "separation" and "great difference" in the physical world. This is also the unrepresentable inner point in which the "nothing" as "vast" can make us alive, as meditators, to a transformed *now* of coexistent being.

We can begin to offer a penultimate understanding of the significance of grafting in *The Winter's Tale*. Camillo pictures the chiastic workings of the natural grafting of roots and branches of the houses of Sicilia and Bohemia: "In their childhoods … there *[A]* rooted betwixt them then *[B]* such an affection *[B]* which cannot choose but *[A]* branch now." The grafted roots are Leontes and Polixenes. The branches that will be produced by the grafting of Sicilia-Bohemia (Camillo does not know) will be Florizel and Perdita. Indeed, as we have begun to see, Camillo's words will turn out to be an oracular prophecy of everything that is destined to happen in *The Winter's Tale*, including Camillo's own being coupled with Paulina, and even, as we shall soon explain, encompassing the spectator's shared responses from a vantage point outside the play. Here is Camillo:

> Sicilia cannot show himself over-kind to Bohemia. They were trained together in their childhoods; and there rooted betwixt them then such an affection which cannot choose but branch now. Since their more mature dignities and royal necessities made separation of their society, their encounters, though not personal, have been royally attorneyed with interchange of gifts, letters, loving embassies; that they have seemed to be together, though absent; shook hands, as over a vast; and embraced as it were from the ends of opposed winds. The heavens continue their loves! (1.1.18–21)

Camillo thus sets out his understanding of a life-determining chiasmus in the way Leontes and Polixenes were thus "trained," in horticultural terms, in accordance with having a root grafting "betwixt them": "*[A]* they have seemed to be together though absent, *[B]* shook hands *[B]* as over a vast, and *[A]* embraced as it were from the ends of opposed winds" (24–5). Yet Camillo has no grasp of the "vast" of "separation," the unrepresentable nothing, that lies waiting within this chiasmus and in which an atemporal now is disclosed, that is, at the intersecting point of chiasmus figured as grafting.[25]

Paulina and Pauline Grafting

Given the heaven-directed relation of Camillo's and Paulina's own branching to the continuity of grafting in *The Winter's Tale,* we should not be surprised to discover that Paulina has an important role in placing the trope of grafting at the centre of this play. In fact, her role is even greater than Camillo's in disclosing, within the trope of grafting itself, both the special temporality that it generates and its ultimate fruit of blessing.

It has long been suggested that Shakespeare's naming of Paulina – a character who is Shakespeare's own invention – is meant to inject ideas of Paul's Epistle to the Romans into *The Winter's Tale.* A Pauline echo has been heard in Paulina's exhortation to the assembled company in the play's final scene: "It is required / You do awake your faith. Then all stand still" (5.3.94–5).[26] In *King Lear*, Cordelia invokes Christ's words at Luke 2:49, saying to Lear, "O dear father, / It is thy business that I go about" (4.4.23–4). I propose that in *The Winter's Tale* Paulina's exhortation to stand in awakened faith not only recalls Romans 11:20, "because of unbelief they were broken off, and thou standest by faith," but brings with it the creative power of Paul's extended simile of grafting in which "thou standest by faith" is the core:

> *If the root be holy, so are the branches.... If some of the branches be broken off, and thou, being a wild olive tree, wert graffed in among them, and with them partakest of the root* and fatness of the olive tree ... *thou standest by faith.... And they also, if they abide not still in unbelief, shall be graffed in*: for God is able to graff them in again.... How much more shall these, which be the natural *branches*, be graffed into their own olive tree?... So all Israel shall be saved: as it is written, There shall come out of Sion *the Deliverer.... For of him, and through him, and to him, are all things*: to whom be glory for ever.
>
> (*King James Version*, 11:16–36; emphases added)

Paul's simile lays out the condition of redemption or blessing that will be created in Christ's grafting of Gentile believers onto Jewish believers.[27] Paulina further echoes this intent in verses that have seemed to commentators oddly vague. Soon after she has said, "It is required / You do awake your faith. Then all stand still" and "'Tis time," she adds, as if to Hermione alone,

> Bequeath to death your numbness, for from him
> Dear life redeems you. (5.3.102–3)

Editors of the play have usually glossed the perplexing pronoun "him" as *death*. Yet the word "redeems" suggests far heavier freight for this "him." I suggest that, in fact, it takes us back to the resounding transcendental coda of Paul's elaboration of the efficacy of grafting in faith. Paulina's "from him" points, once again, to the above passage from Paul where he ends with the Deliverer's power to redeem, to save, to give "dear life" in place of death, specifically redeeming the death of the spirit: "For of him, and through him, and to him, are all things." Through Paulina's invoking of this "him" we have exited theatre and entered a transcendental realm of redeemed "dear life" that is beyond worldly time and earthly representation. Yet not even the Pauline Paulina could see the further Shakespearean intention in the art of chiasmus that configures grafting as an intersection at a point of "great difference" or *epoché*. This takes place in the point of intersection between *King Lear* and *The Winter's Tale*. At the unrepresentable inner point within this chiastic object of reflection – made from reflection on the two artefacts together – the "nothing" as "vast" makes us alive, as meditators, to coexistent being, not least to intersubjective coexistence with Shakespeare. This ultimate blessing of a grafting between the two plays is therefore realized in the chiastic point of a mere *nothing* that now affords the onlooker spectator, with onlooker Shakespeare, the realized experience of the *now* that is beyond theatre.

Appendix: Stanley Cavell and Christoph Menke on Spectatorship and Presentness in *King Lear*

Stanley Cavell writes,

> The perception or attitude demanded in following this drama [*King Lear*] is one which demands a continuous attention to what is happening at each here and now, as if everything of significance is happening at this moment, while each thing that happens turns a leaf of time. I think of it as an experience of *continuous presentness*. Its demands are as rigorous as those of any spiritual exercise....
>
> Catharsis ... is a matter of purging attachment from everything but the present, from pity for the past and terror of the future.... What is revealed is my separateness from what is happening to [the protagonists of the tragedy and to fellow spectators]; that I am I, and here. It is only in this perception of them as separate from me that I make them present.... I have no present apart from theirs.[28]

Christoph Menke challenges Cavell's claims for presentness and spectatorship in *King Lear* by expanding upon Nietzsche's perceptions of irony in *Hamlet*. In Menke's understanding of both *Hamlet* and *King Lear* the "theatrical spectatorship" of the protagonist and the audience entails a "doubly ironic reflection" that causes the "dissolution of presentness" even in the "experience of action." The "double irony" that Menke sees here is "the (theatrical) irony of the player over against his role, which, according to his whims, he puts on or takes off like a mask" and "the (dramatic) irony of fate, over against the agent's intentions, which themselves give rise to what turns against them." Thus in Menke's view spectatorship in *King Lear*, as in *Hamlet*, interrupts "absorption in the presentness of dramatic events and characters" by "adhering to the rebukes of an irony that dissolves the dramatic present."[29]

Cavell and Menke are both describing different stages of an experience of presentness that is embedded in a linear temporality. Such a presentness continuously "turns a leaf of time" (Cavell), while accompanying the "experience of action" (Menke). Menke's recording of a "dissolution of presentness" in "theatrical spectatorship" can even be seen as a fulfilment of Cavell's description of theatrical "catharsis" as the preliminary step of "purging attachment from everything but the present." I have turned to Cavell and Menke both to acknowledge that the experience of presentness in *King Lear* has important temporal dimensions and to note elements of both of their accounts that point beyond temporal presentness. Cavell's idea of a purged present, the demands of which are "as rigorous as those of any spiritual exercise," requires an attention to worldly objects that is paradoxically detached from worldly impingements, detached as well, therefore, from the time of contingency in which pity and terror are occasioned. So, too, the picture of double irony that Menke observes in Shakespeare's spectatorship constitutes, on the concrete level of configured language, a four-way cancellation of polarities that has at least one important possibility that Menke has left out: in the very space or instant of the dissolution of chronological present time one might experience an inward presentness that is beyond the reach of time – that is atemporal. For achieving this atemporal presentness, too, the initial movement, emphasized by Cavell, of alternately being with, and being separate from, others is indispensable. Once achieved, the inward authenticity of this atemporal presentness returns us to the world and to the other.

NOTES

1 Frank Kermode, "Introduction," *The Winter's Tale* (New York: New American Library, 1998), lxxvii.

2 Emily Sun, *Succeeding King Lear: Literature, Exposure, and the Possibility of Politics* (New York: Fordham University Press, 2010), 63 (where Sun notes the chiastic form of Edgar's spectatorship) and 75. Tzachi Zamir, *Double Vision: Moral Philosophy and Shakespearean Drama* (Princeton, NJ: Princeton University Press, 2007) explores "the epistemological role(s) of literary experiences" in forming

moral values (11–14 and throughout). In *King Lear* he describes "rhetorical forms that create openness and response to propositional content" and "the reader's own modified perception of such content" (200–1).

3 A fascinating and instructive parallel to Shakespeare's ways of proceeding in these matters is to be found in Emily Dickinson's different ways of reaching similar goals. On Dickinson's achievement of timelessness in her representations of space and time, see Emily Miller Budick, *Emily Dickinson and the Life of Language: A Study in Symbolic Poetics* (Baton Rouge: Louisiana State University Press, 1985), 197–228.

4 Edmund Husserl, *Ideas: General Introduction to Pure Phenomenology*, trans. W.R. Boyce Gibson (London: George Allen & Unwin, 1952), 110–11, 116–19. In *Being and Time*, trans. John Macquarrie and Edward Robinson (Oxford: Blackwell, 1962), 62 and 65, Heidegger highlights his disagreement with Husserl's conception of the now by pointedly commencing his exposition of the now of *Dasein* exactly as does Husserl his exposition of the now of inner human consciousness that is disclosed by the *epoché*. Thereafter Heidegger's claims for the now of *Dasein* as a "primordial" or originary temporality work to displace Husserl's human now. Derrida's well-known critiques of a "metaphysics of presence" underlie much of his work. They are set out in a large variety of deconstructive contexts, such as, extensively, in *Margins of Philosophy*, trans. Alan Bass (Chicago: University of Chicago Press, 1982). Derrida's views of temporality are heavily influenced by Heidegger's disagreements with Husserl, but Derrida is critical of Heidegger even for his implicit affirmation of vestigial elements of a metaphysics of presence. On these issues see Frank Schalow, *The Renewal of the Heidegger-Kant Dialogue: Action, Thought, and Responsibility* (Albany: SUNY Press, 1992).

5 I will have a further word to say about Heidegger and presence below. I refer here to Benjamin's highly compressed invocation of a *Jetztzeit* in his "Theses on the Philosophy of History," in *Illuminations: Essays and Reflections*, ed. Hannah Arendt, trans. Harry Zohn (New York: Schocken, 1969), 253–64; and Agamben's building upon Benjamin's term in his *The Time That Remains: A Commentary on the Letter to the Romans*, trans. Patricia Dailey (Stanford, CA: Stanford University Press, 2005).

6 In viewing Kant's transcendental deduction and the inward actuality of a transcendental ego, an important way station and provocation to Husserl was Johann Gottlieb Fichte's view of the actuality of an "original," "productive" "I" laid down in *The Science of Knowledge*, trans. Peter Heath and John Lachs (Cambridge: Cambridge University Press, 1982), 206–8 and elsewhere. On these relations see Thomas M. Seebohm," Fichte's and

Husserl's Critique of Kant's Transcendental Deduction," *Husserl Studies* 2 (1985): 53–74. For the Kantian places, see *Critique of Pure Reason*, A 181, B 224, A 218, B 265, A 225, B 273. I will return to this point near the close of this chapter. Citations of Kant in German are from *Kants Werke: Akademie-Textausgabe* (Berlin: de Gruyter, 1968). Quotations from Kant in English translation are from the *Critique of Pure Reason*, trans. Norman Kemp Smith (London: Macmillan, 1993); and *Critique of the Power of Judgment*, trans. Paul Guyer and Eric Matthews (Cambridge: Cambridge University Press, 2000). Page numbers for citations within my text are according to the Akademie edition. For suggestive remarks on Kant's and Husserl's overlapping conceptions of a transcendental ego, see Karl Ameriks, "From Kant to Frank: The Ineliminable Subject," in *The Modern Subject: Conceptions of the Self in Classical German Philosophy*, ed. Karl Ameriks and Dieter Sturma (SUNY Press: Albany, 1995), 223–4. On possible connections between Husserl and Kant in these matters see, among many others, Mark Kingwell, "Husserl's Sense of Wonder," *Philosophical Forum* 31 (2000): 85–107; and Danielle Lories, "Remarks on Aesthetic Intentionality: Husserl or Kant," *International Journal of Philosophical Studies* 14 (2006): 31–49.

7 To be sure, not everyone will agree that such a bracketing, antecedent to a reaffirmation and reclaiming of the world, is either credible or possible. Jacques Maritain, for example, remarked that Husserl's *epoché* involved the flat contradiction of "*thinking of being while refusing to think of it as being.*" See *Distinguish to Unite, Or, The Degrees of Knowledge*, trans. Gerald B. Phelan (South Bend, IN: University of Notre Dame Press, 1995; first English language edition 1937), 108. Yet we should recall that a large part of the thinking of both Heidegger and Derrida directly begins with Husserl's *epoché* or bracketing. Derrida, following Heidegger, parted ways with Husserl on what the *epoché* leaves behind. Derrida's many engagements with Husserl's philosophy refer frequently to Eugen Fink's Husserl-approved presentation of Husserl's philosophy in his highly influential article, "Die phänomenologische Philosophie Edmund Husserls in der gegenwärtigen Kritik," in *Kant-Studien* 38 (1933): 319–83; translated by R.O. Elveton as "The Phenomenological Philosophy of Edmund Husserl and Contemporary Criticism" in *The Phenomenology of Husserl: Selected Critical Readings*, ed. Elveton, 2nd ed. (Seattle, WA: Noesis, 2000), 70–139.

8 On these last points see Dermot Moran's lucid exposition in *Husserl's Crisis of the European Sciences and Transcendental Phenomenology: An Introduction* (Cambridge: Cambridge University Press, 2012), 60–2.

9 In *Kant and Milton* (Cambridge, MA: Harvard University Press, 2010) I have commented extensively on Kant's interest in the experience of the sublime in encounters with both nature and art.

10 Cited from "Hospitality, Justice, and Responsibility: A Dialogue with Jacques Derrida," in *Questioning Ethics: Contemporary Debates in Philosophy*, ed. Richard Kearney and Mark Dooley (London: Routledge, 1999), 81.

11 On Heidegger's applications of his view of negativity to chiasmus, among other things, in order to disclose *Dasein* or non-human being, see Jean-François Mattéi, "The Heideggerian Chiasmus," in *Heidegger: From Metaphysics to Thought*, ed. Dominique Janicaud and Jean-François Mattéi, trans. Michael Gendre (Albany: SUNY Press, 1995), 39–150. Paul de Man, *Allegories of Reading: Figural Language in Rousseau, Nietzsche, Rilke, and Proust* (New Haven, CT: Yale University Press, 1979), 49, offered the oft-quoted (though largely unexplained) observation that "chiasmus … can only come into being as the result of a void, of a lack that allows for the rotating motion of the polarities." De Man's location of a terminal void within chiasmus has been questioned by Brian Vickers, "Deconstruction's Designs on Rhetoric," in *Rhetoric as Pedagogy: Its History, Philosophy, and Practice – Essays in Honor of James J. Murphy*, ed. Winifred Bryan Horner and Michael Leff (London: Routledge, 1995), 304; and Frank B. Farrell, *Why Does Literature Matter?* (Ithaca, NY: Cornell University Press, 2004), 88–90. For a survey of thinking about chiasmus in post-structuralism, especially in de Man and Derrida, see Rodolphe Gasché's "Reading Chiasms," his introduction to Andrzej Warminski's *Readings in Interpretation: Hölderlin, Hegel, Heidegger* (Minneapolis: University of Minnesota Press, 1987), ix–xxvi, as well as Warminski's own comments on the topic.

12 Joel Fineman, *Shakespeare's Perjured Eye: The Invention of Poetic Subjectivity in the Sonnets* (Berkeley: University of California Press, 1986). Marion Trousdale, "Reading the Early Modern Text," in *Shakespeare and Language*, ed. Stanley Wells, Shakespeare Survey (Cambridge: Cambridge University Press, 1997), 50:137, criticizes Fineman's "essentializing of verbal patterns," as in his reading of *The Rape of Lucrece* where chiasmus is inherently identified with rape. Harold Bloom, whose own distinctive project in *Shakespeare: The Invention of the Human* (New York: Riverhead Books, 1998), shares many of Fineman's goals, praises his "authentic insight into the link between Shakespeare's portraits of the ever-growing inner self and Shakespeare's preternatural awareness of bisexuality and its disguises," but disagrees with Fineman's ascribing "everything to 'language,'" 714.

13 Lisa Freinkel, *Reading Shakespeare's Will: The Theology of Figure from Augustine to the Sonnets* (New York: Columbia University Press, 2002), 22–3.

14 Freinkel, *Reading Shakespeare's Will*, 30.

15 Stephen Greenblatt, *Will in the World: How Shakespeare Became Shakespeare* (New York: Random House, 2012), 302–3, 323. Greenblatt's phrase is

adapted from Brutus's saying, "All the interim is / Like a phantasma" (*Julius Caesar*, 2.1.64–5).

16 Sanford Budick, "Hamlet's 'Now' of Inward Being," in *Shakespeare's Hamlet: Philosophical Perspectives*, ed. Tzachi Zamir, 133–56 (New York: Oxford University Press, 2018).

17 I will reserve for another occasion an explanation of the relation of chiasmus, in apostrophe, to intentionality.

18 Lest the reader feel put upon, I wish to acknowledge that the detailed mapping of chiasmata is always to some extent arbitrary, even if, as I believe, the experiential impact of these chiastic movements of sameness and difference is undeniable.

19 The first occurrence of the word "now" in these lines is absent at this point in the second quarto but appears there in both the first quarto and the Folio.

20 Citations from Shakespeare's plays are from *The Norton Shakespeare*, ed. Stephen Greenblatt et al. (New York: Norton, 1997). Unless otherwise indicated, citations from *King Lear* are from the collated text.

21 Shakespeare, *The Winter's Tale*, ed. John Pitcher (London: Bloomsbury, 2010), 19.

22 See Alfred Schütz, "The Problem of Transcendental Intersubjectivity in Husserl (with Comments of Dorion Cairns and Eugen Fink)," trans. Fred Kersten, in *Schutzian Research* 2 (2010): 47. In this achievement of a "second *epoché*" in the double mirroring of intersubjectivity Fink and Schütz see an indispensable role of the mutual directedness of an awareness of death, in both self and other, in which "the transcendental subject must constitute itself and Others" in consciousness of "the finitude of human being, the human fate of death" (51). This, too, is clearly in evidence, in the ever-present awareness of past or imminent death (e.g., of Cordelia, Mamillius, Antigonus) that hangs over both *King Lear* and *The Winter's Tale* and that frequently finds expression in the *epochés* of their chiasmata.

23 Eugen Fink, *Sixth Cartesian Meditation: The Idea of a Transcendental Theory of Method*, trans. Ronald Bruzina (Bloomington: Indiana University Press, 1988), 48, describes a second-order "phenomenology of the phenomenological reduction" in "making of the action of reduction the object of reflection."

24 Mascall, *A booke of the arte and maner, howe to plant and graffe all sortes of trees*, 74.

25 Editors have glossed the "over-kind"-ness of which Camillo speaks in many ways. I suggest that it most naturally points to the inescapable bond of nature in which they are mutually intertwined. This "kind"-ness equally rules the lives of Leontes and Polixenes and will rule, as well – Camillo

cannot yet know – the lives of their offspring. In addition, as we have noted, Camillo cannot yet know that the branch grafting from the root branching that he has described will include the "match" of himself with Paulina. Shakespeare makes these larger connections unmistakable by inscribing a host of ancillary, smaller connections. In the first scene of the play Archidamus predicts to Camillo that "we will be justified in our loves" (1.1.8). In the last scene of the play Leontes makes the match of Camillo and Paulina, saying, that it is "here justified / By us, a pair of kings." Similarly, in the first scene Camillo ends his account of the root grafting of Leontes and Polixenes "that cannot choose but branch now," with the prayer, "The heavens continue their loves." In the last scene we hear from Leontes that the root grafting by this "pair" here branches yet further – in the attained "now" of chiastic grafting – by "heavens directing" (5.3.145–6, 150).

26 An extended argument in this vein is provided by Ken Jackson, "'Grace to Boot': St. Paul, Messianic Time, and Shakespeare's *The Winter's Tale*," in *The Return of Theory in Early Modern English Studies*, ed. Paul Cefalu and Bryan Reynolds (New York: Palgrave, 2011), 192–210. Jackson relies heavily on Agamben's *The Time That Remains: A Commentary on the Letter to the Romans*, which, as I have noted, reads Romans through the lens of Walter Benjamin's concept of messianic time – a concept that was itself influenced by Husserl's exposition of the *epoché*. On significant points of correspondence between Shakespeare's thinking and Paul's, see Julia Reinhard Lupton, *Citizen-Saints: Shakespeare and Political Theology* (Chicago: University of Chicago Press, 2005), 21–48. I am grateful for her comments on this chapter.

27 It has been observed by biblical commentators that Paul has here borrowed an early Jewish midrash that was later recorded in the Talmud (tractate Yibamoth 63a). That midrash glosses the phrase from Genesis 12:3 in which Abraham is told by God, "And in thee shall all families of the earth be blessed." The Hebrew word for *and shall be blessed* is ונברכו. The midrash turns on reading the root of this word, ב ר כ, as that of the Hebrew word for grafting, הרכבה, which thus yields the astounding meaning not that the grafting will lead to blessing but that the grafting is blessing itself. "R. Eleazar … stated: What is meant by the text, *And in thee shall the families of the earth be blessed?* The Holy One, blessed be He, said to Abraham, 'I have two goodly shoots to engraft on you: Ruth the Moabitess and Naamah the Ammonitess.'" In Romans, Paul's eleven packed verses laying out his extended simile of the grafting of Gentile and Jewish believers is thus itself a grafting of Christian and Jewish texts as well as of all who stand

by faith. In Judaism, spiritual identity is passed on matrilineally. From Naamah the Ammonitess, wife of Solomon, righteous queen of Israel, will come Solomon's royal successor Rehoboam. From Ruth the Moabitess will come the prophesied Deliverer. Neither Rabbi Eleazar nor Saint Paul spelled out how grafting might in itself be blessing or deliverance. Whether or not Shakespeare knew the grafted Jewish origin of Paul's metaphor of grafting, Shakespeare finds his way, resonating with Paul, to produce blessing from the structures of grafting.

28 Stanley Cavell, *Must We Mean What We Say? A Book of Essays* (Cambridge: Cambridge University Press, 1976), 322, 338–9 (italics in original).

29 Christoph Menke, "Tragedy and Skepticism: On *Hamlet*," in *Varieties of Skepticism: Essays after Kant, Wittgenstein, and Cavell*, ed. Andrea Kern and James Conant, 377–83 (Berlin: De Gruyter, 2014).

chapter ten

Hegel with Hamlet: Questions of Method

ANSELM HAVERKAMP

He had perfected the means
to represent inwardness.[1]

– For Stephen, 7 November 2018

An Anecdote: Entertaining the Idea

Hegel's first biographer, Karl Rosenkranz, begins his portrait of the philosopher, one of whose best-known students he was, with an anecdote: Hegel's schoolteacher, Löffler (no first name known), had given to his talented student, the eight-year-old Hegel, Wieland's new translation of Shakespeare's plays. He would not understand them yet, but learn to understand them soon.[2] The prediction proved true and the recommendation valid: Hegel's philosophy did develop by learning how to read Shakespeare. Not only the conventional pillars of instruction, Greek tragedy and the church fathers, were formative in Hegel's education (all of classical literature, Greek and Latin, in fact),[3] but their modern antipode Shakespeare – a commonplace illustrated by *Wilhelm Meister*, the educational novel par excellence, and still part of the agenda in Joyce's portrait of the young man in *Ulysses*.

Anecdotes have a point, and since Rosenkranz's is closely tied to the literary pretexts of Hegel's philosophical development, the point seems simple enough. Rather than adding to Hegel's picture a curiously fashionable accent, the story is to compensate some flaw, which asks for an explanation in a genius like Hegel. The crux Rosenkranz has to master in his biography and does indeed master with the Shakespeare anecdote is the improbability of the modern philosopher as genius. It is not that Hegel had read Aristotle or Kant as an eight-year-old boy or that he excelled in mathematics like Pascal or Leibniz. The celebrated philosopher of history had read Shakespeare for a start. He was no prodigy in his profession, but a shy, amiable young man and a friendly, unassuming professor later on, about whom the biographer had to confess that all who had known him in his younger years were utterly surprised to hear about the fame of his later years. The only consistency Rosenkranz elaborates in his presentation of the biographical sources, as if it were the cunning of reason itself, is the parallel development of Hegel as a philosopher and lover.[4] Notoriously shy in his way with women – gifted with an unusual respect for the weaker sex, but without success in courting the admired ones – Hegel married late, Rosenkranz reports, as a surprise almost, and it was a "beau marriage" in the substantial sense that characterized his life and philosophy throughout. Thus, why and in what respect Shakespeare?

Rosenkranz states the case of his admired teacher with utmost care and cleverness; it is the case of the exemplary philosopher of enlightened times in a bourgeois society. As an institution of dialectical self-understanding, the theatre provides – asks for and supports – the enlightened subject's frame of a public consciousness. In the *Phenomenology of the Mind*, which has also been translated as one *of Spirit*, Shakespeare does not simply mirror the world-historical process of the Enlightenment. He does not just illustrate this process, but the stage is the medium of what came to happen. It is not easy, but philologically rather difficult, to prove this point of Rosenkranz's anecdote. And precisely this is the merit of an anecdote: to point within the context of a life – a life's text – to vicissitudes that would otherwise escape, since they are beyond the biographer's means. Which does not mean they would escape his mind. Ominously, Rosenkranz carried, and was certainly conscious of it, a name from *Hamlet* – an involvement of the biographer in his anecdote that would need an anecdote of its own.

Witnesses: Kierkegaard and Solger

There are few developments in Shakespeare criticism from its eighteenth-century's beginnings to the New Historicism of the twentieth century that remained untouched or un-prefigured by Hegel's reflections on Shakespeare. His reading of Shakespeare is an unrivalled (although mostly unacknowledged) paradigm for the post-Romantic academic discipline of literary criticism as a "critique" in the post-Kantian sense.

Prominent successors in the history of philosophy like Kierkegaard and Nietzsche followed his reading of Shakespeare more closely than the explicit Hegelian aftermath admits. Nietzsche's "Dionysian Man" is a barely disguised response to Hegel's *Hamlet*, as was Kierkegaard's resistance to Goethe's "aesthetic" life. As a model for Hegel's reading, Wilhelm Meister's encounter with *Hamlet* in Goethe's novel remained the backdrop of a critical stage-setting that is still effective – no longer, maybe, in the analytically advanced discipline that calls itself still philosophy, but in the study of literature and its lead model for literary modernity, Shakespeare Studies.

A well-informed, philosophically competent witness beside former students of Hegel like Rosenkranz is Kierkegaard, who was familiar with Hegel's philosophical milieu, though not part of his school. He begins the second part of his timely dissertation (if there ever was a timely dissertation, it was this one) with an unmistakable reference to Hegel's infatuation with Shakespeare. The topic is irony and the philosophical key in the title, *The Concept of Irony*, was Hegel's bone of contention: "the truth of irony." The irony implied – beside the one thematized in Kierkegaard's title, like in the sequel, *The Concept of Anxiety* – is due to a conceptual paradox of terms, states of mind like irony and anxiety that do not depend on being conceptualized. The starting point is Hegel's colleague Karl Wilhelm Ferdinand Solger's conception of irony. Hegel had dismissed, disqualified, even denounced Friedrich Schlegel's irony, but had given in to Solger's mediating attempt to rescue the concept. Without detour, Kierkegaard comes to the exemplary case, crucial for Hegel, as it was for the Schlegels, Tieck and Solger alike. Right from the start (third sentence of part 2, "The Truth of Irony") Shakespeare is first on the agenda: "There is an extra-ordinary degree of *objectivity* in his madness," Kierkegaard explains: "When Shakespeare is related ironically to what he writes, it is precisely in order *to let the objective dominate.* Irony is everywhere present [in his work]; it sanctions every single line so that there will be neither too much nor too little."[5]

"Let the objective dominate" was Hegel's judgment on Shakespeare's "dramatic irony." Kierkegaard reports Hegel "in der Sache" and the "Sache's" name is "the objective," or, in Solger's more cautious way of putting it, "so-called objectivity."[6] The subjectivity effect of irony brings out what is objectively happening and not due to just subjective imagination – an objective state of affairs opposed to the imaginary freedom proposed by Friedrich Schlegel. For Kierkegaard, Shakespeare's role in the irony debate was still evident, and his testimony of a by now opaque state of affairs is all the more valuable. The point from which Kierkegaard proceeds is Hegel's positive reaction to Solger's rescue of an objective irony from Friedrich Schlegel's (as Hegel feared) nihilism *avant la lettre.* Kierkegaard ironically restages Hegel; he "mimes" Hegel, one might say, whose answer to Solger he cites.[7] In this response Shakespeare is always present, beginning with Solger's review of *Lectures on Dramatic Art and Literature* by Friedrich Schlegel's brother, August Wilhelm Schlegel, a work whose authority would become the starting point for Nietzsche's *Birth of Tragedy.* In Nietzsche, Shakespeare's importance for Hegel returns with, but unhappily reduced to, August Wilhelm's analysis – a twisted story, which reverberates up to now.[8]

I shall concentrate on what is underestimated in this story, Hegel's substantial interest in Shakespeare, for which "dramatic irony" remained a dubious denominator. The alternative, in which Hegel agreed with Solger's discussion of irony, is "objective humor" as an ingredient already of Hegel's appreciation of *Wilhelm Meister.* A key of Hegel's philosophy of art in general, this term owes everything to his reading of Shakespeare, and Rosenkranz points in this direction. But it does more than give a clue for future historians of ideas; it initiates questions of method rather than of content. Writing with Shakespeare on the side meant more for Hegel than registering humour in Shakespeare's plays. Responding to Solger, the objectivity of Hegel's humour transcends dramatic irony in that it reveals itself in the process called "phenomenology." There, the objectivity is a matter not of content, but of cognitive performance within the genealogy of the "subject." After Aristotle reading Greek tragedy and Saint Augustine reading Vergil (a disaster barely mended by Dante), Hegel's reading of Shakespeare may be the foremost instance of what it means philologically, in terms of method, to read literature philosophically. In order to demonstrate the intricate interlacing of allusions to Shakespeare's texts and their reflective transformation in Hegel's own text, I proceed along a series of longer passages from the *Phenomenology.* I take the additional complication of a Hegel translation that does not know about the implicitly transported Shakespeare as an opportunity to clarify and highlight the relevant points in the order of their occurrence.[9]

Hamlet's Progress: The *Phenomenology*

The *Phenomenology* reads best from the end – Hegel's long preface is the proof, since there he does exactly this: instead of an outline, he looks back from the result. Thus, it seems only appropriate to begin with the role of art in the perspective of the book's ending, in the penultimate chapter of the penultimate part, "Religion" (CC). "Religion in the Form of Art" (b) is the chapter's title, which takes the decisive step towards "The revealed religion" (c), and to the last part, "Absolute Knowing" (DD).[10] The multilayered design of the book was and is still subject to much controversy; suffice it here to say that literature has a significant part in it, especially near its riddled ending, where empirical history enters into what seemed to be at first a purely cognitive affair, but becomes more and more intertwined with historically concrete manifestations of the mind in its self-conscious development. In this development, in which it is philosophy's part of re-flection in the sense of looking back, in the retrospect of a higher perspective, literature manifests the growth of the mind's intellectual capacity.[11] The winding way of what happens in that process is in parts opaque and far less obvious than that it happens. Literature does not simply illustrate the process for Hegel, but is a medium of what actually comes to happen through it.

A first decisive step for the phenomenological project is thus retraced and documented as late as § 733, "Religion in the form of art." This step is of a purely linguistic nature and takes shape in the institution of Greek tragedy. In tragedy (Aeschylus and Sophocles) rather than in philosophy (Socrates and Plato), the decisive threshold was reached and crossed. *The Birth of Tragedy* will imitate and emulate this Hegelian move and reach farther back, beyond the institution of tragedy, to its performative origins. Like Hegel, Nietzsche will find the perfect instance of the Dionysian primal scene incorporated in Hamlet instead of Socrates – but this, it is important to realize, was already a crucial insight in Shakespeare's drama itself.[12] Not to forget Freud, whose intuition of an "Oedipus complex," found the primordial scene fully represented in *Hamlet:* It is Hamlet who first had the Oedipus complex – not Oedipus, who could not know, but Hamlet, who came to know. Here, Hegel did more than Nietzsche and Freud would or could admit and most readers suspect.[13] Not unexpectedly, he closely followed (and presupposed for his readers silently) the analysis of tragedy in Aristotle's *Poetics,* but with a twist as yet unheard of. The silent conversation between Aristotle and his distant other Shakespeare is the hidden challenge of Hegel's argument (my emphases and amendments added):

> § 733. A higher language, that of Tragedy, gathers closer together the dispersed moments of the inner essential world and the world of action [of

> the inner essence and action of the world]: the substance of the divine, in accordance with the nature of the Notion [Hegel's *Begriff*], sunders itself into its shapes [i.e., differentiates itself conceptually into different literary characters – *Gestalten*], and their movement is likewise in conformity with the Notion [the characters correspond in their movement to their conception]. In regard to form, the language ceases to be narrative [as is already Aristotle's point], because it enters into the content, just as the content ceases to be one that is imaginatively presented [and consequently imagined – *vorgestellt*]. The hero is him- [or her-] self the speaker, and the performance [*Vorstellung* – both "show" and "idea" – a conscious pun on Hegel's part] displays to the audience, who are as spectators also self-conscious human beings, who know their rights and purposes, the power and the will of their specific nature and know how to assert them [to speak for themselves]. They are artists who do not express with unconscious naturalness and naivety the external aspect of their resolves and enterprises, as it happens in the language accompanying ordinary actions in actual life. Lastly [in the end], these characters exist as actual human beings [their being – *Dasein* – as characters makes them finally – *endlich* – like "real people" – into *wirkliche Menschen* – two more puns: *end-lich* – in the *end,* and *wirk-lich* – *acting* like in real life], who impersonate the heroes and portray them, not in the form of a narrative, but in the actual speech of the actors themselves.

The linguistic turn, which occurs on the phenomenological way to "absolute knowledge," leads from the religiously bound participation of the audience in the rite to the awakening of a self-conscious community from its narrative embeddedness in the cult. The rite had re-enacted the mythical foundations of the community as an unquestionable order of things: imposition of power by the mighty, related and re-enforced by the epic singer. This stage is resumed and left behind, not reiterated in Aeschylus, Sophocles, and Euripides. Hegel rephrases Aristotle's genealogy of literary genres: the transition from the epic tradition to the tragic performance of that tradition in the institution of the theatre.[14] He revises the mimetic functioning of art from a quasi-natural embeddedness and binding force to a medium in the process of a shared consciousness towards its self-conscious perfection in "absolute knowing." The text is difficult, to say the least (especially, if one is not aware of the implied Aristotle), and Hegel's translators had a hard time. That much, however, seems safe to say in a first summary: Hegel avoids the topicality of the *Querelle* between ancients and moderns and the question about the extent to which the moderns are more advanced in their art than the ancients. In accordance with the contemporary (Young's and Herder's) pairing of Sophocles with Shakespeare as his modern equal, Hegel's analysis seems closer to the Shandean motif of the dwarfs on the shoulders of giants.[15]

Unlike Jacob Bernays and Nietzsche, Hegel takes the Aristotelian *catharsis* as a symptom, rather than as the original essence of tragedy. He is not interested in the effect, but in the peculiar "illocutionary force" (to use J.L. Austin's term) of a spectator-consciousness that is reached in Greek tragedy and enabled and supported by the chorus. After Herder, August Wilhelm Schlegel, ultimate *Hamlet*-translator (Kierkegaard read *Hamlet* in his translation), had elaborated this point with acuteness and remained the relevant authority for Nietzsche. Hegel's conclusion was different; it reached farther – not in spite of, but because he gave Shakespeare a closer reading than the usual references had in stock. Every reader of *Hamlet* knows the riddled outcome of the mouse-trap scene and the Hecuba speech, where *catharsis* is the theme, not the effect – and that is part of the trap. For Hegel, it is the starting point of a deeper analysis (my emphases and amendments added):

> § 736. The content and movement of the Spirit which here is object to itself has already been considered as the nature and [that is, the] realization of the ethical substance. In its religion [Latin *religio,* "binding force"], it attains to a consciousness of itself, or exhibits itself to consciousness in its purer form and its simpler embodiment. If, then, the ethical substance, in virtue of its Notion [in its conception, being conceived of as itself], splits itself as regards its content into powers which were defined as divine and human law, or law of the nether and of the upper world – the one the Family, the other the State power, the first being the feminine and the second the masculine character [both kind and mask] – ... the previously multiform circle of gods with its fluctuating characteristics [and determinations] confines itself to these powers, which are thereby brought closer to genuine individuality [individuality, undivided in the "proper" sense as *eigent-liche Individualität*].

"Closer to individuality" in its "proper" sense means here in the sense of Goethe's *Meister,* in which the undivided self comes into its "own" (becomes *eigent*-lich). It is Hamlet who makes the difference in a maze of complicated analytical respects:

> § 737. At the same time [in equal parts – *zu-gleich*] the ethical substance is divided with respect to its form or to knowing [i.e., it splits itself up

> according to its form or knowing]. The doer finds himself thereby in the antithesis of knowing and not-knowing.... The present reality is, therefore, one thing in itself, and another thing for consciousness [for the conscious actor between knowing and not-knowing]; the upper and the nether law come to signify in this connection the power that knows and reveals itself to consciousness, and the power that conceals itself and lies in ambush. The one ... knows all and reveals all – Phoebus, and Zeus who is his father. But the commands of this truth-speaking god and his announcements of what is, are really [in fact] deceptive. For this knowing is, in its principle, immediately a not-knowing [in its unmediated conception by the therein deceived subject, subjected to this deceptive truth that is not a knowing – *in seinem Begriffe unmittelbar das bloße Nichtwissen*].

The stage, on which this conflict of knowledge is exposed, is ruled from the start by dramatic irony, as a Hegelian critic of the nineteenth century, Connop Thirwall, observed as early as 1833.[16] It presents the audience with a specific type of "negative knowledge" – Cavell calls it a "disowning knowledge" – that sharpens the negativity in Hegel's Shakespeare. For Hegel, the radicalization of this point in *Hamlet* is the latent thrust of the play. It emerges already in Sophocles as the "power that conceals itself and lies in ambush," and looms large in duplicitous "equivocation." We may note here the typological shorthand used by Hegel in his dense account, firmly modelled upon *Oedipus Rex*, but moving on to *Hamlet*, in the mutual illumination of the antithesis of "upper and lower law." Hamlet uncovers and masters the latent "ambush" with a consciousness more advanced than the one deceived in Greek tragedy – a consciousness that Laertes, like a remnant of Greek tragedy, is lacking.

> § 737 (*continued*). The priestess through whom the beautiful god [Apollo] speaks [in *Oedipus*] is in no way different from [is the exact same as – *nichts anders als*] the equivocating sisters of Fate [the "weird sisters"], who by their promises drive [Macbeth] to crime, and who by the double-tongued character of what they announced as a certainty deceive him, who relied on the obvious meaning. The consciousness, therefore, that is purer [Hamlet's] than the latter, which believes in witches [Macbeth's], and is more prudent [*besonnener*], more solid [more profound – *gründlicher*] than the former [Oedipus's], which trusts the priestess and the beautiful god [Apollo], tarries with his revenge, even though the very spirit of his father reveals to him the crime by which he was murdered, and institutes still other proofs – for the reason that this revelatory spirit [the ghost of Hamlet father] could also be the devil.

The consciousness "that is purer," Hamlet's, does not fall for the mythic fallacy, which inescapably dominates Greek tragedy and carries the tragic implication of an "ethical order," in which it is embedded and remains trapped in total deception. Hamlet's narrow escape from this deception is conceived of in Shakespeare as a "turning point of history," Solger concluded, himself a translator of Sophocles, in his *Lectures on Aesthetics.*[17] Congenial to the spirit of the *Phenomenology*, Solger praises Shakespeare for the "sphere of the *purest,* highest subjectivity," which is the sphere of the "*purer* consciousness" demonstrated by Hamlet. Included in Hegel's patchwork is Orestes as the one "who trusted with childlike confidence" (§ 737 continued). Orestes took on the divinely imposed duty to exact a most vicious revenge – the analogy had been discussed early on, already by Nicholas Rowe, and was repeated by Herder before Hegel. Orestes suffers the tragic fate that Hamlet evades; he pays a price for what seems to run down to the same deadly result, but whose remedy lies open in Hamlet's "coming to know," as Cavell has put it in terms of a striking Hegelian negativity, "of what we cannot just not know" (Freud's analysis broadened).[18] Orestes fell prey to a deep tragic necessity, while Hamlet died (as Hegel explains in greater detail in his *Aesthetics*) in a scene of purest contingency, through the fatal "change of rapiers" (5.2.306). There was no tragic mistake (*harmatéma*) that would be culpable, Hegel realizes, nor any mere mishap (*a-tuchéma*).[19] All is under control, and Hamlet acts (in an act of inverted irony) "most royal," as even Fortinbras admits (5.2.403).

In order to highlight Hamlet's exemplary surplus for the conception of the *Phenomenology*, Hegel came up with an extraordinary reading of *Hamlet's* plot structure, which emerges in contrast to the classical Greek background. The intuition "that this revelatory spirit could also be the devil" is not only in the face of all Shakespeare readings and interpretations of his time, it goes against the grain of Hamlet reception in general, which must insist on the seriousness of the true father's father-name and on the truth of his commandment. Hegel, however, had learned through Shakespeare to read Sophocles, which enabled him to recognize in turn how Shakespeare had answered the classical standard of dramatic irony. A devil enters, who seems to have no place in Shakespeare's play, but whose absence is the stronger. "It" – like Hamlet's father ghost an It – impersonates the "objective" within the irony of History, the flip side of the total allegory that salvation history had presented up to Shakespeare. Hegel specifies: "The negative of the object, or its self-supercession, has a positive meaning for the self-consciousness" as "the indivisible unity of being-for-itself" – its individuality. On these negative grounds Hegel enters the last part, "Absolute Knowing" (§ 788), which leads up to the "Calvary of Absolute Spirit" (§ 808). The allegory of History had always been its irony or, from the point of view of the "*absolute* spirit," "*objective* humour." Objectivity in itself is historical; it remains to be investigated, needs to be traced in the epistemological substructure of the process. Again, *Hamlet* is key.

Calvary: The Paradox of the Skull-Bone

In *Hamlet* we witness how tragedy comes to an alternative end: "History comprehended" is the *Phenomenology's* last word (§ 808). *History comprehended* means "at once the recollection and the Golgotha of the Absolute Spirit," Hegel clarifies, recollecting and containing in his conception of history Hamlet with the skull of Yorick in his hands, the most famous theatrical scene of his time. Paradoxically, this baroque image of a *meditatio mortis* prefigures a new sense of escape, one that emerges in *Hamlet,* from tragedy's fatal classical limitation. In the dispute with Hamlet's father ghost, Hegel recognizes a consciousness that is "purer" (closer to "absolute"), because it is up for dialectical reconciliation – *Versöhnung des Gegensatzes mit sich.* The false but popular etymology of *Versöhnung* echoes the fate of sons (*Söhne*) as the Christian Christ Son's prime matter of reconciliation. Thus, Klopstock's *Messias* had answered the Shakespeare adept Milton's *Paradise Lost* (a hot debate in the generation before Hegel).[20] In *Hamlet* the "purer consciousness" transcends "the Lethe of the nether world of death," Hegel recalls in his *Lectures on Aesthetics,* and he renders old Hamlet's invocation of "Lethe's wharf" (1.5.33), that had prompted him from the grave, as the "strand of finitude." He clearly saw that this could not "satisfy" Hamlet: *sie genügt ihm nicht.*[21]

In the *Phenomenology,* this achievement gained attention and momentum in the graveyard scene, when Hamlet awaits the beloved Ophelia's maimed rites. The sophistry of the witty gravedigger lends Hamlet's behaviour a baroque significance last but not least in the light of the most notorious of monologues, "To be or not to be" (3.1.56). Hegel takes the notoriety for granted and proceeds immediately to a subtle analysis that must have impressed Kierkegaard. In his *Smuler,* "philosophical bites" translated as *Fragments,* he entitles one "metaphysical caprice" of bites "The Absolute Paradox," and in response to the conception of the "Absolute" at the end of the *Phenomenology,* he identifies the absoluteness of the metaphysical paradox as "Hamlet's dialectic."[22] In view of Calvary,

Hamlet's encounter with the graveyard skulls offers the occasion for a doubled reflection on objectivity, its necessary reliance on irony and the urgent demand for a humour facing history's impossible reconciliation.

In *Phenomenology's* progress, Yorick "the court jester" had raised the standard of reflection long before tragedy's achievement enters explicitly into Hegel's design (§§ 733*ff.*). He enters Hegel's account in the early phase of "self-observation," which begins with "the relation of self-consciousness to its immediate actuality" (as early as §§ 309*ff.*).[23] As seat of the mind, the brain is "not a *physical* part," but "the *being* of a self-conscious individuality," and thus positioned against, and confronted with, the external "natural thing," which is, "as the actuality and existence of man ..., his skull-bone" (§ 331) – the emphasis falls on the "factual being" of the bone as the lifeless substructure for the brain as seat of the living individuality of the conscious self:

> § 333. [No matter, what] may occur to us in connection with a skull, like the thoughts of Hamlet over Yorick's ..., the skull-bone just by itself is such an indifferent, natural thing that nothing else is to be seen in it, or fancied about it than simply the bone itself. It does indeed remind us of the brain and its specific nature, and of skulls of different formation, but not of a conscious movement, since there is impressed on it neither a look nor a gesture, nor anything that proclaims itself to have come from a conscious action, but another sort of aspect of the individuality, that would no longer be a self-reflected, but a purely *immediate* being.

The "*immediate* being" of the skull-bone (Hegel's emphasis), its absolute objectivity, is disconnected from all possible internal significance or, as he puts it, stressing the dramatic genre, "speaking movement" (§ 333), as it is thematized in Hamlet's meditation on the skull. As an arbitrary given, the skull-bone in particular is not recognizable as part of an individual, since the speaking faculty is missing: the skull is "chop-fallen" (5.1.178).[24] At this early point before all historical concretion, the first Hamlet reference is implicitly "planted" by Hegel. It was William Empson who called such planting "a standard piece of Shakespearian technique" and found it foremost in *Hamlet.*[25] Already Hegel recognized and indeed adapted the technique in order to bridge the precarious gap in the phenomeno-logical development between the earlier epistemological stages (one might say, the anthropogenetic substructure) and the historical telos of the manifest forms of "Religion in the Form of Art" (part CC, section b). In his later *Lectures on Aesthetics* Hegel will credit Juliet along with Hamlet explicitly with the dramatic surfacing of "dialectics" as method.[26] In the *Phenomenology*, Shakespeare is introduced as a source of technique rather than of motifs. The issues that Hegel finds in *Hamlet* and addresses as tragedy's cognitive achievement are issues of method rather than content. He adapts Shakespeare's "planting" as a method of enabling a dialectics in progress.

The decisive step on the way to "absolute knowing," which is prefigured in Yorick's skull as emblem of the absolute phenomenological paradox, is taken up by Kierkegaard as the self-reflective moment of a theatre – the theatre as an institution – on the theatre. It continues the mouse-trap that was intended to catch the conscience of the guilty king. But famously the trap did not work or, rather, the drama does not tell how it worked. Instead it leads up to Hamlet's conundrum of "To be or not to be," ironically cited from a *Quodlibet*, a scholastic exercise of Logic.[27] It masks Shakespeare's departure from Greek tragedy in the decisive moment, since it is in "To be or not to be" that Hamlet leaves behind the famous Silenus's wisdom that it were better "not to be born" than "to be born."[28] "That it were better my mother had not borne me," Hamlet echoes only a little later (3.1.123). The citation was promptly recognized by Nietzsche, classical scholar, who went on to sharpen the Dionysian bent in *Hamlet* from "not to be" to "being nothing" in *The Birth of Tragedy*.[29]

The mouse trap returns on the graveyard, and the gravedigger has the appropriate keyword ready for Hegel, since it is Hamlet who exclaims, "How absolute the knave is" (5.1.133). The gravedigger's absoluteness indicates the paradoxical apex of "absolute knowing" that is approached: Calvary is professionally no news for the gravedigger, who makes many a rude point about it. He certainly knows about "factual being," and Johannes Climacus, Kierkegaard's "John of the Ladder," acknowledges the dialectic's paradox: the skull as the non-speaking point zero of representation. The gravedigger has no problem to identify the individual skull in question and connects this one instantly with his own bad memories of "the King's jester" (5.1.175). Both the digger and the jester are contrary exponents of the same absoluteness in knowing or – in the medical terminology of humours – of melancholy vs. irony.[30] Skull in hand, Hamlet illustrates Hegel's intricate analysis of the skull-bone with an equally intricate speech. Hegel's reflection at this point of *Phenomenology*'s progress performs a subtle emulation of Hamlet's monologue long before the dead end of the process is reached and "History is comprehended."

The Yorick scene exposes a first step beyond the dramatic state of art that is reached in Greek tragedy, and it foreshadows early on the much later stage that is reached with *Hamlet* the play's technical achievement and reach beyond dramatic irony. It shows the delusion of the consciously "speaking movement" as the tragic trap left behind in *Phenomenology's* reflection on its way to objective humour. The subjectivity effect is reason for a last laugh: "Alas, poor Yorick," Hamlet addresses the mute bone (5.1.178–89). The power of vivid imagination prevails, but it turns into horror – "how abhorred" – in the decomposition that detaches the bone, which the skull "quite chop-fallen" is: "That skull had a tongue in it" (5.1.74) – detaches it piece by piece from all that may have been connected with it in recollection. Hamlet is left with the bone alone, without the lips he often kissed (5.1.182). A glimpse of a theatre after tragedy, Beckett's *Endgame*, is not far off. The skull has to put on "paint an inch thick" in order to mask death at the ultimate point of the play, a death as senseless a contingency as a "chopless" skull without expression: "Make her laugh at that" is Hamlet's last wish to the dead maiden. The desperate laughter of comedy topples the tragedy of error that is left behind.[31]

Immanence: A Bone of Contention

An unresolved philological problem of Hegel criticism is the uneven trajectory of ever-changing degrees of implication in the *Phenomenology*'s way to full explicitness of knowledge.[32] Or, as Hegel had announced in his preface, "The True, not as *substance*, but equally as *subject*" (§ 17) – not as a sub*stance*, but sub*jected* to the process of its coming to be: Truth is the truth of the subjected subject's coming to know. Only a few turns in the developmental progress of consciousness are marked in Hegel's text through highlights like Yorick's skull; mostly they appear in passing and vanish soon. One historical aspect that is implicit in the advancement to consciousness is the supercession or "burial" of stages in textual crypts difficult to access.[33] The literary sphere plays its role as a depository of former achievements on the road to an absoluteness of knowing that obliterates the relativity of its gradual coming to know. Shakespeare's dramatic personae loom large in this cryptic account. As a consequence of the dialectical crux, classical and modern characters appear telescopically blended into each other. This amounts to more than the usual *paradiastolé* of Renaissance "re-description" that would turn Greek tragedy into something better, morally improved. Hobbes's rigid rhetoric, in which ambiguity and ambivalence are on the brink of hypocrisy, is Quentin Skinner's best example.[34] Hegel, on the contrary, refashions the epochal break with a Hamlet knowing not "seems" (1.2.77). For him, the abysmally deepened ambiguity of "not to be" relates to nothing morally relevant, whether achieved or missing. The tragically exposed "substance" is lifted to a higher level of knowing, one that leaves behind the "seems," which inflicts deception and deepens the deceit that is embedded in an "ethical order" that is literally, in its letters, living on and working with equivocation.

The philological predicament of reconstructing the steps along the lines of Hegel's *Logic* consists in the difficulty of reassessing, at each new step, the respective state of affairs.[35] Calvary on the last level marks the absolute limit of lived recognition, a cognition whose historical shadow is reflected in language and dramaturgy. The substructure of the phenomenological trajectory appears on stage in *Hamlet* the play; there it is thematized *in actu* and pointed out by Hegel as a dramatic achievement rather than an effect of mere performance. According to principles of cognitive structure, rather, than the lively description of characters, Shakespeare was read by Hegel. As for Aristotle, the *enargeia* is proof of a heightened cognitive mobility rather than of emotive response. The natural-historical genealogy is left behind by a purer consciousness, which becomes aware in Hamlet, post-tragic hero, not of life's natural limitation, but of the mind's dialectical absolution from life's logic.[36] Hegel's commentary on the limits of observation – on the mix-up of "high and low" in the "organ of generation and urination" – is overcome by the idea of a "life that comprehends itself" (§ 346).

While individuals get lost or linger in a limbo of memories, characters steadfastly remain as an inscription of what they etymologically (*character* means "writing") indicate: a kind of writing to be read – no *catharsis* of emotion, but an archaeology of knowledge. Following Aristotle's lead, Hegel deciphered in Shakespeare's theatre an epistemological drama of objective history, rather than of lived experience. It amounts to a conception of the world *as* History. The "beginning and end of art" can anticipate only what remains enclosed until the end in a state of reflected anticipation; the mere (could it be more?) entertainment of an idea, whose name may be "freedom" (for Hegel it was), and whose embeddedness in life includes a process designed to transcend the historical forms of the "objective mind."[37] Their objectivity in the varying content of Shakespeare's dramas is of a conflictual nature that does not lend itself easily to consensual living. It needs a sense of objective humour *in spite* of the impossibility of achieving such a thing in any other way than subjectively or in the fleeting second-degree objectivity of art. In its prospect, Shakespeare's art may almost necessarily lead beyond Hegel. If it does so, Hegel on his part pointed to the idea of an objectively inbuilt transcendence that lies buried in the paradoxical (call it "dialectical") immanence of a life facing Calvary.

3 John Philipp Kemble as Hamlet, Sir Thomas Lawrence, 1801.
Tate Gallery, London. Wikimedia.

Sir Thomas Lawrence's picture of the actor, "John Philipp Kemble as Hamlet," was unknown to Hegel when he worked on the *Phenomenology* but gives an idea of what Hegel had theorized at about the same time. The illuminated actor's face – we need not know (and would be rather irritated, if we knew) what he is imagined to think; it does not matter – corresponds to the well-lit skull-bone, shining in the gloom of its materiality, while Hamlet's hand holds it, his fingers locked in its face exactly where the jaw that made the jester jest is missing. Not much of a laugh is ours and wasn't Ophelia's, but a sense of objective humour is needed and may carry a promise (of consolation). This, instead of a *catharsis* like pissing, is *Hamlet's* truth beyond irony in Hegel.

NOTES

1 Stephen Greenblatt, *Will in the World: How Shakespeare Became Shakespeare* (New York: Norton, 2004), 299, on Shakespeare's "epochal breakthrough" with *Hamlet.*

2 Karl Rosenkranz, *Georg Wilhelm Friedrich Hegels Leben: Supplement zu Hegels Werken* (Berlin: Duncker & Humblot, 1844), 7; cited from Hegel's brief school diary from 1785–7, appendix, 434. Looking back in 1785, after the beloved preceptor's untimely death, Hegel acknowledges in his mourning remembrance the gift of "8 volumes Shakespeare already in 1778." Löffler's recommendation (my paraphrase) is Rosenkranz's well-meaning invention.

3 For the educational context, compare John H. Smith, *The Spirit and Its Letters: Traces of Rhetoric in Hegel's Philosophy of Bildung* (Ithaca, NY: Cornell University Press, 1988), 90*ff.*

4 For a more accurate account of the young student Hegel and the rather precarious phase preceding his marriage (discretely bypassed by Rosenkranz), see Hans Friedrich Fulda, *Georg Wilhelm Friedrich Hegel* (Munich: Beck, 2003), 28–31, 271*ff.*

5 Soren Kierkegaard, *The Concept of Irony* (1841), ed. Howard V. Hong and Edna H. Hong (Princeton, NJ: Princeton University Press, 1989), 324 (emphasis added). The translation is academic, it does not match Kierkegaard's style. But one has to admit that the double bind, in which any translation of his texts is caught, of conceptually pointed wit and learned allusion, is hard to cope with.

6 See Rüdiger Bubner, "Die 'Sache selbst' in Hegel's System" (1978), *Zur Sache der Dialektik* (Stuttgart: Reclam, 1980), 48.

7 Hong and Hong's note, *The Concept of Irony,* 551, refers to Solger's *Vorlesungen über Ästhetik* (1819) and Hegel's reference to Solger in the

Philosophy of Right (1821), trans. T.M. Knox (Oxford: Clarendon, 1952), § 140, 101–2; in the original *Grundlinien der Philosophie des Rechts*, ed. Johannes Hoffmeister (Hamburg: Meiner, 1955), § 140, 137–8. Here Solger's critical review of August Wilhelm Schlegel's *Vorlesungen über dramatische Kunst und Literatur* (1809–11) plays the central role, reprinted in Solger's *Nachgelassene Schriften und Briefwechsel* 1–2, ed. Ludwig Tieck and Friedrich von Raumer (Leipzig: Brockhaus, 1826), 2:514. For Hegel, this collection was the occasion for an extensive appreciation of the tragically deceased,"Ueber Solger's nachgelassene Schriften und Briefwechsel" (1828), in Hegel's *Berliner Schriften 1818–1831*, ed. Johannes Hoffmeister (Hamburg: Meiner, 1956), 157 and 185. See my memorial lecture "Solgers Ironie: Der idealische Jüngling und die Misere der Universität" (2006), *Diesseits der Oder: Frankfurter Vorlesungen* (Berlin: Kadmos, 2008), 197–211.

8 See, for example, Henry Sussman, *The Hegelian Aftermath* (Baltimore, MD: Johns Hopkins University Press, 1982), 97*ff.* and 105*ff.* But compare also Donald Barthelme's infamous "Kierkegaard Unfair to Schlegel" (1968) from his collection *City Life* (New York: Farrar, Straus and Giroux, 1970), which resonates in the posthumous essay collection, into which the Kierkegaard story would have perfectly fitted, *Not Knowing*, ed. Kim Herzingen (New York: Random House, 1997).

9 A separate subject of investigation would be Hegel's use of the Wieland translation. The linguistic intricacies involved in this bilingual affair are far from sufficiently researched; suffice it here that Hegel's understanding of Shakespeare was evidently as competent as one could hope. See my essay "Pyrrhus' Sieg: Shakespeare. Wieland. Hegel," in *Wieland / Übersetzen*, ed. Bettine Menke and Wolfgang Struck, 43–56 (Berlin: De Gruyter, 2010).

10 I cite from the critical German Hegel edition with the help of A.V. Miller's translation and his useful subdivision of the text in paragraphs: Georg Wilhelm Friedrich Hegel, *Phänomenologie des Geistes* (1807), ed. Hans-Friedrich Wessels and Heinrich Clairmont (Hamburg: Meiner, 1988); trans. as *Hegel's Phenomenology of Spirit* by A.V. Miller with an analytical overview by J.N. Findlay (Oxford: Oxford University Press, 1977). See also the predecessor, J.B. Baillie's translation, *The Phenomenology of Mind* (London: Macmillan, 1910, 1931). I use Miller, but in critical cases I include also the by no means outdated Baillie translation. A new translation by Terry Pinkard (Cambridge: Cambridge University Press, 2018) appeared after this text went into print.

11 I recommend and follow here the conception of "formal analysis" developed in Pirmin Stekeler-Weithofer's reading of *Phenomenology* and *Philosophy of Right* in particular, *Philosophie des Selbstbewußtseins: Hegels System*

als Formanalyse von Wissen und Autonomie (Frankfurt/M: Suhrkamp, 2005), 10*ff.* and 297*ff.*

12 This is my starting point in the *Hamlet* chapter of *Shakespearean Genealogies of Power: A Whispering of Nothing in Hamlet* &c. (London: Routledge, 2011), 32*ff.*

13 Walter Benjamin included – a point I cannot discuss here in detail. But compare Rainer Nägele, *Theater, Theory, Speculation: Walter Benjamin and the Scenes of Modernity* (Baltimore, MD: Johns Hopkins University Press, 1991), chap. 8; and Julia Reinhard Lupton and Kenneth Reinhard, *After Oedipus: Shakespeare in Psychoanalysis* (Ithaca, NY: Cornell University Press, 1993), chap. 2.

14 See Francis M. Cornford's first masterpiece (which is, in fact, a theory of tragedy), dedicated to Jane Ellen Harrison, *Thucydides Mythistoricus* (Oxford: Clarendon, 1907), 138, citing Hegel implicitly and almost verbatim: "the thing said comes straight from the lips of the actors."

15 For the surrounding evidence, see Edna Purdie's introduction to her canonical edition of *Von Deutscher Art und Kunst*, 25–9 (Oxford: Clarendon, 1924, 1948, 1960, 1964), including Herder's "Shakespear" [*sic*]. In addition to this classical piece of information, Kristin Gjesdal proposed a useful juxtaposition of "Hegel, and Herder on Art, History, and Reason," *Philosophy and Literature* 30 (2006), 17–32. However, when it comes to historically concrete phenomenological stages, most prominently Greek tragedy and Shakespeare, the proposed alternative of "non-essentialist" and "teleology" is no longer valid; it is deconstructed in Hegel's use of the literary as a demonstration of what "actually" – *actualiter*, as in "der Sache" – happened with each step.

16 See here and in the following Christoph Menke, *Die Gegenwart der Tragödie: Versuch über Urteil und Spiel* (Frankfurt am Main: Suhrkamp, 2005), 63*ff.*; trans. as *Tragic Play: Irony and Theater from Sophocles to Brecht* (New York: Columbia University Press, 2009), 47*ff.*

17 Karl Wilhelm Ferdinand Solger, *Vorlesungen über Ästhetik*, ed. Karl Wilhelm Ludwig Heyse (Leipzig: Brockhaus, 1819), 320 (emphasis added). Compare the recent republication of the introduction to Solger's Sophocles translation, "Über Sophokles und die alte Tragödie" (1808) in éd. bilingue par Noemi Angehrn, *Sur Sophokles et la tragédie antique* (Lausanne: L'Age d'Homme, 2010).

18 Stanley Cavell, *Disowning Knowledge in Six Plays of Shakespeare* (Cambridge: Cambridge University Press, 1987), 191. Compare also André Green's Hegel reference in his Hölderlin-titled *Un Oeil en trop: Le complexe d'Oedipe dans la tragédie* (Paris: Minuit, 1969), 84.

19 Richard Sorabji, *Necessity Cause and Blame: Perspectives on Aristotle's Theory* (Chicago: University of Chicago Press, 1980), appendix "Tragic Error," 296*ff.*

20 See Anselm Haverkamp, *Klopstock / Milton: Teleskopie der Moderne* (Stuttgart: Metzler, 2018), 70, 231.

21 Georg Wilhelm Friedrich Hegel, *Ästhetik*, ed. Friedrich Bassenge, (Berlin: Aufbau, 2nd ed., 1962), 2:581. See Dirk Quadflieg, "Die Sandbank des Vergessens," in *Denkfiguren: Figures of Thought*, ed. Eva Horn and Michèle Lowrie, 175–7 (Berlin: August 2013).

22 Soren Kierkegaard / Johannes Climacus, *Philosophical Fragments* (1844), ed. Hong and Hong (Princeton, NJ: Princeton University Press, 1985), 41n.

23 The context of this long and tedious part on contemporary "Physiognomy and Phrenology" (§§ 309–46) is of no immediate interest for the invocation of *Hamlet*. In the last of these paragraphs, however (§ 346), Hegel's adaptation ends on an almost Shakespearean tone, when he compares the "ignorance" of a consciousness limited to the surface of the observed matter without "depth" (*Vorstellung* – mistranslated by Miller as "picture-thinking") with the mistaking of "the organ of [Nature's] highest fulfilment, the organ of generation, with the organ of urination" (Hegel more drastically says "pissing"). The consciousness that remains in the lower realm of *Vorstellung* works like *Pissen*.

24 The Arden edition of *Hamlet*, 2nd ser., ed. Harold Jenkins (London: Methuen, 1982; Nelson, 1997), 5.1.87, has "chopless," specified at 5.1.186, "quite chop-fallen." The 3rd ser. *Hamlet*, ed. Ann Thompson and Neil Taylor (London: Thomson, 2006), prefers an undistinguished flat "chapless" in both places.

25 William Empson, *The Structure of Complex Words* (1951), ed. Jonathan Culler (Cambridge, MA: Harvard University Press, 1989), 67*ff*.

26 Compare the forgotten essay – a small book, in fact, worth being republished – by Emil Wolff, "Hegel und Shakespeare," *Vom Geist der Dichtung* (Gedächtnisschrift für Robert Petsch), ed. Fritz Martini (Hamburg: Hoffmann und Campe, 1949), 135*ff*.

27 Margareta de Gracia, "Soliloquies and Wages in the Age of Emergent Consciousness," *Textual Practice* 9 (1995): 74, 77; also her *Hamlet without Hamlet* (Cambridge: Cambridge University Press, 2007), 199*ff*.

28 The relevant reference is Sophocles's *Oedipus at Colonus*, 1225, but the literary evidence includes also the ethics of Aristotle via Plutarch and handbooks like Diogenes Laertius. R.C. Jebb, in the commentary to his edition of *Oedipus Coloneus* (Cambridge: Cambridge University Press, 1928), 194, highlights the Epicurean reception of the motif, which throws additional light on the proverbial nature of Silenus's wisdom as a common *legómenon* that is cited in *Hamlet* (Jebb's translation is "Not to be born"). For the context of Nietzsche's interest, see James I. Porter, *Nietzsche*

and the Philology of the Future (Stanford, CA: Stanford University Press, 2000), 217.

29 Friedrich Nietzsche, *The Birth of Tragedy*, chap. 3. See in greater detail *Shakespearean Genealogies of Power*, 32 with long note 30.

30 See Jean Starobinski, "L'encre de la mélancolie," *La Nouvelle Revue Française* 123 (1963), 410–23, ending with Shakespeare's "black ink."

31 Katrin Trüstedt, *Die Komödie der Tragödie* (Konstanz: Konstanz University Press, 2011), 47*ff.*, 237*ff.*

32 See in greater analytical detail Dieter Henrich, *Hegel im Kontext* (Frankfurt/M: Suhrkamp, 1971), 145*ff.*

33 Emanuel Hirsch, "Die Beisetzung der Romantiker in Hegels Phänomenologie" (1924), on the implicitly cited ("buried") poets in the *Phenomenology*; repr. in *Materialien zu Hegels Phänomenologie des Geistes*, ed. Hans Friedrich Fulda and Dieter Henrich (Frankfurt/M: Suhrkamp, 1973), 249.

34 Quentin Skinner, *Reason and Rhetoric in the Philosophy of Hobbes* (Cambridge: Cambridge University Press, 1996), 172*ff.*

35 Hans Friedrich Fulda, *Das Problem einer Einleitung in Hegels Wissenschaft der Logik* (Frankfurt am Main: Klostermann, 1965), 24, 94, 256.

36 Compare Christoph Menke's subtle distinction of the "genealogy" within the phenomenological process, "Geist und Leben: Von der Phänomenologie zur Genealogie" (2007), *Autonomie und Befreiung: Studien zu Hegel* (Berlin: Suhrkamp, 2018), 101*ff.*

37 Thomas Khurana, *Das Leben der Freiheit: Form und Wirklichkeit der Autonomie* (Berlin: Suhrkamp, 2017), 16, for Hegel's "idea"; 517*ff.* for the post-Hegelian "complication."

chapter eleven

Bliss Unrevealed: The "Trial" in Shakespeare's *The Winter's Tale*

PAUL A. KOTTMAN

In his reading of *The Winter's Tale*, René Girard notes that the play can "affect those even with no particular interest in religion in a manner that can only be defined as religious, or bordering on the religious."[1] Other discussions of *The Winter's Tale*'s also note its "religious" dimension. Special attention has been paid to the themes of "forgiveness" (Beckwith, Lupton), "faith" (McCoy), and "resurrection" (Cavell, Girard).[2] Given the emphasis on forgiveness and resurrection, "religious" here seems to mean Christian. Then again, as Cavell notes, the issue of "adult life struggling toward happiness from within its own 'debris'" also occupies Freud and the Romantics. And they openly acknowledge this occupation as part of their debt to Shakespeare.[3] If these are Christian issues, then they are not exhausted by any Christian or religious or artistic treatment of them.

Still, Shakespeare does seem to have in mind not only the recognizably Christian themes of forgiveness, "faith" awakened, artistic devotion, and vocation – but also those of maternal love and grief for a dead son. In this chapter I will discuss the latter elements in the play's trial scene, where the scepticism of the first half of the play reaches its fever pitch, as a prelude to returning to the former issues on another occasion for a fuller discussion. At the same time – to state one more orienting generality – the story of *The Winter's Tale*, already in Shakespeare's sources, clearly revises key elements of the Christian narrative: for a start, like Mary, Hermione's conception is a matter of some speculation and concern – although it is not portrayed as immaculate. Like Mary, Hermione's love for her children is maternal – but it is also perhaps rooted in sexual love for a man. Like Mary, Hermione will grieve the loss of her son – but she will also grieve for a daughter. What to make of all this?

I

In what follows, I also want to offer some thoughts about the inseparability of form and meaning in the trial scene of *The Winter's Tale.* For the moment, we can leave open the issue of whether this form should be taken as artistic or religious; *The Winter's Tale* bears upon the fates of both art and religion in the years since Shakespeare's death. For some initial help, let me first turn to what I see as the most ambitious and far-reaching reflections on the fate of art and religion: the lectures of Hegel. Elsewhere I have argued that it was Shakespeare, not Hegel, who first registered the pastness of art's highest vocation – and that it was Hegel who recognized that Shakespeare was the first artist to see art's highest vocation as a thing of the past.[4] Here I want to begin considering *The Winter's Tale* in light of Hegel's remarks on Christian art, starting with Christian painting. Because Hegel sees modern (what Hegel calls "romantic") art as essentially Christian art – not post-seventeenth-century art – it is worth considering what it means for Hegel to see Shakespeare as the culmination or fullest development of modern art, and as the moment of art's registration of its own loss of highest vocation.

It is difficult to state Hegel's views on painting economically. But the first thing to be said is that, for Hegel, Christian painting makes visible (makes "shine") the liveliness of subjectivity as self-relatedness, or "inwardness" (*volle Innigkeit*). Christian painting does this, moreover, by showing something of general-universal significance in its portrayal of concrete, particular self-conscious, inwardly self-related human beings. For Hegel, Christian paintings attract our gaze such that we learn something about our own subjectivity; in looking at portrayals of particular human beings posed in particular ways, as well as landscapes or still lifes, we learn something about ourselves as self-consciously self-related.[5]

Second, painting makes human self-consciousness *affectively*, compellingly visible – in a "lively" way. That is, minimally, Christian paintings are not mere illustrations of narrative episodes that can be called to mind whether or not they are sensuously apprehended, as if pictorial illustration merely aided such calling to mind. Whatever is theoretically grasped *is* grasped affectively by the beholder.

Third, what is sensuously grasped – the subject matter or content – is self-related subjectivity or, more broadly, the human heart, feeling, *Innigkeit.* And Hegel specifies that this self-related subjectivity must result from a withdrawal from external suffering into self-repose. That is, this self-relation appears where a human being overcomes not some external obstacle but some *internal* obstacle.[6] Hegel calls this "bliss" – as distinct from "happiness" or "good fortune," since it also entails broken-heartedness. Hegel also refers to this bliss as "religion alone" – "the peace of the individual who has a sense of himself but finds true satisfaction only when, self-collected, his mundane heart is broken so that he is raised above his mere natural existence and its finitude, and in this elevation has won a universal depth of feeling."[7] Hegel offers several examples of what he means, including a treatment of Correggio's Mary Magdalene that would be worth a separate discussion.

However – and the thesis is so astonishing that it has yet to receive the commentary it deserves – the paradigm of such painterly bliss for Hegel is the religious love, the passionless love, of Mary for her son, Christ: "As the most perfect subject for painting, I have already specified the [blissful] love, the object of which is not a purely spiritual 'beyond' but is present, so that we can see love itself before us in what is loved. The supreme and unique form of this love is Mary's love for the Christ-child ... the most beautiful subject to which Christian art in general, and especially painting in its religious sphere has risen."[8]

For Hegel, religious or passionless (*leidenschaftslos*) love is the true, ideal subject matter of painting. We could, I think, call it the ideal of parental love, which is what Hegel sees validated in Christian religion, too, in its inversion whereby the privileged adoration of a transcendent God by his "children" is superseded by the adoration of a concrete, imminent child by his mother.[9] Hegel sees this realized in the history of painting, as Christian painting overcomes the iconoclasm according to which the Divine (as transcendent) cannot be represented pictorially, in favour of *seeing* and being affected by seeing the Divine as "love reconciled and at peace with itself ... above all as the Madonna's love for her child, as the absolutely suitable ideal subject for this sphere" (*LFA* 819). Painting, that is, brings about a new view of the "divine" as passionless love for a child, rather than the iconoclastic (non-artistic) adoration of a Divine beyond. And this new view is not just a mirroring illustration of a practice (of parental love) that lies outside painting; the paintings are a matrix for understanding, and hence for intervening in, the reality of the love that they depict. Think of how parents often gaze upon photographs or images of their children, not as mere representations to be dispassionately studied, but with a devotion that is dialectically entwined with historical shifts in the practical forms that devotion to children takes.

As Hegel points out elsewhere, love as "mutual subjectivity" cannot flourish in modernity unless parents love their children more than children love their parents.[10] Perhaps it is helpful here to recall, too, that artists often regard their works as their "children" – and that painting is often figured as a kind of "giving birth" or "labour of love." These metaphors – for they cannot be literally true (to destroy an artwork is a travesty, but it is not a murder) – might be taken as a clue to grasping the way in which paintings can demand a form of attentiveness that is significantly akin to the attentiveness required for the devotional love of children, in the sense that beholding fine paintings entails the attribution of an absolute value and passionless devotion to what is beheld. *Lovingly* passionless, not merely disinterested (in Kant's sense) – without the expectation that the love be "returned" in kind from the artwork (or the child). This, I take it, is also part of Hegel's critique of the role that disinterestedness plays in Kant's account of aesthetic judgment.

We should note that while Hegel emphasizes that the passionless devotion entailed in beholding "Christ the child" is the most "important object of love in paintings" (*LFA* 820), he nevertheless does not see this as adequate to comprehend loving "subject-subject" relations *tout court.* Hegel is clear that the "mutual subjectivity" of love cannot be restricted to such passionless devotion; he goes on to discuss the "heat of passion" in dramatic and poetic presentations of love (*LFA* 566–8). The Madonna's passionless love is, in other words, only how the art of *painting* best grasps love-as-divine – inadequately and incompletely with respect to the fuller modern logic of mutual subjectivity, wherein love goes beyond parental-maternal love and comes to necessarily include passion, caprice, romantic love, the individual's "heart for love and ... right to become happy through it" (*LFA* 568).

Hegel's larger point, then, seems to be that love – superseded through and in parental love – ultimately reveals the insufficiency of the art of painting's analogousness to it. And if Hegel's "science of art" is to be true to its name, then *that* insufficiency must also somehow show up *in* art. That is why Hegel must *then* go on to emphasize the insufficiency of poetry and drama, too, when it comes to the sensuous comprehension of love's intense, passionate contingency. (For example, dramatic art is no longer fine art when it devolves into merely the depiction of the "supreme contingency" of passionate love, as Hegel puts it, "[or] in the ... caprice which has neither universality nor any scope beyond itself ... [and] which freezes us despite all the heat of passion in its presentation" [*LFA* 568].)

In such passages, Hegel seems to be suggesting that it is *dramatic-poetic* presentations of love – and not painting's presentations – that instructively manifest their own failure to sensuously comprehend love as the modern logic of mutual subjectivity or "spirit as infinite subjectivity." Put another way, in part because painting cannot annul itself *from within its own activity*, dramatic poetry is called for – if art is to *bring to an end* (not just be forced by external circumstances to conclude) its task of sensuously embodying the logic of mutual subjectivity – such that our grasp of art's *becoming past* might yet instruct us with respect to the demands of "the modern logic of social subjectivity," the ethical task of shared intelligibility in "subject-subject" loving relations (*ATB* 86).

In other words, art's becoming past with respect to the demands of comprehending "love" is one way that we might continue to learn what love's demands can yet entail.[11]

II

Parental and passionate love are of course at the heart of Shakespeare's *Winter's Tale*, and Hermione bears more than a passing resemblance to representations of Mary in Christian painting.

Imprisoned by Leontes, from whom she is now estranged, barred from seeing Mamillius, her son, and informed that her newborn daughter is to be burned alive, Hermione is "hurried here, to this place, i'th'open air, before I have got strength of limit" (that is, before fully recovering from giving birth to her daughter) – to a public trial. There, she "lays down" (*WT* 3.2.79) her attachment to her finite life in the very sort of terms used by Hegel to define the "bliss" of Mary's infinitely self-related subjectivity. Hermione is not annulled by having everything she holds dear taken from her. She demands, rather, to be seen and understood as who she is, in this state of bereavement. When Leontes threatens her with death, she replies:

> Sir, spare your threats.
> The bug with which you would fright me I seek.
> To me can life be no commodity….
> But yet hear this – no life,
> I prize it not a straw, but for mine honour
> Which I would free. (3.2.89–109)

It might be objected that Hermione *speaks* these lines; she does not appear, silently, as in a painting of the "blissful" Madonna. But things are more complicated than that. Hermione *will* very shortly fall silent and become – we are eventually asked to believe – a kind of visual artwork. And she follows this speech – with virtually the last words we hear from her for sixteen years – with the following lines:

> The Emperor of Russia was my father.
> O that he were alive, and here *beholding*
> His daughter's trial; that he did but see
> The *flatness* of my misery; yet with eyes
> Of pity, not revenge. (3.2.116–21; my emphasis)

In imagining her trial *beheld* by her father, she sees her misery as "flatness"– as a two-dimensional picture of her state.[12] And in asking for "eyes of pity, not revenge" she seems to be suggesting that the vindication of her suffering is visible, already, in the "flatness" of her appearance. Hence, any further vindication of her honour (by her father) is unnecessary.

One implication of this might be that Hermione also senses that she is not being looked at aright by Leontes, not being rightly *seen* by him, even as she appears in flesh and blood before him, in person, on trial at his behest. We already know that her words are not believed by Leontes, and so – as she herself notes – it makes little sense for her to appear in person at the trial merely in order to *speak* to him in her own defence:

> Since what I am to say must be that
> Which contradicts my accusation, and
> The testimony on my part no other
> But what comes from myself, it shall scarce boot me
> To say 'Not guilty.' Mine integrity
> Being counted falsehood shall, as I express it,
> Be so received. (3.2.20–7)

And yet, we are told, "It is his highness' pleasure that the queen / Appear in person here in court" (3.2.8–9). To what end? Does Leontes want to parade her, as Octavius wants to parade Cleopatra – "a great king's daughter, / The mother to a hopeful prince, here standing / To prate and talk for life and honour, 'fore / Who please to come and hear?" (3.2.38–41)? I do not think so, because I think that Leontes is sincere when he opens the scene by stating his reluctance to bring Hermione, "the daughter of a king, our wife, and one / Of us too much beloved" to trial.[13] Is it then to "catch her conscience" – to see if she will disclose her guilt or innocence as Hamlet hoped Claudius might do when confronted with the Mousetrap? I see no evidence that Leontes regards Hermione's honour or guilt as something to be seen in the spontaneous expressions of her face, or in the bearing of her person.

It clearly does matter to Leontes, on the other hand, that the trial could clear him of any accusation of "tyranny."[14] That is, it matters to him not only that the indictment and verdict be read with Hermione present, in front of witnesses; it matters that the truth be revealed to be something other than his tyrannical domination of others, especially of Hermione. He asks her to stand trial so as *not* to dominate her, so as to submit to the same verdict to which she will submit. He does not want the truth to be authorized *by* him, or by his fantasies and suspicions. He wants to the truth to come out, to be revealed *to* him and Hermione alike in such a way that they are both bound to it. And the sincerity of this desire, on its own, means that he is not a tyrant in his own eyes. It may indeed mean that Leontes is also not the radical sceptic that he has been taken to be – at least, insofar as Leontes *also* seems to crave a revelation that he can believe in, that he can take as authoritative for him.[15]

The accusation seemed to have been provoked by Leontes's suspicion that Perdita is not his "issue." And the trial seems to have resulted from Leontes's further view that the confirmation of his suspicion needs to be resolved by some external determination *other* than what might be had by looking at the child, by studying the child's physical features. It has been supposed that what Leontes needs is some super-sensible or ahistorical verification, a truth that – like Iago's quip about Desdemona's honour – amounts to an "essence that's not seen." In our current era, a DNA test might take the place of such verification; modern scientific truth is also an essence that need not be seen to be believed. But I do not think that this adequately gets at the *form* of the truth Leontes craves, or why he wants the oracle to be read in public, with Hermione standing trial. What Leontes wants, I think, is not just the ahistorical objectivity of scientific data – its irreducibility to subjective sense-perception, its "divine" authority. What he wants from the trial, I mean, is a sensuous *form* of authority – the formal revelation of a truth, of a fact of the matter – which both he and Hermione would be bound to accept.

We could say that he craves the *form* of authority proper to the highest vocation of drama or dramatic representation.[16] And for drama to have that kind of authority, it must facilitate the suspension of disbelief. The question – the open question for Shakespeare, I think – is whether dramatic revelation is (still) up to that task. Another way of pressing the question: Can dramatic revelation reflect meaningfully on its own capacity to help us suspend our disbelief, in the face of the new demands on mutual acknowledgment that the world throws up? I see Shakespeare's late works grappling with these questions.

As with any performed drama, its director or sponsor (Leontes) cannot fully govern the result, although he can rightly insist on elements of the mise-en-scène, such as the reading of the oracle. If the witness of the oracle were to pronounce Hermione guilty, then she might of course still protest her innocence – but she would have lost the ability to claim that her plight resulted merely from Leontes's jealous tyranny. She would have to at least answer the oracle's testimony as well, taking seriously *its* form of authority. Indeed, it is Hermione – not Leontes – who declares "Apollo be my judge" (3.23.114). By the same token, if the witness of the oracle pronounces Leontes "a jealous tyrant," then Leontes might still protest his innocence; but he would be unable to do so unless he could find a way to disbelieve the testimony of oracle, without rejecting the dramatic revelation as a whole – without disbelieving *everything.*

As it turns out, this is precisely what he tries to do. Leontes does not – as most interpreters conclude – persist in ever more radical doubt; instead, he doubts the oracle (doubts his own tyranny) in order to keep alive the suspension of disbelief, in the hope of further revelation.

> There is no truth at all i'th'oracle
> The sessions shall proceed – this is mere falsehood. (3.2.136–7)

In rejecting the oracle, therefore, Leontes is not rejecting the continuation of the trial itself. Leontes wants the sessions to proceed, wants the truth to be revealed – somehow – by whatever follows. If he calls for the trial's continuance by rejecting the veracity of the oracle's testimony – "there is no truth at all in'th'oracle … this is mere falsehood" – then he is not necessarily behaving tyrannically. As already noted, Leontes has reason to say that the oracle – which brands him a "jealous tyrant" – is false.[17]

We should try to better understand this impasse. The trial's drama has been now brought to a point, I want to say, at which it is no longer clear what could count as evidence or a "sensuous form of authority" about the past that might compel Leontes and Hermione, and those gathered, to accept the same present reality. Put another way, the dramatic presentation of a truth or reality that can be shared by Leontes and Hermione alike, and by everyone around them, can no longer come from unveiling evidence of *past deeds*, from achieving agreement about the historical record or a shared understanding of "what really happened" between Polixenes, Camillo, and Hermione. Such agreement, such a shared understanding, will never be achievable – that much is now clear. And facing up to *that* is something that Hermione, Leontes, Paulina, and the rest must now do.

But how?

The sensuous *form* that a compelling revelation might take is now open, no longer governed by the dramatic form that Leontes had called for.

It is only when the trial is brought to *that* point, I want to say, that Leontes and Hermione are thrown back into the historical present. It is no longer a matter of determining the truth of what has happened; what happens *next* suddenly matters.

The issue might be stated this way: Could any new reality be presented to Leontes and Hermione in such a way that they both accept it, share it, face up to it – suspend their disbelief?

III

Whatever the answer to that question, it must take the form of testing whether Leontes and Hermione can share any reality whatsoever – any objective, independent fact or feature of the world which they both cannot deny. As noted earlier, this is also the question for drama's highest vocation – for the fate of religious revelation as well as dramatic art's highest vocation.

So, what is *most* real to Leontes and Hermione? What facilitates their suspension of disbelief?

At one level, the question might be one of psychological motivation or bedrock desire. Whatever is most real to Leontes and Hermione will be revealed, in their self-relation, by a reality by which they cannot stop being motivated on pain of self-annihilation. In other words – with the same Cartesian echoes that Cavell hears – this motivation can be revealed only in the crucible of a radical effort to deny it, to throw it into radical doubt. The *failure* of the radical denial of a motivation is the *form* that its revelation takes.[18]

With this in mind, Cavell began to offer his own answer to the question just posed: "what is *most* real" to Leontes and Hermione? Cavell's method locates the answer to this in what, he thinks, Leontes works hardest to deny: that he is the father of his children, that his children are "his." Cavell suggests that Leontes's "disowning his issue is more fundamental than, or causes, his jealousy of his friend and brother," his denial of Hermione's – and everyone else's – fidelity and veracity.[19] I hasten to add that Cavell, significantly, also conflates the question of Leontes's denial of "his children" with the denial that Mamillius is his "son" (more on that in a moment).[20]

As evidence, Cavell turns to the very moment of the play under discussion here. That is, he pursues this question by asking how "Leontes' 'diseased opinion' (1.2.197) drops its disease."[21] And he answers, "It vanishes exactly upon learning that his son is dead." Allow me to quote Cavell in full, since I will want to contrast my own understanding to his:

> The sequence is this: Leontes refuses the truth of Apollo's oracle; a servant enters, crying for the king. Leontes asks, 'What's the business?' and is told the prince is gone. Leontes questions the word and is told that it means 'Is dead.' Leontes' response is at once to relent: 'Apollo's angry, and the heavens themselves / Do strike at my injustice'; whereupon Hermione faints. (*Disowning Knowledge*, 195)

I agree with Cavell that it is upon learning of Mamillius's death that Leontes seems to drop his denial of his own paternity, seems to (re)suspend his disbelief. But I do not see, as Cavell does, that the denial and acceptance – the reality – at issue here can be adequately grasped by focusing primarily on Leontes's denial that his son is his, or that "Leontes' ... suffering has a cure, namely to acknowledge his child as his, to own it."[22] At least, it seems to me significant that such an acknowledgment is not what Shakespeare focuses on in this moment. Cavell, by contrast, thinks that it's "*here* that [Leontes] buckles, lets himself feel the shock" (195). But in fact, Leontes's first response makes no mention of his children – neither Mamillius nor his daughter. This *in spite of the fact that he has just learned that his son is dead.* His lengthy speech, which begins "Apollo, pardon ..." (3.2.150–69) makes no mention of Mamillius; he focuses on reconciliation to Polixenes, recalling Camillo, wooing Hermione.

For Cavell, Leontes's failure at self-awareness, his failure to "see" Hermione aright, is finally rooted in Leontes's denial/acceptance of his children as his own. He suggests that Leontes's relationship to Hermione (his jealousy of Polixenes, too) is determined and predicated upon his acceptance of his own paternity. Here is Cavell's train of thought:

> The matter for [Shakespeare's] drama ... is to investigate the finding of a wife *not* in empirical fact lost, but, let me say, transcendentally lost, lost just

> because one is blind to her – as it were conceptually unprepared for her – because that one is blind to himself, lost to himself. Here is what becomes, at some final stage, of the great Shakespearean problematic of legitimate succession: Always seen as a matter essential to the flourishing state, recognizing (legitimizing) one's child now appears as a matter essential to individual sanity, a discovery perhaps begun in Hamlet, and developed in Lear. (*Disowning Knowledge*, 204)

So, for Cavell, shoring up one's own sanity, by conceptually preparing to "find" one's sexual lover, is done by acknowledging one's parenthood. And that acknowledgment entails not just the transmission of name/property/legitimacy to one's child, but in something like the realization ("at some final stage" of Shakespeare's career) of parental love as a condition of human self-knowledge. Cavell – like Christianity, and Christian painting, I am tempted to say – sees the passionless loving parental bond as prior to, in the sense of being the conceptual condition of possibility for, the passionate *sexual-love* bond. Although it should be again emphasized that Cavell also sees this as a primarily *paternal* problem (*Leontes's* problem) – the issue of paternity *as* the acknowledgement of sons, especially, as one's own (I will return to this).

Now, perhaps the parental bond *is* prior, in the sense that perhaps the conceptual articulation of the significance of parental love in Christian painting or Christian religious or human experience writ large – Mary's blissful love of, grief for, her son – is a precondition for any emergent actualization and valorization of a culturally authoritative sexual-love bond between a man and a woman, as mother and father, and perhaps of any love affair (gendered in this way or not). There is no way to settle that large issue here, but it can remain on the table.[23]

But *if* parental love is prior, then we should look again at what Christian painting *and* Shakespeare's play are at pains to show, and is elided in Cavell's summary: *maternal* grief and maternal love. Yes, Leontes recognizes his own "injustice" when he learns that his son has died. But he learns what that injustice *is* – it is revealed to Leontes, I want to say – even as he says the very word: "my injustice [*Hermione faints*] / How now there?" (3.2.144).

IV

Let us then pick up the sequence on which Cavell focuses, but at the point at which he leaves off: Hermione's collapse.

PAULINA: This news is mortal to the queen. Look down
And see what death is doing (3.2.145)

Like Mary, Hermione loses her son. And Paulina – like the churches which display paintings– instructs us to *look* at this, to register Hermione's grief.

Consider Annibale Carracci's *Lamentation of Christ* (1604, National Gallery London), not as an illustration of this moment but as an effort that might help us to make sense of what Shakespeare is making sense of. If Mary Magdalene (*bottom right*) responds to Christ's death by throwing up her hands, then the woman behind stretches her hands out – directing our gaze and her care to Mary. (This visible contrast between the position of these four hands makes me see the former as an act of raising arms, rather than stretching them out.) The limbs of the others, on the left, intertwine and fall into one another. Christ's weight is not borne in Mary's arms so much as he is splayed in her lap. If anything, it is Mary whose weight seems borne in the arms of the woman behind her. I imagine her – and the woman whose arms are outstretched – saying something (both their mouths are open, as if in speech) along the lines of Leontes's words: "Beseech you, tenderly apply to her / Some remedies for life" (3.2.149–50).

Mary's face mirrors Christ's dead visage, distinctly unbeautiful in its slack-jawed colourlessness. The death of the son is registered in what *looks like* the death of his mother. "I say she's dead – I'll swear it," says Paulina of Hermione:

If word nor oath
Prevail not, go and see. If you can bring
Tincture or lustre in her lip, her eye,
Heat outwardly or breath within, I'll serve you
As I would do the gods. (3.2.200–4)

Later in the *Winter's Tale*, we are all taken to "go and see" – in the gallery that Paulina arranges, wherein Hermione will appear like stone. I will have to save a discussion of that scene for another time. Here I want to see whether Carracci's tableau might help us to understand Hermione's collapse in act 3, scene 2 of the *The Winter's Tale*. For help, let me turn again to Hegel:

> Mary sees Christ carry his cross, she sees him suffer and die on the cross, taken down from the cross and buried, and no grief of others is so profound

4 Annibale Carracci, *Lamentation of Christ*, ca 1604. National Gallery, London. Wikimedia.

as hers. Yet, even in such suffering, its real burden is not the unyieldingness of grief or of loss only, nor the weight of necessary imposition, nor complaint about the injustice of fate, and so a comparison with the characteristic grief of Niobe is especially appropriate. Niobe too has lost all her children and now confronts us in pure sublimity and unimpaired beauty.... Mary's grief is of a totally different kind. She is emotional, she feels the thrust of the dagger into the center of her soul, her heart breaks, but she does not turn into stone. She did not only *have* love; on the contrary, her whole inner life *is* love, the free concrete spiritual depth of feeling which preserves the absolute essence of what she has lost, and even in the loss of the loved on she ever retains the peace of love. Her heart breaks; but the very substance and burden of her heart and mind which shines through

5 Michelangelo, *Pietà*, 1498–9. Vatican Museum. Wikimedia.

> her soul's suffering with a vividness never to be lost is something infinitely higher. This is the living beauty of *soul* in contrast to the abstract *substance* which, in its ideal existence in the body perishes, remains imperishable, but in stone. (*LFA* 825–6)

I want to draw attention to the way in which Hegel sees Mary's love as "totally different" from the classical "pure sublimity and unimpaired beauty" of Niobe. Mary's impaired beauty in Carracci's painting achieves something that differs, say, from Michelangelo's efforts in the Vatican *Pietà*: the revelation of "the very substance and burden" – *not* of her dead son, of *his* weight – but "of *her* heart and mind which shines through."

6 Michelangelo, *The Deposition*, 1547–55. Museo dell'Opera del Duomo, Florence. Wikimedia.

Hegel expressed his admiration for the *Pietà* (see *LFA* 790). Michelangelo's later (unfinished) version of the Pietà seems to have followed this same thought – making Christ's weight in the "deposition" central to its figuration.

At issue, I want to say (with Hegel, I think), is not only how to apprehend the weight of what is lost. If the magnitude of the loss were what most needed depicting, then – Hegel suggests – something more like Niobe's tears or Laocoon's grimace would be more appropriate. But – as Christian depictions of Mary's lamentation often suggest – Mary is best seen in her acceptance of this painful reality, the acceptance and realization of the depth of her love. She "is emotional, she feels the thrust of the dagger into the center of her soul, her heart breaks, but she does not turn into stone."

Can we see Mary *as she sees herself*? The depth of her self-relation – her view of herself – is born in her unbeautiful appearance, not only as weighed by the dead son she bears in her arms. Not just the magnitude of Mary's loss, not just that burden – but *Mary* herself, in the profundity of her unbeautiful grief?

V

Cavell, I noted, makes Leontes's acceptance of his paternity the condition of possibility for a self-relation that would enable him to begin to acknowledge Hermione. But if we pursue the scene as Shakespeare presents it, beyond the sequential summary given by Cavell, some important alternatives present themselves.

First, although Leontes does emphatically deny that Perdita is his daughter, contrary to Cavell's suggestion, he never denies that Mamillius is his son. Whereas Cavell, again, conflates the question of Leontes's denial of "his children" with a denial that Mamillius is his "son," Shakespeare keeps the two apart: the pair of children never meet each other, and Leontes's initial refusal of the newborn daughter is adamant.[24] Moreover, rather than struggle with accepting Mamillius as his (as Cavell has it), Leontes struggles to accept Mamillius as *theirs* – as his *and* Hermione's son, an object of *their* love. He does not so much deny his paternal bond to Mamillius as deny Hermione's maternal bond to him – he keeps the two of *them* apart.

Second, it should be remembered that one reason for a father to acknowledge a son rather than a daughter is that – in a patriarchal world – a son can bear the legitimacy of the *paternal* (but not necessarily the maternal) acknowledgment in ways that a daughter cannot.[25] In such a world, to acknowledge a son and to acknowledge a daughter must be two different forms of acknowledgment. One way of looking at this is to consider that, in barring Mamillius from his mother, Leontes is not banishing Mamillius from the throne – or from future ascension. With *King Lear* in mind, for example, we could say that such a patriarchal structure allows fathers to acknowledge relations to sons in myriad ways without thereby acknowledging, with respect to the mother, anything other than having once had sexual-biological relations with her.[26] That is, Leontes can acknowledge his "physical" dependence on Hermione for his own paternity – every child must have a mother, of biological necessity – without acknowledging his dependency on *Hermione's* acknowledgment or love of the child, or of him. His dependence on *her* "blissful" love of their child – her self-relation – has yet to be acknowledged. And it is far from clear how they can begin to rightly see each other, as lovers, in the absence of that acknowledgment.

In saying this, I do not mean that the issue of acknowledging children in *The Winter's Tale* remains merely a matter of legitimacy, paternal prerogatives, or patriarchal-monarchical inheritance. But Shakespeare includes a son and a daughter, in ways the Christian narrative avoids. So I wanted to indicate that the patriarchal context matters to the vicissitudes of mutual acknowledgment between Leontes and Hermione in ways that Cavell does not adequately address. The difference between acknowledging a son and acknowledging a daughter is unavoidable in this context, since the structural inequality of son and daughter is repeated in the inequality between husband and wife – especially if the latter's maternal and sexual self-relation can be made to "stand trial."

Indeed, this difference between sons and daughters presses the question: What would it mean for a father to acknowledge or love a child as his own *irrespective of the child's gender*, and beyond matters of political or economic legitimacy? And *how* could the meaning of that very question ever get a grip from within an extreme patriarchy like Leontes's Sicilia? If, as I have been emphasizing, parental *love* – devotion to children as one's *own* in some sense not captured by seeing them as bearers of one's title or property or prerogatives – is to come into view, then it must emerge from *this* background.

Consider again Carracci's painting. It hangs in the National Gallery in London, which remains open until 9 p.m. on Fridays – when the gallery is empty enough to allow a special kind of intimacy with the canvases. The bustle of Trafalgar Square outside, the hum of London, the empty darkness of the gallery, thoughts of Shakespeare living in this city some generations back – all this, and the lack of an explicitly religious setting, provoke me to look at the Carracci painting not as the image of death of God's son and his grieving mother. I see, instead, two dead children – a brother and a sister – attended only by women, perhaps themselves the mothers or grandmothers.

Faced with the sight of his two dead children, a father – a King, a Gloucester, a Leontes – may have reason to lament, first, the death of his son. But to which dead child would a mother first turn her gaze, stretch out her arms?

And what about us? Faced with such a tableau … to whom would we look first, reach for first?

Leontes, it seems, needed to be told where to look. "This news is mortal to the queen," says Paulina, "Look down / And see what death is doing."

As he looks upon Hermione – upon a scene something like the one Carracci offers – Leontes's response differs markedly from the women in Carracci's canvas. Leontes denies the depth of his wife's grief, her self-relation, her "bliss":

> Take her hence.
> Her heart is but o'ercharged. She will recover. (3.2.146–7)

Why does Leontes think that Hermione will "recover" from the death of their son? Does he think that he can measure her grief because it cannot possibly outweigh his own? That her parental love (her self-relation) cannot equal his? That he can out-grieve her, out-grieve them all?

There is evidence for this:

> Prithee bring me
> To the dead bodies of my queen and son.
> One grave shall be for both. Upon them shall
> The causes of their death appear, unto
> Our shame perpetual. Once a day I'll visit
> The chapel where they lie, and tears shed there
> Shall be my recreation. So long as nature
> Will bear up with this exercise, so long
> I daily vow to use it. Come, and lead me
> To these sorrows. (3.2.231–9)

It is difficult to escape the sense that a religion is being articulated here, a cult of paternal grief forged in self-pitying interment of mother and child, mother with child, as if covering over maternal love – "one grave shall be for both." The first part of *The Winter's Tale* indeed concludes with the erasure of maternal love's appearance – as if to tally the cost of displacing the cult of the Madonna, say.

Contrary to Cavell, what Leontes most damagingly denies is not that his children are his. Most damagingly, Leontes denies that what it means for his children to be his – in a loving sense not captured by patriarchal prerogatives or issues of legitimacy – also depends on whether Hermione loves and grieves, and on how *her* love and self-relation are seen by him. It is not therefore, as Cavell has it, that Leontes's failure to see Hermione is rooted in his denial/acceptance of his children. Whether and how Hermione loves her children, rather, must bear on whether Leontes, too, can see their children are *theirs* – as the objective existence of their love – in any way not captured the demands of patriarchal-economic power relations, or biological processes. And after all, doesn't Leontes desperately want to see the children as *theirs*, to be able to suspend his disbelief about that?

A last comment:

One way of looking at the myth of the immaculate conception is to consider God's acknowledgment that Christ is Mary's child, too. Not just biologically – via a patriarchal appropriation of her womb, as in Simone de Beauvoir's reading of the immaculate conception – but in the sense that God acknowledges his dependence on Mary's self-related love (her love for God himself, as well for the child).[27] But of course, from a religious viewpoint, Mary's love and conception were not sexual. So the questions facing Leontes and Hermione are different.

How can Leontes acknowledge his dependency on Hermione's *self-relation*, on her maternal love – and not just on her womb? And can this be done in ways that take on board the vicissitudes of passionate sexual love, the possibility that parental love and passionate love might not only co-exist but be co-dependent?

Can any meaningful revelation about this still take artistic or religious form; or do such hopes remain things of the past?

NOTES

1 René Girard, *Theater of Envy* (Oxford: Oxford University Press, 1991), 335–6.

2 Julia Reinhard Lupton, "Judging Forgiveness: Hannah Arendt, W.H. Auden, and *The Winter's Tale*," *New Literary History* 45, no. 4 (Autumn 2014): 641–3; Richard C. McCoy, "*The Winter's Tale* and the Recovery of Faith," in *Faith in Shakespeare*, 113–45 (Oxford: Oxford University Press, 2013); Sarah

Beckwith, *Shakespeare and the Grammar of Forgiveness* (Ithaca, NY: Cornell University Press, 2011); René Girard, *A Theater of Envy: William Shakespeare* (Oxford: Oxford University Press,1991); Stanley Cavell, *Disowning Knowledge in Seven Plays of Shakespeare* (Cambridge: Cambridge University Press, 1987).

3 Cavell, *Disowning Knowledge,* 193.

4 Paul A. Kottman, "Hegel and Shakespeare on the Pastness of Art," in *The Art of Hegel's Aesthetics: Hegelian Philosophy and the Perspectives of Art History,* ed. Paul A. Kottman and Michael Squire, 263–301 (Munich: Fink, 2018).

5 Portraits of animals, too. See Robert Pippin, "Hegel on Painting," in Kottman and Squire, *The Art of Hegel's Aesthetics,* 211–37.

6 Not, like Hercules, "dragons outside him or Lerneaen hydras" – that is – but rather "the dragons and hydras of his own heart, the inner obstinacy and inflexibility of his own self." Hegel, *Aesthetics: Lectures on Fine Art,* trans. T.M. Knox (Oxford: Clarendon, 1975), 1:816.

7 Hegel, *LFA,* 1:816.

8 Hegel, *LFA,* 1:824.

9 See Hegel, *LFA,* 1:816–27.

10 "On the whole, children love their parents less than their parents love them." Hegel, *Elements of the Philosophy of Right,* ed. Allen Wood (Cambridge: Cambridge University Press, 1991), §175, Addition, 213. For more, see my *Love as Human Freedom* (Stanford: Stanford University Press, 2017), 168–9.

11 In *Love as Human Freedom,* I track ways in which "love" finds its reflective form in artworks – especially poetic-literary works – but in a way that (I hope) also demonstrates that art is not, finally, entirely adequate to this task, and hence that love ought to be seen as itself a dimension of Absolute Spirit, reflectively but incompletely grasped in artistic (or religious or philosophical) presentations.

12 John Pitcher, editor of the third Arden edition, glosses this word as "absoluteness" – citing the *Oxford English Dictionary,* which, however, refers to this very same line from Shakespeare as the only evidence for its definition.

13 "This session, to our great grief we pronounce / Even pushes 'gainst our heart" (3.2.1–2). I take it that "of us too much beloved" is meant to refer as much to the people of Sicilia as to Leontes himself.

14 "Let us be cleared / Of being tyrannous, since we so openly / Proceed in justice" (3.2.4–5).

15 In saying this, I want also to agree with two claims made by Cavell. For Cavell, "Descartes' discovery of skepticism shows … what makes Leontes' madness possible, or what makes his madness representative of the human

need for acknowledgment" (203). I agree, and I also agree that, like Descartes, Leontes is searching in the trial for a *method* for curing his doubt (whether he knows that what he's doing is, or not). Cavell writes next, "The depth of this madness, or of its possibility, is revealed by *The Winter's Tale* to measure, in turn, the depth of drama, or of spectacle, or of showing itself, in its competition with telling or narrative, because, as suggested, even after believing the truth proclaimed by an oracle Leontes is not brought back to the world (supposing he ever is) except by the drama of revelation and resurrection at the end of this work for theater" (204). I also agree that drama is presented here – by *both* Leontes and Shakespeare, as it were – as a kind of antidote to scepticism. Whether drama's revelations are (still) adequate to that task is another question – one tied to the fate of religion as well.

16 Agnes Heller puts it well when she notes that Shakespeare "preserves and reinforces one essential feature of mystery plays" – the "revelatory" truth of what happens. "One is confronted with the question of what exactly this truth is, not with the question of whether this is the truth." See her "Poetic Truth and Historical Truth," in *Philosophers on Shakespeare*, ed. Paul A. Kottman (Stanford: Stanford University Press, 2009), 186.

17 To those who would argue that Leontes will only accept an outcome of the trial that validates his accusations, I point simply to the fact that this is not at all how the scene ends.

18 Cavell is careful to note – and I agree – that Descartes's own method is not necessarily exportable, psychologically or otherwise. "The cure in Descartes' case is not so readily describable [as that of Leontes]; and perhaps it is not available. I mean, acknowledging that the world exists, that you know for yourself that it is yours, is not so clear a process" (203). Agreed. But this makes it all the more significant that Cavell *does* think the cure presents itself in *The Winter's Tale* in the form of an acknowledgment, by Leontes, of his paternity. So I shall turn to that question now, and contest much of what Cavell has to say about that.

19 It is worth recalling that Leontes does not only deny that Hermione and Polixenes are faithful or honest; he calls *everyone* a liar: "You're liars all!" (2.3.144). I am citing from Cavell, *Disowning Knowledge*, 195. Along the way, Cavell indirectly takes a jab at René Girard's famous thesis about the fundamental role played by mimetic rivalry or mimetic desire in human culture and psychology: "The idea of his fearing to be a father would make his jealousy of Polixenes suspicious – not merely because it makes the jealousy empirically baseless, but because it makes it psychologically derivative. This is worth saying because there are views that would take the

jealousy between brothers as a rock-bottom level of human motivation." But Girard's own reading of *The Winter's Tale*, published a few years after Cavell's own essay, sees the play as Shakespeare's own "deepening awareness that his past ferocity with sufferers of mimetic desire was still fueled by the virulence of the disease in himself" (*Theater of Envy*, 338). Girard's use of the word "disease" here echoes Shakespeare's own reference to Leontes's "diseased opinion" (1.2.297) and indicates that Girard, as if responding to Cavell's jab, sees *The Winter's Tale* as Shakespeare's effort to refute the notion that jealousy is a rock-bottom level of human motivation.

20 See Cavell, *Disowning Knowledge*, 194–5.

21 Cavell's way of describing the tension is this: "Chaos seems to have come again; and what chaos looks like is the inability to say what exists; to say whether, so to speak, language applies to anything." Cavell, *Disowning Knowledge*, 197.

22 Cavell, *Disowning Knowledge*, 203

23 For a framework within which to at least begin thinking about such issues, see my *Love as Human Freedom.*

24 See Cavell, *Disowning Knowledge*, 194–5.

25 For a meditation on the social insufficiency of the maternal acknowledgment of sons, in a patriarchal setting, consider that Gertrude's motherly claims on Hamlet are enough to keep him from being assassinated by Claudius, enough to keep him and alive and at court, but not enough to open much else in the way of a future for either of them.

26 I am thinking of Gloucester's remarks about the begetting of Edmund at the very beginning of the play. See my discussion in *Tragic Conditions in Shakespeare: Disinheriting the Globe* (Baltimore, MD: Johns Hopkins University Press, 2009), 84–6.

27 Simone de Beauvoir, *The Second Sex*, trans. Constance Borde and Sheila Malovanz-Chevallier (New York: Vintage, 2011). Beauvoir's point is, of course, well taken. And yet in Luke's Gospel, Mary *does* say, "Let it be so," even as her troubles are registered. Mary did not intend to get pregnant, but she nevertheless experiences her maternity not as the result of sexual-biological reproduction (she is a virgin), but of love.

Afterword

CHARLES McNULTY

King Lear, widely regard as the pinnacle of Shakespeare's achievement in the drama, presents us with a vexing paradox. The play usurped the position of *Hamlet* as Shakespeare's pre-eminent tragedy in the middle of the twentieth century. (Two world wars, the threat of nuclear annihilation, and the blasted theatrical landscapes of Samuel Beckett primed audiences for the play's apocalyptic vision.) Yet *King Lear* poses such formidable challenges in the theatre that some of the most prominent Shakespeare scholars, critics, and theatre practitioners have doubted whether the stage, any stage, can contain its vastness.

Those who engage in such heresy, typically after a surfeit of mediocre productions, usually take cover behind one of three prominent critics: Samuel Johnson, Charles Lamb, and A.C. Bradley. I should know because after a string of disappointments with the play in performance, I consulted these sceptics for an article I was writing for the *Los Angeles Times* questioning whether the play may indeed be "unreachably sublime."[1] The production under review was Daniel Sullivan's scattershot 2014 New York Public Theater staging at Central Park's Delacorte Theatre starring John Lithgow, but a career of professional theatregoing had left me well stocked with examples.

Johnson's famous misgivings about the ending of *King Lear* ("I might relate that I was many years ago so shocked by Cordelia's death I know not whether I ever endured to read again the last scenes of the play till I undertook to revise them as an editor")[2] are sometimes dismissed as a fussy Shakespearean footnote, but this was hardly an off-the-cuff remark. Aware of the artistic arguments against Nahum Tate's adaptation, which supplanted Shakespeare's tragedy with a happier version that was to hold the English stage for 150 years starting in 1681, he was nevertheless unable to dismiss his reservations: "A play in which the wicked prosper, and the virtuous miscarry, may doubtless be good, because it is a just representation of the common events of human life: but since all reasonable beings naturally love justice, I cannot easily be persuaded that the observation of justice makes a play worse; or, that if other excellencies are equal, the audience will not always rise better pleased from the final triumph of persecuted virtue."[3] Johnson wasn't arguing simply from the standpoint of the delicate sensibilities of his theatregoing contemporaries; he was aware that hardier Elizabethan audiences had made *King Leir*, an earlier and more conventional version of the drama, popular enough for Shakespeare to attempt his own radical reworking of it. Commercial success and artistic merit are hardly coterminous, but Johnson was unable to dismiss enduring qualities of dramatic satisfaction.

Charles Lamb thought the glory of *King Lear* was intellectual and could be corrupted only by what he called the "contemptible machinery" of the theatre.[4] Lamb held early nineteenth-century British stagecraft in low regard. But he questioned whether the character of Lear could be represented on even an ideal stage. "So to see Lear acted – to see an old man tottering about the stage with a walking-stick, turned out of doors by his daughters in a rainy night, has nothing in it but what is painful and disgusting."[5] For Lamb, the "tamperings," and by this he means Tate's audience-pandering revisions (the romantic scenes between Edgar and Cordelia, the happy ending for Lear and his good daughter) prove to him that this "hard and stony" play is "beyond all art."[6] "On the stage we see nothing but corporeal infirmities and weaknesses, the impotence of rage: while we read it, we see not Lear, but we are Lear – we are in his mind, we are sustained by a grandeur which baffles the malice of daughters and storms."[7] In short, the only way to know *King Lear* is to commune with the play privately in one's study.

Finally, A.C Bradley, in his published lectures on *King Lear*, pondered the reasons "Shakespeare's greatest" tragedy is the least popular of the "famous four."[8] Bradley's lectures were published in 1904, long before Peter Brook and Jan Kott helped us to recognize Shakespeare as Beckett's contemporary. Boldly contending that *King Lear* is "too huge for the stage," Bradley located "the peculiar greatness" of the play in its immense scope, "the mass and variety of intense experience which it contains."[9] Thus, in his view, "its comparative unpopularity is due, not merely to the extreme painfulness of the catastrophe, but in part to its dramatic defects," which are a consequence of the play's appeal "to a rarer and more strictly poetic kind of imagination."[10] Bradley's case, synthesizing the objections of Johnson and Lamb, offers the most comprehensive critique of the play's stage-worthiness, even if it fails to anticipate how revolutions in twentieth- century stagecraft wrought by modernism and postmodernism might open new possibilities for theatrical confrontation.

To summarize these historic objections, *King Lear* eludes us in the theatre because (1) the unwieldy plot presents formidable dramatic roadblocks; (2) the ending rebuffs our moral wishes; (3) performance can only debase the play's intellectual and poetic grandeur. These points are sometimes indulgently entertained before they are dismissed as examples of antiquated thinking that have no relevance to our ostensibly braver age. Yet anyone courageous enough to undertake staging the play would be advised to spend some time contemplating the theatrical qualms of these scholarly critics, who not only stood in awe of Shakespeare's genius but also helped us to better appreciate its peculiar lineaments in *King Lear.*

Kenneth Tynan, who as drama critic for the *Observer* and the *New Yorker* had the opportunity to see the greatest twentieth-century actors tackle Lear, once described the play as "a labyrinthine citadel, all but impregnable."[11] In a 1953 review of Donald Wolfit's performance, he memorably compared the challenge of playing Lear in "the last unearthly act" to landing "as it were by parachute on the top of Parnassus."[12] My last major Lears – Lithgow in Sullivan's Shakespeare in the Park production; Glenda Jackson in Deborah Warner's Old Vic production; and Antony Sher in Gregory Doran's Royal Shakespeare production – all, understandably, fell short of this level of daredevil athleticism. Anthony Hopkins, in the attenuated BBC television production, delivered a savage performance of excerpts that, were it not for the slick contemporary design, might have resembled a nineteenth-century actor-manager's spotlighted stroll through the tragedy.

Sullivan's production corroborated Bradley's view of the play as being too vast for the stage. Bradley, of course, wasn't referring to the drama's length (*Hamlet, Richard III, Antony and Cleopatra* and *Othello* are all longer) as much as its poetic scale. Sullivan's revival suggested that *King Lear* may be too logistically cumbersome for the inflexible producing confines of the American theatre. Simply put, the four-week rehearsal allotment of the typical non-profit theatre isn't sufficient to prepare a cast for the monumental task of scaling *King Lear.* Sullivan clearly didn't have adequate time to thread his disparate actors into a unified company. How could he be expected to rigorously probe the text with them line by resonantly ambiguous line? The ensemble was overmatched by the demands of Shakespeare's mind and music. At the centre was Lithgow, a supremely intelligent actor, working exceedingly hard to live up to this casting opportunity in a production that was unfortunately too caught up in its own survival to become more than a prestigious acting credit on a veteran actor's résumé.

The Warner and Doran productions, employing actors more conversant with Shakespearean diction, stumbled in different ways. The meeting of modern stagecraft and early-modern dramaturgy seemed unsettled in both revivals, as though the directors were grappling on the fly with how to produce the play in our post–Peter Brookian universe. Warner designed her approach around her star, a two-time Oscar-winner who had resumed her theatrical career after more than two decades in politics to play the title role. Jackson's early stage career included Brook's landmark 1964 production of *Marat/Sade*, and it appeared as if Warner were vying for a similar mélange of Brecht's epic theatre and Artaud's theatre of cruelty. There was detachment, marked by gestural italics, which over time transmuted into raw anguish, but not in a way that was easy to emotionally or aesthetically parse. Warner's boldness too often came across as busyness, draining the tragedy of a good deal of the angry pathos generated by the production's fiery star. Jackson, when I interviewed her in New York while she was performing in Edward Albee's *Three Tall Women* on Broadway, pointedly described Warner's direction as "fashionable." But the octogenarian actor is not growing less risk-averse: she took another crack at the role in a 2019 Broadway production directed by Sam Gold, an American auteur whose freewheeling approach to classics gave Warner's vogueishness a run for its money.

At the RSC there were signs of disconnection between the director (Doran) and his lead actor (Sher), who happen to be marital partners. Sher's language-centred approach to playing Lear shone a spotlight on his own fluency. This was above all a beautifully articulated, if at times theatrically barnstorming, performance. Curiously though, as the play wore on, Doran seemed to become more tantalized by silences than Shakespearean sounds. As Lear's losses mounted, the production opted for a kind of Beckettian dishabille. A barren tree reminiscent of the one in *Waiting for Godot* shifted the theatrical period from the late nineteenth to the mid-twentieth century. Brook's landmark staging of *King Lear* cast its mammoth shadow, but instead of Paul Scofield's archaic majesty there was Sher's elocutionary finesse. The production, operating at cross-purposes, failed to arrive at a détente between actor-manager and auteur.

Once again *King Lear* overwhelmed its interpreters, though to their credit these directors didn't throw up the white flag in the way of Richard Eyre's television presentation, which was curtailed for the shortened attention spans of viewers and the privileged schedules of screen stars. The experimental push of the stage productions seemed at least to be reckoning, however unevenly, with some of the issues raised by Johnson, Lamb, and Bradley. The expectation of poetic justice is no longer ingrained, but what are the challenges that even the most jaded modern audience confronts in a play that so ruthlessly withholds consolation? Does Lear's journey need to be filtered through a contemporary lens (Brecht, Beckett, Artaud, Brook, or perhaps some postmodern mélange?) for it to resonate in a theatrical era so far removed from Shakespeare's own? As Brook observed in his seminal treatise *The Empty Space*, "If you just let a play speak, it may not make a sound."[13] Say what you will about the erratic nature of Warner's and Doran's productions, they recognized that Shakespeare's genius requires contemporary mediation.

Directors are still sorting out how to bring the shifting vocabularies of the modern theatre to an earlier tradition that was itself in a state of flux. *King Lear* is a Jacobean tragedy written by the reigning master of the Elizabethan form. Much of the trouble we continue to have in meeting the work on stage is built into the playwriting. Shakespeare was defying precedent. His revisions of earlier versions of the King Lear story suggest his own radical thrust. In *King Leir*, for example, there is no Fool or Gloucester subplot, madness isn't a central theme, and Lear and Cordelia aren't restored to happiness. Shakespeare was testing what the stage could aesthetically, morally, and emotionally withstand, and we are still daunted by his daring.

In the harrowing scene between Gloucester and Lear, the allegorical encounter between a blind man and a madman, there is a hint of just how conscious Shakespeare was of his experiment. Edgar, upon seeing Lear in his ravaged state, mutters, "Oh thou side-piercing sight" (4.6.85).[14] Lear's next line, "Nature's above art in that respect" (4.6.86), is a response to his own previous utterance, "No, they cannot touch me for coining. I am the King himself" (4.6.83–4). But the juxtaposition tells another story – that of a dramatist who is challenging himself to go further than he's gone before. Shakespeare depicts not what we have been conditioned to expect from drama but what the tragedy of life in due course teaches us all: a truth "above" or exceeding what art has hitherto deemed permissible to share.

It's important to bear in mind that Johnson and Lamb would have had occasion to see only versions of the play as reworked to some degree by Tate, and even Bradley would likely not have had many opportunities to encounter an unadulterated version of Shakespeare's tragedy. They understood the magnitude of Shakespeare's accomplishment as keen readers while doubting as theatregoers the stage's capacity to accommodate the work's immense poetic scope. I have been fortunate enough to see the play performed numerous times in versions that, however much a mishmash of quarto and folio texts, strove to be faithful to Shakespeare's ruthless vision. Although I have yet to encounter a production that can live up to the exhilaration of my own periodic confrontations with the play as a solitary reader, I find the case for theatrical viability made by Harley Granville-Barker to be especially cogent. A playwright, director, and critic who combined a knowledge of practical stagecraft with a scholar's textual attentiveness, Granville-Barker begins his irreplaceable preface to *King Lear* by confronting the classic arguments against the drama's stage-worthiness. He feints a concession to the longstanding complaints: "It is possible that this most practical and loyal of dramatists did for once – despite himself, driven to it by his unpremeditating genius – break his promise and betray his trust by presenting to his fellows a play, the capital part of which they simply could not act. Happily for them, they and their audiences never found him out."[15] Granville-Barker, who recognized a consummate man of the theatre when he saw one, explains that Shakespeare relies "very naturally upon his strongest weapon, which by experiment and practice, he has now, indeed, forged to an extraordinary strength and suppleness besides: the weapon of dramatic poetry."[16]

Granville-Barker isn't contesting the difficulty of staging *King Lear*. He is defending the feasibility of the project. How do you create a storm onstage without falling into the cheapening theatrical effects frowned upon by Lamb and Bradley? By concentrating on the language, on "the music and imaginative suggestion," and by above all trusting in the synergy of image and character.[17] As for Lear's trajectory, which has proven so defiant to actors, Granville-Barker calls our attention to the way Shakespeare's canny plotting avoids the obvious traps of anticlimax after the first act and audience exhaustion midway through the play. The working in of the "lower-pitched theme of Edmund's treachery,"[18] Granville-Barker observes, helps to vary the intensity of the storm scene and its immediate aftermath. Careful scrutiny of the text reveals that Lear's movement from "malediction to martyrdom" is motivated by Shakespeare "in terms of humanity, and according to the rubric of drama."[19] Granville-Barker points to Lear's line "O! Reason not the need" as a turning point in "the abandoning of the struggle and embracing of misfortune" – a crucial juncture in the audience's relationship to a character who hitherto hasn't done much to win over our sympathies.[20] When uncertain how to theatrically proceed, Granville-Barker urges a closer inspection of the text, which was written by a playwright who understood only too well the myriad ways actors could be led astray and posted discreet signs to set them right.

The deep reading this requires, however, is part of the practical difficulty of performing *King Lear.* The logistics of contemporary producing militate against the kind of interpretive rigour Granville-Barker prescribes. There simply isn't enough time to thread a company of disparate performers into a seamless ensemble. What's more, there aren't many directors today who can match Granville-Barker's critical acumen, textual sensitivity, and fluency in Shakespearean dramaturgy – or leading actors equipped to take such direction. But the goal is theoretically achievable. Have I given up hope of encountering a production that can at least match, if not transcend, my experiences as an eternal student of the play? Not while Mark Rylance, the greatest of contemporary Shakespeareans, is still around.

NOTES

1 Charles McNulty, "Critic's Notebook: With Age, the Wisdom of Staging 'Lear' Becomes Less Clear,' *Los Angeles Times,* 13 August 2014.
2 From *The Plays of William Shakespeare,* ed. Samuel Johnson (London: J. and R. Tonson et al., 1765), 6:159.
3 *The Plays of William Shakespeare,* 6:159.
4 Charles Lamb, "On the Tragedies of Shakespeare," in *Charles Lamb: Selected Prose* (London: Penguin, 1985), 39.
5 Lamb, "On the Tragedies of Shakespeare," 39.
6 Lamb, "On the Tragedies of Shakespeare," 40.
7 Lamb, "On the Tragedies of Shakespeare," 40.
8 A.C. Bradley, "Lecture VII: *King Lear,*" in *Shakespearean Tragedy: Lectures on* Hamlet, Othello, King Lear *and* Macbeth (London: Penguin, 1991), 224.
9 Bradley, "Lecture VII: *King Lear,*" 228.
10 Bradley, "Lecture VII: *King Lear,*" 229.
11 Kenneth Tynan, *Curtains* (New York: Atheneum, 1961), 53.

12 Tynan, *Curtains*, 39–40.
13 Peter Brook, *The Empty Space* (New York: Atheneum, 1968), 38.
14 All references to *King Lear* are from *The Riverside Shakespeare* (Boston: Houghton Mifflin, 1974).
15 Harley Granville-Barker, *Prefaces to Shakespeare* (Princeton: Princeton University Press, 1947), 263.
16 Granville-Barker, *Prefaces*, 266.
17 Granville-Barker, *Prefaces*, 267.
18 Granville-Barker, *Prefaces*, 275.
19 Granville-Barker, *Prefaces*, 289.
20 Granville-Barker, *Prefaces*, 290.

Works Cited

Adelman, Janet. *Suffocating Mothers: Fantasies of Maternal Origin in Shakespeare's Plays, Hamlet to the Tempest.* New York: Routledge, 1992.

Agamben, Giorgio. *Homo Sacer.* Translated by Daniel Heller-Roazen. Stanford: Stanford University Press, 1998.

– *The Time That Remains: A Commentary of the Letter to the Romans.* Translated by Patricia Dailey. Stanford: Stanford University Press, 2005.

Alexander, Gavin. "Prosopopoeia: The Speaking Figure." In *Renaissance Figures of Speech,* edited by Sylvia Adamson, Gavin Alexander, and Katrin Ettenhuber, 97–112. Cambridge: Cambridge University Press, 2007.

Altman, Joel B. *The Tudor Play of Mind: Rhetorical Inquiry and the Development of Elizabethan Drama.* Berkeley: University of California Press, 1978.

Ameriks, Karl. "From Kant to Frank: The Ineliminable Subject." In *The Modern Subject: Conceptions of the Self in Classical German Philosophy,* edited by Karl Ameriks and Dieter Sturma, 223–4. Albany, NY: SUNY Press, 1995.

Anon. *Wily Beguiled.* London, 1606.

Arendt, Hannah. *Eichmann in Jerusalem: A Report on the Banality of Evil.* London: Penguin, 2006.

– *The Life of the Mind.* San Diego: Harcourt, 1978.

– "Personal Responsibility under Dictatorship." In *Responsibility and Judgement,* edited by Jerome Kohn, 17–48. New York: Random House, 2003.

Aristotle. *Nicomachean Ethics.* Translated by David Ross. Oxford: Oxford University Press, 1980.

– *Nicomachean Ethics.* Translated by H. Rackham. Cambridge, MA: Harvard University Press, 1934.

– *On the Soul. Parva Naturalia. On Breath.* Translated by W.S. Het. Cambridge, MA: Harvard University Press, 1957.

– *Rhetorica.* In *The Works of Aristotle,* vol. 11, edited by W.D. Ross and translated by W. Rhys Roberts. Oxford: Clarendon, 1924.

Augustine. *City of God.* Translated by Henry Bettenson. New York: Penguin Books, 1972.

Badiou, Alain. *In Praise of Love.* Translated by Peter Bush. London: Serpent's Tail, 2012.

Barber, C.L. *Shakespeare's Festive Comedy: A Study of Dramatic Form and Its Relation to Social Custom.* Princeton, NJ: Princeton University Press, 2012.

Barthelme, Donald. "Kierkegaard Unfair to Schlegel." *City Life.* New York: Farrar, Straus, and Giroux, 1970.

– *Not Knowing: The Essays and Interviews of Donald Barthelme,* edited by Kim Herzinger. New York: Random House, 1997.

Barthes, Roland. *A Lover's Discourse.* Translated by Richard Howard. New York: Farrar, Straus, and Giroux, 1978.

Basire, John. *An Excellent Letter from John Basire Doctor of Laws, to His Son Isaac Basire.* London, 1669.

Bate, Jonathan. "The Performance of Revenge: *Titus Andronicus* and *the Spanish Tragedy.*" In *The Show Within: Dramatic and Other Insets: English Renaissance Drama (1550–1642): Proceedings of the International Conference Held in Montpellier, 22–25 November 1990.* Vol. 2. Edited by François Laroque, 267–83. Montpellier: Publications de Université Paul-Valéry, 1992.

Bates, Catherine. *On Not Defending Poetry: Defence and Indefensibility in Sidney's Defence of Poesy.* Oxford: Oxford University Press, 2017.

Beaumont, Francis. *The Knight of the Burning Pestle.* In *English Renaissance Drama: A Norton Anthology,* edited by David Bevington et al., 1067–139. New York: Norton, 2002.

Beauvoir, Simone de. *The Second Sex.* Translated by Constance Borde and Sheila Malovanz-Chevallier. New York: Vintage, 2011.

Beckwith, Sarah. *Shakespeare and the Grammar of Forgiveness.* Ithaca, NY: Cornell University Press, 2011.

– *Signifying God: Social Relation and Symbolic Act in the York Corpus Christi Plays.* Chicago: University of Chicago Press, 2003.

Benjamin, Walter. "Critique of Violence." In *Selected Writings,* edited by Michael Jennings, translated by Edmund Jephcott, 1:236–52. Cambridge, MA: Harvard University Press, 1996.

– *The Origin of the German Tragic Drama.* Translated by John Osborne. London: Verso, 1988.

– "Theses on the Philosophy of History." In *Illuminations: Essays and Reflections,* 253–64. Edited by Hannah Arendt. Translated by Harry Zohn. New York: Schocken, 1969.

Benveniste, Émile. *Indo-European Language and Society*. Translated by Elizabeth Palmer. London: Faber & Faber, 1973.

Berger, John, and Jean Mohr. *A Fortunate Man: The Story of a Country Doctor*. London: Vintage International, 1997.

Bernacer, Javier, and Jose Ignacio Murillo. "The Aristotelian Conception of Habit and Its Contribution to Human Neuroscience." *Frontiers in Human Neuroscience* 8 (2014): 1–10.

Bevington, David, et al., eds. *English Renaissance Drama: A Norton Anthology*. New York: Norton, 2002.

Bloom, Harold. *Shakespeare: The Invention of the Human*. New York: Riverhead Books, 1998.

Blumenberg, Hans. *Work on Myth*. Translated by Robert M. Wallace. Cambridge, MA: MIT Press, 1985.

Blunderville, Thomas. *The Arte of Logicke*. London, 1599.

Boehrer, Bruce. "Economies of Desire in *A Midsummer Night's Dream*." *Shakespeare Studies* 32 (2004): 97–117.

Boose, Lynda E. "Othello's Handkerchief: 'The Recognizance and Pledge of Love.'" *English Literary Renaissance* 5, no. 3 (1975): 360–74.

Bradley, A.C. *Shakespearean Tragedy: Lectures on* Hamlet, Othello, King Lear, *and* Macbeth. London: Penguin, 1991.

Brissenden, R.F. *Virtue in Distress: Studies in the Novel of Sentiment from Richardson to Sade*. New York: Barnes and Noble, 1974.

Brook, Peter. *The Empty Space*. New York: Atheneum, 1968.

Brown, Jane K. "Discordia Concors: On the Order of *A Midsummer Night's Dream*." *Modern Language Quarterly* 48, no. 1 (1987): 20–41.

Brown, Peter. "Introducing Robert Markus." *Augustinian Studies* 32 (2001): 181–7.

Browning, Kirk, dir. *Ian McKellen: Acting Shakespeare*. New York: Entertainment One, 1982.

Bubner, Rüdiger. "Die 'Sache selbst' in Hegel's System." In *Zur Sache der Dialektik*, 40–70. Stuttgart: Reclam, 1980.

Budick, Emily Miller. *Emily Dickinson and the Life of Language: A Study in Symbolic Poetics*. Baton Rouge: Louisiana State University Press, 1985.

Budick, Sanford. "Hamlet's 'Now' of Inward Being." In *Shakespeare's Hamlet: Philosophical Perspectives*, edited by Tzachi Zamir, 133–56. New York: Oxford University Press, 2018.

– *Kant and Milton*. Cambridge: Harvard University Press, 2010.

Bullokar, John. *An English Expositor: Teaching the Interpretation of the Hardest Words in Our Language*. London, 1616.

Calderwood, James. "*A Midsummer Night's Dream*: The Illusion of Drama." *Modern Language Quarterly* 26, no. 4 (1965): 506–22.

Cannadine, David. *The Undivided Past: Humanities Beyond Our Differences*. New York: Alfred A. Knopf, 2013.

"care, n.1." *Oxford English Dictionary Online*. Oxford University Press. http://www.oed.com/view/Entry/27899.

Carlisle, Clare. *On Habit*. London: Routledge, 2014.

Callaghan, Dympna. "Looking Well to Linens: Women and Cultural Production in *Othello* and Shakespeare's England." In *Marxist Shakespeares*, edited by Jean E. Howard and Scott Cutler Shershow, 41–57 (London: Routledge, 2001).

Carroll, William C. *Fat King, Lean Beggar: Representations of Poverty in the Age of Shakespeare*. Ithaca, NY: Cornell University Press, 1996.

Cavell, Stanley. *Disowning Knowledge in Seven Plays of Shakespeare*. Cambridge: Cambridge University Press, 1987.

– *The Claim of Reason: Wittgenstein, Skepticism, Morality, and Tragedy*, updated edition. Oxford: Oxford University Press, 2002.

– *Must We Mean What We Say? A Book of Essays*. Cambridge: Cambridge University Press, 1976.

– *In Quest of the Ordinary: Lines of Skepticism and Romanticism*. Chicago: University of Chicago Press.

Cefalu, Paul. "'Damned Custom ... Habits Devil': Shakespeare's *Hamlet*, Anti-Dualism, and the Early Modern Philosophy of Mind." *ELH* 67 (2000): 399–431.

Cicero. *De Finibus Bonorum et Malorum*. Edited by T.E. Page and W.H.D. Rouse. Translated by H. Rackham. Loeb Classical Library. London: William Heineman, 1914.

Clemen, Wolfgang. *Kommentar zu Shakespeares Richard III: Interpretation eines Dramas*. Göttingen: Vandenhoeck & Ruprecht, 1969.

Cohen, Walter. *Drama of a Nation: Public Theatre in Renaissance England and Spain*. Ithaca, NY: Cornell University Press, 1985.

Cornford, Francis M. *Thucydides Mythistoricus*. Oxford: Clarendon, 1907.

"cure, n.1."*Oxford English Dictionary Online*. Oxford: Oxford University Press. www.oed.com/view/Entry/46000.

Curran, Kevin. "The Face of Judgement in *Measure for Measure*." In *Face-to-Face in Shakespearean Drama: Ethics, Philosophy, Performance*, edited by Matthew J. Smith and Julia R. Lupton, 163–75. Edinburgh: Edinburgh University Press, 2019.

– "Prospero's Plea: Judgment, Invention, and Political Form in *The Tempest*." In *Shakespeare and Judgment*, edited by Kevin Curran, 157–71. Edinburgh: Edinburgh University Press, 2017.

– *Shakespeare's Legal Ecologies: Law and Distributed Selfhood*. Evanston, IL: Northwestern University Press, 2017.

Davey, Nicholas. "On the Polity of Experience: Towards a Hermeneutics of Attentiveness." *Renascence: Essays on Values in Literature* 54, no. 4 (Summer 2004): 217–34.

de Grazia, Margreta. *Hamlet without Hamlet.* Cambridge: Cambridge University Press, 2007.

– "Soliloquies and Wages in the Age of Emergent Consciousness." *Textual Practice* 9 (1995): 67–92.

Dekker, Thomas. *If It Be Not Good, The Devil Is in It. The Dramatic Works of Thomas Dekker,* vol. 3, edited by Fredson Bowers, 113–223. Cambridge: Cambridge University Press, 1953–62.

– *The Whore of Babylon. The Dramatic Works of Thomas Dekker,* vol. 2, edited by Fredson Bowers, 491–592. Cambridge: Cambridge University Press, 1953–62.

de Man, Paul. *Allegories of Reading: Figural Language in Rousseau, Nietzsche, Rilke, and Proust.* New Haven, CT: Yale University Press, 1979.

de Mornay, Philippe. *The True Knowledge of a Man's Owne Selfe.* London, 1602.

Dent, R.W. "Imagination in *A Midsummer Night's Dream.*" *Shakespeare Quarterly* 15, no. 2 (1964): 115–29.

Derrida, Jacques. "Hospitality, Justice, and Responsibility: A Dialogue with Jacques Derrida." In *Questioning Ethics: Contemporary Debates in Philosophy,* edited by Richard Kearney and Mark Dooley, 65–83. London: Routledge, 1999.

– *Margins of Philosophy.* Translated by Alan Bass. Chicago: University of Chicago Press, 1982.

Dictionary of Christianity. Edited by Jean C. Cooper. Chicago: Fitzroy Dearborn, 1996.

Dictionary of Untranslatables: A Philosophical Lexicon. Edited by Barbara Cassin. Translated by Emily Apter, Jacques Lezra, and Michael Wood. Princeton, NJ: Princeton University Press, 2014.

Donnellan, Declan. *The Actor and the Target.* London: Nick Hern, 2002.

Dryden, John. *The Poems of John Dryden.* Vol. 5. Edited by Paul Hammond and David Hopkins. Harlow: Pearson/Longman, 2005.

Dula, Peter. *Cavell, Companionship, and Theology.* Oxford: Oxford University Press, 2011.

Duncan-Jones, Katherine, and Jan van Dorsten, eds. *Miscellaneous Prose of Sir Philip Sidney.* Oxford: Clarendon, 1973.

Elam, Keir. *The Semiotics of Theatre and Drama.* 2nd ed. London: Routledge, 2002.

Eliot, George. *Silas Marner.* New York: Alfred A. Knopf, 1993.

Elyot, Thomas. *The Dictionary of Syr Thomas Eliot Knyght.* London, 1538.

Empson, William. *The Structure of Complex Works.* Edited by Jonathan Culler. Cambridge, MA: Harvard University Press, 1989.

Engle, Lars. "Shakespearean Normativity in *All's Well That Ends Well.*" In *Shakespearean International Yearbook,* edited by Garham Bradshaw, Thomas Bishop, and Mark Tuner, 264–78. Aldershot: Ashgate, 2004.

Enterline, Lynn. *Shakespeare's Schoolroom: Rhetoric, Discipline, Emotion.* Philadelphia: University of Pennsylvania Press, 2012.

Erne, Lukas. *Beyond* The Spanish Tragedy: *A Study of the Works of Thomas Kyd.* Manchester: Manchester University Press, 2001.

Farrell, Frank B. *Why Does Literature Matter?* Ithaca, NY: Cornell University Press, 2004.

Fink, Eugen. "The Phenomenological Philosophy of Edmund Husserl and Contemporary Criticism." In *The Phenomenology of Husserl: Selected Critical Readings,* edited and translated by R.O. Elveton, 70–139. Seattle: Noesis, 2000.

Fischer-Lichte, Erika. *The Semiotics of Theater.* Translated by Jeremy Gaines and Doris L. Jones. Bloomington: Indiana University Press, 1992.

Felski, Rita. *The Limits of Critique.* Chicago: University of Chicago Press, 2015.

Fineman, Joel. *Shakespeare's Perjured Eye: The Invention of Poetic Subjectivity in the Sonnets.* Berkeley: University of California Press, 1986.

Fink, Eugen. *Sixth Cartesian Meditation: The Idea of a Transcendental Theory of Method.* Translated by Ronald Bruzina. Bloomington: Indiana University Press, 1988.

Fitchte, Johann Gottlieb. *The Science of Knowledge.* Translated by Peter Heath and John Lachs. Cambridge: Cambridge University Press, 1982.

Fletcher, K.F.B. "Hyginus' *Fabulae*: Toward a Roman Mythography." In *Writing Myth: Mythography in the Ancient World,* edited by R.S. Smith and S. Trzaskoma, 133–64. Walpole, MA: Peeters, 2013.

Foster, Charles. *Being a Beast: Adventures across the Species Divide.* London: Profile Books, 2016.

Foucault, Michel. *The History of Sexuality.* Vol. 3, *The Care of the Self.* Translated by Robert Hurley. New York: Vintage, 1988.

Fraunce, Abraham. *The Lawyers Logike.* London, 1588.

Freinkel, Lisa. *Reading Shakespeare's Will: The Theology of Figure from Augustine to the Sonnets.* New York: Columbia University Press, 2002.

Fromm, Erich. *The Art of Loving.* New York: Open Road Media, 2013.

Frye, Susan. *Pens and Needles: Women's Textualities in Early Modern England.* Philadelphia: University of Pennsylvania Press, 2010.

Fulda, Hans Friedrich. *Das Problem einer Einleitung in Hegels Wissenschaft der Logik.* Frankfurt am Main: Klostermann, 1965.

– *Georg Wilhelm Friedrich Hegel*. Munich: Beck, 2003.
Garbe, Marjorie. *Shakespeare: From Metaphor to Metamorphosis*. New Haven, CT: Yale University Press, 1974.
Gasché, Rodolphe. "Reading Chiasms." Introduction to *Readings in Interpretation: Hölderlin, Hegel, Heidegger*, by Andrzej Warminski, ix–xxvi. Minneapolis: University of Minnesota Press, 1987.
Gibson, John. *Fiction and the Weave of Life*. Oxford: Oxford University Press, 2007.
Gillette, William. *The Illusion of the First Time in Acting*. New York: Dramatic Museum of Columbia University, 1915.
Girard, René. *A Theater of Envy: William Shakespeare*. Oxford: Oxford University Press, 1991.
Gjesdal, Kristin. "Hegel and Herder on Art, History, and Reason." *Philosophy and Literature* 30 (2006): 17–32.
– "Literature, Prejudice, Historicity: The Philosophical Importance of Herder's Shakespeare Studies." In *The Insistence of Art: Aesthetic Philosophy after Early Modernity*, edited by Paul Kottman, 91–115. New York: Fordham University Press, 2017.
Gosson, Stephen. *Playes Confuted in Five Actions*. London, 1582.
Gottlieb, Derek. *Skepticism and Belonging in Shakespeare's Comedy*. London: Routledge, 2016.
Grady, Hugh. "Shakespeare and Impure Aesthetics: The Case of *A Midsummer Night's Dream*." *Shakespeare Quarterly* 59, no. 3 (2008): 274–302.
Granville-Barker, Harley. *Prefaces to Shakespeare*. Princeton, NJ: Princeton University Press, 1947.
Graybiel, Ann M. "Habits, Rituals, and the Evaluative Brain." *Annual Review of Neuroscience* 31 (2008): 359–87.
Graybiel, Ann M., and Kyle S. Smith. "Good Habits, Bad Habits." *Scientific American* 310, no. 6 (2014): 39–43.
Green, André. *Un Oeil en trop: Le complexe d'Oedipe dans la tragédie*. Paris: Minuit, 1969.
Greenblatt, Stephen. *Shakespearean Negotiations*. Berkeley: University of California Press, 1988.
– *Will in the World: How Shakespeare Became Shakespeare*. New York: Norton, 2004.
Guazzo, Stephen. *The Civile Conversation*. London, 1581.
Hadot, *Pierre*. *Philosophy as a Way of Life*. Edited by Arnold I. Davidson. Malden, MA: Blackwell, 1995.
– *What Is Ancient Philosophy?* Translated by Michael Chase. Cambridge, MA: Harvard University Press, 2002.

Hamilton, J.T. *Security: Politics, Humanity, and the Philology of Care.* Princeton, NJ: Princeton University Press, 2013.

Hampton, Timothy. "Difficult Engagements: Private Passion and Public Services in Montaigne's *Essais.*" In *Politics and Passions, 1500–1850,* edited by Victoria Kahn, Neil Saccamano, and Daniela Coli, 30–48. Princeton, NJ, and Oxford: Princeton University Press, 2006.

Hartmann, Wilfried. *Der Investiturstreit.* Munich: R. Oldenbourg, 2007.

Hausted, Peter. *The Rival Friends.* Edited by Laurens J. Mills. Bloomington: Indiana University Press, 1951.

Haverkamp, Anselm. *Klopstock/Milton: Teleskopie der Moderne.* Stuttgart: Metzler, 2018.

– "Pyrrhus' Sieg: Shakespeare ... Wieland ... Hegel." In *Wieland/Übersetzen: Sprachen, Gattungen, Räume,* edited by Bettine Menke and Wolfgang Struck, 43–56. Berlin: De Gruyter, 2010.

– *Shakespearean Genealogies of Power: A Whispering of Nothing in* Hamlet, Richard II, Julius Caesar, Macbeth, The Merchant of Venice, *and* The Winter's Tale. London: Routledge, 2011.

– "Solgers Ironie: Der idealische Jüngling und die Misere der Universität." In *Diesseits der Oder: Frankfurter Vorlesungen,* 197–211. Berlin: Kadmos, 2008.

Hegel, Georg Wilhelm Friedrich. *Aesthetics: Lectures on Fine Art.* Vol. 1. Translated by T.M. Knox. Oxford: Clarendon, 1975.

– *Ästhetik.* Edited by Friedrich Bassenge. Berlin: Aufbau, 1955, 1962.

– *Elements of the Philosophy of Right.* Edited by Allen Wood. Cambridge: Cambridge University Press.

– *Grundlinien der Philosophie des Rechts.* Edited by Johannes Hoffmeister. Hamburg: Meiner, 1955.

– *Phänomenologie des Geistes.* Edited by Hans-Friedrich Wessels and Heinrich Clairmont. Hamburg: Meiner, 1988.

– *The Phenomenology of Mind.* Translated by J.B. Bailie. London: Macmillan, 1910, 1931.

– *Phenomenology of Spirit.* Translated by A.V. Miller. Analysis of the text and foreword by J.N. Findlay. Oxford: Oxford University Press, 1977.

– *Philosophy of Right.* Translated by T.M. Knox. Oxford: Clarendon, 1952.

– "Ueber Solger's nachgelassene Schriften und Briefwechsel." In *Berliner Schriften 1818–1831,* edited by Johannes Hoffmeister, 155–220. Hamburg: Meiner, 1956.

Heidegger, Martin. *Being and Time.* Translated by John Macquarrie and Edward Robinson. Oxford: Blackwell, 1962.

– *Being and Time.* Translated by Joan Stambaugh. SUNY Series in Contemporary Continental Philosophy, edited by Dennis J. Schmidt. New York: SUNY Press, 1996.

Heller, Agnes. “Poetic Truth and Historical Truth.” In *Philosophers on Shakespeare,* edited by Paul A. Kottman, 184–92. Stanford, CA: Stanford University Press, 2009.

Henrich, Dieter. *Hegel im Kontext.* Frankfurt/M: Suhrkamp, 1971.

Herder, Johann Gottfried. “Shakespear.” In *Von Deutscher Art und Kunst,* edited by Edna Purdie, 97–121 Oxford: Clarendon, 1924, 1948, 1960, 1964.

Herman, Peter C. “Equity and the Problem of Theseus in *A Midsummer Night's Dream*: Or, the Ancient Constitution in Ancient Athens.” *Journal for Early Modern Cultural Studies* 1, no. 4 (2014): 4–31.

Hesk, Jon. “Types of Oratory.” In *The Cambridge Companion to Ancient Rhetoric,* edited by Erik Gunderson, 145–61. Cambridge: Cambridge University Press, 2009.

Heywood, Jasper, trans. *The Second Tragedie of Seneca Entituled Thyestes.* London, 1560.

Hirsch, Emanuel. “Die Beisetzung der Romantiker in Hegels Phänomenologie.” In *Materialien zu Phänomenologie des Geistes,* edited by Hans Friedrich Fulda and Dieter Henrich, 245–75. Frankfurt/M: Suhrkamp, 1973.

Hochshild, Arlie Russel. *The Managed Heart: The Commercialization of Human Feeling.* Berkeley: University of California Press, 1983.

Holzem, Andreas. “Eid und Eidschwörer. Wahrheitssuche und Loyalitätsverpflichtung im frühneuzeitlichen Sendgericht.” In *Eid und Wahrheitssuche. Studien zu rechtlichen Befragungspraktiken in Mittelalter und früher Neuzeit,* edited by Stefan Esders and Thomas Scharff, 211–36. Frankfurt a. M.: Peter Lang, 1999.

Horspool, David. *Richard III: A Ruler and His Reputation.* London: Bloomsbury, 2015.

Hughes, Thomas. *The Misfortunes of Arthur.* Edited by Brian Jay Corrigan. New York: Garland, 1992.

Hunt, Maurice. “Individuation in *A Midsummer Night's Dream.*” *South Central Review* 3, no. 2 (1986): 1–13.

Huntington, Samuel P. *The Clash of Civilizations and the Remaking of World Oder.* New York: Simon & Schuster, 1996.

Husserl, Edmund. *Ideas: General Introduction to Pure Phenomenology.* Translated by W.R. Boyce Gibson. London: George Allen & Unwin, 1952.

Hutson, Lorna. *Circumstantial Shakespeare.* Oxford: Oxford University Press, 2015.

– *The Intervention of Suspicion: Law and Mimesis in Shakespeare and Renaissance Drama*. Oxford: Oxford University Press, 2007.

Hyginus. *Fabulae* 220. In *The Literary Genres in the Flavian Age Canons: Transformations, Reception*. Edited by Federica Bessone and Marco Fucecchi. Boston: De Gruyter, 2017.

"idea, n." *Oxford English Dictionary Online*. Oxford: Oxford University Press.

Ishiguro, Kazuo. *Never Let Me Go*. New York: Vintage, 2005.

Jackson, Ken. "'Grace to Boot': St. Paul, Messianic Time, and Shakespeare's *The Winter's Tale*." In *The Return of Theory in Early Modern English Studies*, edited by Paul Cefalu and Bryan Reynolds, 192–219. New York: Palgrave, 2011.

Jebb, R.C., ed. *Oedipus Colneus*. Cambridge: Cambridge University Press, 1928.

Jenkins, Harold, ed. *Hamlet*. Arden edition. 2nd series. London: Methuen, 1982; Nelson, 1977.

Jones, Ann Rosalind, and Peter Stallybrass. *Renaissance Clothing and the Materials of Memory*. Cambridge: Cambridge University Press, 2000.

Jonson, Ben. *The Cambridge Edition of the Works of Ben Jonson*. 7 vols. Edited by David Bevington et al. Cambridge: Cambridge University Press, 2012.

Kant, Immanuel. *Critique of Pure Reason*. Translated by Norman Kemp Smith. London: Macmillan, 1993.

– *Critique of the Power of Judgement*. Translated by Paul Guyer and Eric Matthews. Cambridge: Cambridge University Press, 2000.

– *Kants Werke: Akademie-Textausgabe*. Berlin: de Gruyter, 1968.

Karlberg, Michael R. *Beyond the Culture of Contest: From Adversarialism to Mutualism in an Age of Interdependence*. Oxford: George Ronald, 2004.

Kearney, James. "'This Is Above All Strangeness' *King Lear*, Ethics, and the Phenomenology of Recognition." *Criticism* 54, no. 3 (June 2012): 455–67.

Kearney, Richard, and Mark Dooley, eds. *Questioning Ethics: Contemporary Debates in Philosophy*. London: Routledge 1999.

Kermode, Frank. Introduction to *The Winter's Tale*, lxiii–lxxvii. Edited by Frank Kermode. New York: New American Library, 1998.

– *Shakespeare, Spenser, Donne: Renaissance Essays*. Routledge, 2005.

Kezar, Dennis. "Shakespeare's Addiction." *Critical Inquiry* 30 (2003): 31–62.

Khurana, Thomas. *Das Leben der Freiheit: Form und Wirklichkeit der Autonomie*. Berlin: Suhrkamp, 2017.

Kierkegaard, Soren. *The Concept of Irony*. Edited by Howard V. Hong and Edna H. Hong. Princeton, NJ: Princeton University Press, 1989.

– *Philosophical Fragments and Johannes Climacus*. Edited and translated by Howard V. Hong and Edna H. Hong. Princeton, NJ: Princeton University Press, 1985.

Kingwell, Mark. "Husserl's Sense of Wonder." *Philosophical Forum* 31 (2000): 85–107.

Knapp, Jeffrey. "Shakespeare's Pains to Please." In *Forms of Association: Making Publics in Early Modern Europe*, edited by Paul Yachnin and Marlene Eberhart, 256–71. Amherst: University of Massachusetts Press, 2015.

Korda, Natasha. *Shakespeare's Domestic Economies: Gender and Property in Early Modern England*. Philadelphia: University of Pennsylvania Press, 2002.

Kottman, Paul A. "Duel." In *Early Modern Theatricality*, edited by Henry Turner, 402–22. Oxford: Oxford University Press, 2013.

– "Hegel and Shakespeare on the Pastness of Art." In *The Art of Hegel's Aesthetics: Hegelian Philosophy and the Perspectives of Art History*, edited by Paul A. Kottman and Michael Squire, 263–301. Munich: Fink, 2018.

– *Love as Human Freedom*. Stanford, CA: Stanford University Press, 2017.

– *Tragic Conditions in Shakespeare: Disinheriting the Globe*. Baltimore, MD: Johns Hopkins University Press.

– "What Is Shakespearean Tragedy?" In *Oxford Handbook of Shakespearean Tragedy*, edited by Michael Neill and David Schalkwyk. Oxford: Oxford University Press, 2016. Oxford Handbooks Online, DOI: 10.1093/oxfordhb/9780198724193.013.1.

Kselman, John S. "Curse and Blessing." In *Harper's Bible Dictionary*, edited by Paul J. Achtermeier, 198–9. San Francisco: Harper & Row, 1985.

Kuzner, James. *Shakespeare as a Way of Life: Skeptical Practice and the Politics of Weakness*. New York: Fordham University Press, 2016.

Kyd, Thomas. *The Spanish Tragedy*. In *English Renaissance Drama: A Norton Anthology*, edited by David Bevington et al., 3–73. New York: Norton, 2002.

Lally, Phillipa, Cornelia H. M. van Jaarsveld, Henry W.W. Potts, and Jane Wardle. "How Are Habits Formed: Modelling Habit Formation in the Real World." *European Journal of Social Psychology* 40 (2010): 998–1009.

Lamb, Charles. "On the Tragedies of Shakespeare." In *Charles Lamb: Selected Prose*. London: Penguin, 1985.

Lemon, Rebecca. *Addiction and Devotion in Early Modern England*. Philadelphia: University of Pennsylvania Press, 2018.

Levine, Laura. "Rape, Repetition, and the Politics of Closure in *A Midsummer Night's Dream*." In *Feminist Readings of Early Modern Culture: Emerging Subjects*, edited by Valerie Traub, M. Lindsay Kaplan, and Dympna Callaghan 210–28. New York: Cambridge University Press, 1996.

Lindsay, Tom. "'Which First Was Mine Own King': Caliban and the Politics of Service and Education in *The Tempest*." *Studies in Philology* 113, no. 2 (22 March 2016): 397–423.

Little, Lester K. *Benedictine Maledictions: Liturgical Cursing in Romanesque France.* Ithaca, NY: Cornell University Press, 1993.

Lories, Danielle. "Remarks on Aesthetic Intentionality: Husserl or Kant." *International Journal of Philosophical Studies* 14 (2006): 31–49.

Lupton, Julia Reinhard. *Citizen-Saints: Shakespeare and Political Theology.* Chicago: University of Chicago Press, 2005.

– "Judging Forgiveness: Hannah Arendt, W.H. Auden, and *The Winter's Tale.*" *New Literary History* 45, no. 4 (Autumn 2014): 641–63.

– *Shakespeare Dwelling: Designs for the Theater of Life.* Chicago: University of Chicago Press, 2018.

– *Thinking with Shakespeare: Essays on Politics and Life.* Chicago: University of Chicago Press, 2011.

Lupton, Julia Reinhard, and Kenneth Reinhard. *After Oedipus: Shakespeare in Psychoanalysis.* Ithaca, NY: Cornell University Press, 1993.

Lyons, John. "Deixis, Space, and Time." *Semantics* 2 (1977): 636–724.

Mack, Peter. *Elizabethan Rhetoric: Theory and Practice.* Cambridge: Cambridge University Press, 2002.

Manley, Lawrence. "Folie à Deux." In *Face-to-Face in Shakespearean Drama: Ethics, Performance, Philosophy,* edited by Matthew J. Smith and Julia Reinhard Lupton, 52–76. Edinburgh: Edinburgh University Press, 2019.

Maritain, Jacques. *Distinguish to Unite, or, The Degrees of Knowledge.* Translated by Gerald B. Phelan. South Bend, IN: University of Notre Dame Press, 1995.

– *The Range of Reason.* New York: Scribner, 1952.

Markus, Robert A. *Christianity and the Secular.* Notre Dame, IN: University of Notre Dame Press, 2006.

Marlowe, Christopher. *Doctor Faustus.* In *English Renaissance Drama: A Norton Anthology,* edited by David Bevington, Katharine Eisaman Maus, and Eric Rasmussen, 250–85. New York: Norton 2002.

Marshall, David. "Exchanging Visions: Reading *A Midsummer Night's Dream.*" *ELH* 49, no. 3 (1982): 543–75.

Marston, John. *Jack Drum's Entertainment.* In *The Plays of John Marston.* Vol. 3. Edited by H. Harvey Wood. Edinburgh: Oliver and Boyd, 1939.

– *Parasitaster, or the Fawn.* Edited by David A. Blostein. Manchester: Manchester University Press, 1978.

Mascall, Leonard. *A booke of the arte and maner, howe to plant and graffe all sortes of trees.* London, 1590.

Mattéi, Jean-François. "The Heideggerian Chiasmus." In *Heidegger: From Metaphysics to Thought,* edited by Dominique Janicaud and Jean-François Mattéi. Translated by Michael Gendre, 39–150. Albany, NY: SUNY Press, 1995.

Mayeroff, Milton. *On Caring.* New York: Harper and Row, 1971.

McCoy, Richard C. *Faith in Shakespeare.* Oxford: Oxford University Press.

McMillin, Scott, and Sally-Beth MacLean. *The Queen's Men and Their Plays.* Cambridge: Cambridge University Press, 1998.

Menke, Christoph. *Die Gegenwart der Tragödie: Versuch über Urteil und Spiel.* Frankfurt am Main: Suhrkamp, 2005.

– "Geist und Leben: Von der Phänomenologie zur Genealogie." In *Autonomie und Befreiung: Studeien zu Hegel*, 82–116. Berlin: Suhrkamp, 2018.

– "Tragedy and Skepticism: On *Hamlet*." In *Varieties of Skepticism: Essays after Kant, Wittgenstein, and Cavell*, edited by Andrea Kern and James Conant, 377–83. Berlin: De Gruyter, 2014.

– *Tragic Play: Irony and Theater from Sophocles to Brecht.* New York: Columbia University Press, 2009.

The Merry Devil of Edmonton. Edited by William Amos Abrams. Durham, NC: Duke University Press, 1942.

Miller, Ronald F. "*A Midsummer Night's Dream*: The Fairies, Bottom, and the Mystery of Things." *Shakespeare Quarterly* 26, no. 3 (1975): 254–68.

Minar, Edward. "Living with the Problem of the Other: Wittgenstein, Cavell, and Other Minds Scepticism." In *Wittgenstein and Scepticism*, edited by Denis McManus, 218–39. London: Routledge, 2004.

Moi, Toril. *Revolution of the Ordinary: Literary Studies after Wittgenstein, Austin, and Cavell.* Chicago: University of Chicago Press.

Montagu, Ashley. *The Anatomy of Swearing.* Philadelphia: University of Pennsylvania Press, 2001.

Montrose, Adrian. "'Shaping Fantasies': Figurations of Gender and Power in Elizabethan Culture." *Representations* 2 (1983): 61–94.

Moran, Dermot. *Husserl's Crisis of the European Sciences and Transcendental Phenomenology: An Introduction.* Cambridge: Cambridge University Press, 2012.

Morgan, Edmund Sears. *Visible Saints: The History of a Puritan Idea.* Ithaca, NY: Cornell University Press, 1963.

Moriarty, Michael. "Principles of Judgement: Probability, Decorum, Taste, and the *je ne sais quoi*." In *The Cambridge History of Literary Criticism.* Vol 3, *The Renaissance,* edited by Glyn P. Norton, 522–8. Cambridge: Cambridge University Press, 1999.

Nägele, Rainer. *Theater, Theory, Speculation: Walter Benjamin and the Scenes of Modernity.* Baltimore, MD: Johns Hopkins University Press, 1991.

Nazar, Hina. *Enlightened Sentiments: Judgment and Autonomy in the Age of Sensibility.* New York: Fordham University Press, 2012.

Nevo, Ruth. *Comic Transformations in Shakespeare.* London: Methuen, 1980.

Newcombe, David Gordon. *Henry VIII and the English Reformation.* London: Routledge 2003.

Nunberg, Geoffrey. "Indexality and Deixis." *Linguistics and Philosophy* 19 (1993): 1–43.

Nussbaum, Martha C. *The Fragility of Goodness: Luck and Ethics in Greek Tragedy and Philosophy.* Cambridge: Cambridge University Press, 1986.

– *Love's Knowledge: Essays on Philosophy and Literature.* Oxford: Oxford University Press, 1990.

Panofsky, Erwin. *Idea: A Concept in Art Theory.* Translated by Joseph S. Peake. New York: Harper & Row, 1968.

Parker, John. "Persona." In *Cultural Reformations: Medieval and Renaissance in Literary History,* edited by James Simpson and Brian Cummings, 591–608. Oxford: Oxford University Press, 2010.

Pavis, Patrice. *Languages of the Stage: Essays in the Semiology of the Theatre.* New York: Performing Arts Journal Publications, 1982.

– "Performance Analysis: Space, Time, Action." Translated by Sinéad Rushe. *Gestos* 22 (1996): 11–32.

Pippen, Robert. "Hegel on Painting." In *The Art of Hegel's Aesthetics: Hegelian Philosophy and the Perspectives of Art History,* edited by Paul A. Kottman and Michael Squire, 211–37. Munich: Fink, 2018.

Pitcher, John. Introduction to *The Winter's Tale* by William Shakespeare, 1–136. London: Bloomsbury, 2010.

Porter, James I. *Nietzsche and the Philology of the Future.* Stanford, CA: Stanford University Press, 2000.

Purdie, Edna, ed. *Von Deutscher Art und Kunst.* Oxford: Clarendon, 1924, 1948, 1960, 1964.

Quadflieg, Dirk. "Die Sandbank des Vergessens." In *Denkfiguren: Figures of Thought,* edited by Eva Horn and Michèle Lowrie, 175–7. Berlin: August Verlag, 2013.

Quiring, Björn. *Shakespeare's Curse, The Aporias of Ritual Exclusion in Early Modern Royal Drama.* Translated by Michael Winkler and Björn Quiring. New York: Routledge, 2014.

Rainer, Naegele. *Theater, Theory, Speculation: Walter Benjamin and the Scenes of Modernity.* Baltimore, MD: Johns Hopkins University Press, 1991.

Rainolds, John. *Th'overthrowe of Stage-Playes.* London, 1599.

Rawlins, Thomas. *The Rebellion.* London, 1640.

Regino of Prüm. *Libri duo de synodalibus causis et disciplinis ecclesiasticis.* Leipzig: Engelmann, 1840.

Reich, Thomas Warren. "History of the Notion of Care." In *Encyclopedia of Bioethics.* Rev. ed. New York: Simon & Schuster Macmillan, 1995.

Rieger, Gabriel. "'I woo'd thee with my sword, / And won thy love doing thee injuries': The Erotic Economies of *A Midsummer Night's Dream.*" *Upstart Crow* 28 (2009): 70–87.

Rokem, Freddie. *Philosophers and Thespians: Thinking Performance.* Stanford, CA: Stanford University Press, 2010.

Rosalind, Ann Jones, and Peter Strallybrass. *Renaissance Clothing and the Materials of Memory.* Cambridge: Cambridge University Press, 2002.

Rosenkranz, Karl. *Georg Wilhelm Friedrich Hegels Leben: Supplement zu Hegels Werken.* Berlin: Duncker & Humblot, 1844.

Rossiter, A.P. *Angel with Horns and Other Shakespeare Lectures* London: Longmans, 1961.

Rutter, Carol Chillington. "Learning Thisby's Part – or – What's Hecuba to Him." *Shakespeare Bulletin* 22, no. 3 (2004): 5–30.

Sanchez, Melissa E. "Seduction and Service in *The Tempest.*" *Studies in Philology* 105, no. 1 (2008): 50–82.

Santer, Eric. *On Creaturely Life: Rilke, Benjamin, Sebald.* Chicago: University of Chicago Press, 2006.

Schalow, Frank. *The Renewal of the Heidegger-Kant Dialogue: Action, Thought, and Responsibility.* Albany, NY: SUNY Press, 1992.

Schütz, Alfred. "The Problem of Transcendental Intersubjectivity in Husserl (with Comments of Dorion and Eugen Fink)." Translated by Fred Kersten. *Schutzian Research* 2 (2010): 9–12.

Seebohm, Thomas M. "Fichte's and Husserl's Critique of Kant's Transcendental Deduction." *Husserl Studies* 2 (1985): 53–74.

Semenza, Gregory M. Colón. "*The Spanish Tragedy* and Revenge." In *Early Modern English Drama: A Critical Companion*, edited by Garrett A. Sullivan Jr. et al., 50–60. Oxford: Oxford University Press, 2006.

Seneca. *Thyestes.* In *Seneca: Tragedies II.* Translated by John G. Fitch. Cambridge, MA: Harvard University Press, 2004.

Sidney, Philip. *The Defense of Poesy.* In *Miscellaneous Prose of Sir Philip Sidney*, edited by Katherine Duncan-Jones and Jan van Dorsten. Oxford: Clarendon, 1973.

Shakespeare, William. *The First Part of Henry VI.* In *The Pelican Shakespeare*, edited by William Montgomery. General editors Stephen Orgel and A.R. Braunmuller. New York: Penguin, 2002.

– *King Lear.* Edited by Grace Ioppolo. New York: W.W. Norton, 2008.

– *King Richard III.* Edited by Anthony Hammond. London: Arden/Thomson, 2002.

– *Macbeth.* In *The Pelican Shakespeare*, edited by Stephen Orgel. General editors Stephen Orgel and A.R. Braunmuller. New York: Penguin, 2002.

– *The New Oxford Shakespeare: The Complete Works.* Edited by Gary Taylor et al. Oxford: Oxford University Press, 2016.

– *Othello.* Edited by E.A.J. Honigmann. The Arden Shakespeare. London: Thomson Learning, 1997.

– *Othello, the Moor of Venice.* Edited by Michael Neill. Oxford: Oxford University Press, 2006.

– *Romeo and Juliet.* In *The Pelican Shakespeare,* edited by Peter Holland. General editors Stephen Orgel and A.R. Braunmuller. New York: Penguin, 2002.

– *The Tempest.* Edited by Peter Hulme and William H. Sherman. New York: W.W. Norton, 2004.

– *The Tragedy of King Richard the Second.* In *The Complete Pelican Shakespeare,* edited by Frances Dolan. General editors Stephen Orgel and A.R. Braunmuller. New York: Penguin, 2002.

– *Twelfth Night, or What You Will,* edited by Keir Elam. The Arden Shakespeare, London: Cengage Learning, 2008.

Shirilan, Stephanie. *Robert Burton and the Transformative Powers of Melancholy.* London: Routledge, 2016.

Shuger, Debra K. "Subversive Fathers and Suffering Subjects: Shakespeare and Christianity." In *Religion, Literature, and Politics in Post-Reformation England, 1540–1688,* edited by Donna B. Hamilton and Richard Strier, 46–69. Cambridge: Cambridge University Press, 1996.

Shulman, Jeffrey. "Bottom Is Up: The Role of Illusion in *A Midsummer Night's Dream.*" *Essays in Arts and Sciences* 16 (1987): 9–21.

Skinner, Quentin. *Forensic Shakespeare.* Oxford: Oxford University Press, 2015.

– *Reason and Rhetoric in the Philosophy of Hobbes.* Cambridge: Cambridge University Press, 1996.

Smith, Ian. "Othello's Black Handkerchief." *Shakespeare Quarterly* 64, no. 1 (2013): 1–25.

Smith, John H. *The Spirit and Its Letters: Traces of Rhetoric in Hegel's Philosophy of Bildung.* Ithaca, NY: Cornell University Press, 1988.

Smith, William, and John Lockwood. *A Smaller Latin-English Dictionary.* 3rd ed. London: John Murray, 1933.

Solger, Karl Wilhelm Ferdinand. Review of *Vorlesungen über dramatische Kunst und Literatur* (1809–11), *Nachgelassene Schriften und Briefwechsel,* by August Wilhelm Schlegel, I–II, edited by Ludwig Tieck and Friedrich von Raumer. Leipzig: Brockhaus, 1826, II: 493–628.

– "Über Sophokles und die alte Tragödie." Éd. bilingue par Noemi Angehrn, *Sur Sophokles et la tragédie antique.* Lausanne: L'Age d'Homme, 2010.

– *Vorlesungen über Ästhetik.* Edited by Karl Wilhelm Ludwig Heyse. Leipzig: Brockhaus, 1829.

Solomon, Robert C. *About Love: Reinventing Romance for Our Times.* Indianapolis, IN: Hackett, 2006.

Soni, Vivasvan, ed. "The Crisis of Judgement." Special issue, *Eighteenth Century: Theory and Interpretation* 51 (2010): 261–88.

Sorabji, Richard. *Necessity Cause and Blame: Perspectives on Aristotle's Theory.* Chicago: University of Chicago Press, 1980.

Spenser, Edmund. *The Faerie Queene.* Edited by Thomas P. Roche. New York: Penguin, 1987.

Stanislavski, Constantin. *Creating a Role.* Edited by Hermine I. Popper. Translated by Elizabeth Reynolds Hapgood. London: Eyre Methuen, 1981; repr. London: Bloomsbury, 2013.

Starobinski, Jean. "L'encre de la mélancolie." *La Nouvelle Revue Française* 123 (1963): 410–23.

Stekeler-Weithofer, Pirmin. *Philosophie des Selbstbewußtseins: Hegels System als Formanalyse von Wissen und Autonomie.* Frankfurt/M: Suhrkamp, 2005.

Stendhal. *Love.* Translated by Gilbert and Suzanne Sale. New York: Penguin 2004.

St. John, Christopher, ed. *Ellen Terry and Bernard Shaw: A Correspondence.* London: Reinhardt and Evans, 1931.

Sun, Emily. *Succeeding King Lear: Literature, Exposure, and the Possibility of Politics.* New York: Fordham University Press.

Sussman, Henry. *The Hegelian Aftermath.* Baltimore, MD: Johns Hopkins University Press, 1982.

Targoff, Ramie. *Common Prayer: The Language of Public Devotion in Early Modern England.* Chicago: University of Chicago Press, 2001.

Thomas, Keith. *Religion and the Decline of Magic: Studies in Popular Beliefs in Sixteenth- and Seventeenth-Century England.* London: Penguin 1991.

Thompson, Ann, and Neil Taylor, eds. *Hamlet.* Arden edition, 3rd series. London: Thomson Learning, 2006.

Thwaites, Thomas. *GoatMan: How I Took a Holiday from Being Human.* New York: Princeton Architectural, 2016.

Tillich, Paul. *The Courage to Be.* New Haven, CT: Yale University Press, 2014.

Tillyard, E.M.W. *Shakespeare's History Plays.* London: Chatto & Windus, 1959.

Tomkis, Thomas. *Albumazar.* Edited by Hugh G. Dick. Berkeley: University of California Press, 1944.

Trousdale, Marion. "Reading the Early Modern Text." In *Shakespeare Survey,* edited by Stanley Wells, 50:135–46. Cambridge: Cambridge University Press.

Truestedt, Katrin. *Die Komödie der Tragödie.* Konstanz: Konstanz University Press, 2011.

Tynan, Kenneth. *Curtains.* New York: Atheneum, 1961.

Vickers, Brian. "Deconstruction's Designs on Rhetoric." In *Rhetoric as Pedagogy: Its History, Philosophy, and Practice – Essays in Honor of James J. Murphy,* edited by Winifred Bryan Horner and Michael Leff, 295–315. London: Routledge, 1995.

–, ed. *English Renaissance Literary Criticism.* Oxford: Oxford University Press, 1999.

Watson, Robert N. "The Ecology of Self in *Midsummer Night's Dream.*" In *Ecocritical Shakespeare,* edited by Lynne Dickson Bruckner and Daniel Brayton, 33–58. Burlington: Ashgate, 2011.

Weiner, Andrew D. "'Multiformitie Uniforme': *A Midsummer Night's Dream.*" *ELH* 38, no. 3 (1971): 329–49.

Whyman, Rose. "The Actor's Second Nature: Stanislavski and William James." *New Theatre Quarterly* 23, no. 2 (2007): 115–23.

Williams, Bernard. *The Sense of the Past: Essays in the History of Philosophy.* Princeton: Princeton University Press, 2006.

– *Shame and Necessity.* Los Angeles: University of California Press, 1993.

Williams, Grant. "Being Seen Is Believing: Spectacle, Ethics, and the Others of Belief in Elizabethan Revenge Tragedy." *Theta VIII, Théâtre Tudor* (2009): 253–74.

Williams, Raymond. *Keywords: A Vocabulary of Culture and Society.* London: Fontana, 1976.

Wittgenstein, Ludwig. *Philosophical Investigations.* Translated by G.E.M. Anscombe, P.M.S. Hacker, and Joachim Schulte. 4th ed. Oxford: Wiley-Blackwell, 2009.

Wolff, Emil. "Hegel und Shakespeare." In *Vom Geist der Dichtung* (Gedächtnisschrift für Robert Petsch), edited by Fritz Martini, 122–79. Hamburg: Hoffman und Campe, 1949.

Woolf, Rosemary. *The English Mystery Plays.* Berkeley: University of California Press, 1980.

Wright, Thomas. *The Passions of the Minde in Generall.* London, 1601.

Younge, Richard, *The Drunkard's Character.* London, 1638.

Yachnin, Paul. "Magical Properties: Vision, Possession, and Wonder in Othello." *Theatre Journal* 48, no. 2 (1996): 197–208.

Zamir, Tzachi. *Acts: Theater, Philosophy, and the Performing Self.* Ann Arbor: University of Michigan Press, 2014.

– *Double Vision: Moral Philosophy and Shakespearean Drama.* Princeton, NJ: Princeton University Press, 2006.

Contributors

J.K. Barret is associate professor of English at the University of Texas at Austin and the author of *Untold Futures: Time and Literary Culture in Renaissance England* (Cornell University Press, cloth and e-book 2016, paperback 2019). Her essays have appeared in edited collections and journals including *Shakespeare Quarterly*, *ELH*, and *English Literary Renaissance*. Her current research has received fellowship support from sources including the Huntington Library.

Sarah Beckwith is the Katherine Everett Gilbert Professor of English and Theater Studies at Duke University. She is the author of *Christ's Body: Identity, Culture and Society in Late Medieval Writing* (Routledge, paperback, 1996), *Signifying God: Social Act and Symbolic Relation in York's Corpus Christi Play* (University of Chicago Press, 2001), and most recently *Shakespeare and the Grammar of Forgiveness* (Cornell University Press, 2011). She is writing a book on Shakespeare's late tragedies and ethics, and another on versions of *The Winter's Tale*, called *The Book of Second Chances*. She is a founding editor of *Re-Formations* (University of Notre Dame Press), along with James Simpson and David Aers, and a co-editor of the *Journal of Medieval and Early Modern Studies*.

Sanford Budick is professor of English emeritus at the Hebrew University, where he continues to teach. He was formerly professor of English at Cornell University. He is the recipient of Guggenheim and NEH Fellowships. He has written books on Dryden, on eighteenth-century poetry, on Milton, on Kant's relation to Milton, and on the Western theory of tradition. He has edited collections of essays with Geoffrey Hartman and Wolfgang Iser. He is writing a book on Shakespeare.

Kevin Curran is professor of early modern literature at the University of Lausanne in Switzerland and editor of the book series Edinburgh Critical Studies in Shakespeare and Philosophy. He is the author of *Shakespeare's Legal Ecologies: Law and Distributed Selfhood* (Northwestern University Press, 2017) and *Marriage, Performance, and Politics at the Jacobean Court* (Ashgate, 2009). He is the editor of *Shakespeare and Judgment* (Edinburgh University Press, 2016) and *Renaissance Personhood: Materiality, Taxonomy, Process* (Edinburgh University Press, 2019), and co-editor with James Kearney of "Shakespeare and Phenomenology," a special issue of the journal *Criticism* (2012). In 2017 Curran was named Distinguished International Visiting Fellow at the Center for the History of Emotions in Australia. He is also the founder and president of the Lausanne Shakespeare Festival.

Lowell Gallagher is professor of English at the University of California, Los Angeles, where he teaches courses in Renaissance literature, critical theory, and queer and feminist approaches to biblical studies. He is author of *Medusa's Gaze: Casuistry and Conscience in the Renaissance* (Stanford University Press), *Sodomscapes: Hospitality in the Flesh* (Fordham University Press), and editor or co-editor of several essay collections, including *Redrawing the Map of Early Modern English Catholicism* (University of Toronto Press), *Catholic Figures, Queer Narratives,* with Frederick S. Roden and Patrician Juliana Smith (Palgrave Macmillan), and *Knowing Shakespeare: Senses, Embodiment, and Cognition,* with Shankar Raman (Palgrave Macmillan). Gallagher's current research examines the long history of Catholic speculative fiction, from Counter Reformation–era romances to twentieth-century Catholic theological and aesthetic insights into the sacramental character of post-human ethics.

Anselm Haverkamp is emeritus professor of English at New York University, New York, and honorary professor of philosophy at Ludwig-Maximilians-Universität, Munich. His more recent books include *Shakespearean Genealogies of Power* (2011); *Baumgarten-Studien,* with Rudiger Campe, Christoph Menke (2014); *Productive Digression: Theorizing Practice* (2016); *Philosophie de la métaphore,* with Jean-Claude Monod (2017); *Klopstock/Milton* (2018); *Metapher Mythos Halbzeug* (2018); and *Latenz* (2019).

Sheiba Kian Kaufman is a research associate in the School of Humanities at the University of California, Irvine. Her book project, *The Hospitable Globe: Persia and Early Modern English Drama,* examines how English representations of Persia and its legendary kings present models of interreligious and intercultural hospitality for early modern and Shakespearean drama. Her work appears in *Shakespeare and Hospitality: Ethics, Politics, and Exchange* (2016).

James Kearney is associate professor of English at the University of California, Santa Barbara. He is the author of *The Incarnate Text: Imagining the Book in Reformation England* (University of Pennsylvania Press), and co-editor of "Shakespeare and Phenomenology,"a special issue of the journal *Criticism.* He is currently working on a research project that addresses ethical experience in Shakespeare's late plays. His work has appeared in a variety of journals and collections, including *Arden Shakespeare: The State of Play, ELR, Shakespeare Studies, Criticism, JMEMS, The Oxford Handbook of Shakespeare, The Cambridge Guide to the Worlds of Shakespeare, Shakespeare and Hospitality,* and *Cultural Reformations.*

Jeffrey Knapp is the Eggers Professor of English at the University of California, Berkeley, and the author of four books: *An Empire Nowhere: England and America from* Utopia *to* The Tempest (1992); *Shakespeare's Tribe: Church, Nation, and Theater in Renaissance England* (2002); *Shakespeare Only* (2009); and *Pleasing Everyone: Mass Entertainment in Renaissance London and Golden-Age Hollywood* (2017).

Paul A. Kottman is associate professor of comparative literature at the New School for Social Research. He is the author, most recently, of *Love as Human Freedom* (Stanford, 2017). He also edits the book series Square One: First Order Questions in the Humanities for Stanford University Press.

James Kuzner is associate professor of English at Brown University. He is the author of *Shakespeare as a Way of Life* (Fordham, 2016), *Open Subjects* (Edinburgh, 2011), and of essays that have appeared in journals such as *ELH, Shakespeare Quarterly, Criticism,* and *Exemplaria.*

Julia Reinhard Lupton is professor of English at the University of California, Irvine, where she co-directs the New Swan Shakespeare Center. She is the author or co-author of five books on Shakespeare, including *Shakespeare Dwelling: Designs for the Theater of Life, Thinking with Shakespeare: Essays on Politics and Life,* and *Citizen-Saints: Shakespeare and Political Theology.* She has edited and co-edited many volumes, including *Face-to-Face in Shakespearean Drama: Ethics, Performance, Philosophy* (with Matthew J.

Smith) and *Shakespeare and Hospitality: Ethics, Politics, and Exchange* (with David Goldstein). She is a former Guggenheim Fellow and a former trustee of the Shakespeare Association of America.

Charles McNulty, a recipient of the George Jean Nathan Award for Dramatic Criticism, is the chief theatre critic for the *Los Angeles Times.* He teaches playwriting and dramaturgy at the California Institute of the Arts.

Björn Quiring is assistant professor at the School of English, Trinity College Dublin. He has written *Shakespeare's Curse: The Aporias of Ritual Exclusion in Early Modern Royal Drama* (Routledge, 2014).

Tzachi Zamir is a philosopher and a literary critic (professor of English and comparative literature) and directs the Honours Program at the Hebrew University of Jerusalem. Zamir is the author of *Double Vision: Moral Philosophy and Shakespearean Drama* (Princeton, 2006), *Ethics and the Beast* (Princeton, 2007), *Acts: Theater, Philosophy and the Performing Self* (University of Michigan Press, 2014), *Ascent: Philosophy and Paradise Lost* (Oxford, 2017), and *Just Literature: Philosophical Criticism and Justice* (forthcoming from Routledge). He is also the editor of *Shakespeare's Hamlet: Philosophical Perspectives* (Oxford, 2017).

Index

THE UCLA CLARK MEMORIAL LIBRARY SERIES

1. *Wilde Writings: Contextual Conditions*, edited by Joseph Bristow
2. *Enchanted Ground: Reimagining John Dryden*, edited by Jayne Lewis and Maximillian E. Novak
3. *Culture and Authority in the Baroque*, edited by Massimo Ciavolella and Patrick Coleman
4. *Ritual, Routine, and Regime: Repetition in Early Modern British and European Cultures*, edited by Lorna Clymer
5. *Momigliano and Antiquarianism: Foundations of the Modern Cultural Sciences*, edited by Peter N. Miller
6. *Monarchisms in the Age of Enlightenment: Liberty, Patriotism, and the Common Good*, edited by Hans Blom, John Christian Laursen, and Luisa Simonetti
7. *Thinking Impossibilities: The Intellectual Legacy of Amos Funkenstein*, edited by Robert S. Westman and David Biale
8. *Discourses of Tolerance and Intolerance in the European Enlightenment*, edited by Hans Erich Bödeker, Clorinda Donato, and Peter Hanns Reill
9. *The Age of Projects*, edited by Maximillian E. Novak
10. *Acculturation and Its Discontents: The Italian Jewish Experience between Exclusion and Inclusion*, edited by David N. Myers, Massimo Ciavolella, Peter H. Reill, and Geoffrey Symcox
11. *Defoe's Footprints: Essays in Honour of Maximillian E. Novak*, edited by Robert M. Maniquis and Carl Fisher
12. *Women, Religion, and the Atlantic World (1600–1800)*, edited by Daniella Kostroun and Lisa Vollendorf
13. *Braudel Revisited: The Mediterranean World, 1600–1800*, edited by Gabriel Piterberg, Teofilo F. Ruiz, and Geoffrey Symcox
14. *Structures of Feeling in Seventeenth-Century Cultural Expression*, edited by Susan McClary
15. *Godwinian Moments*, edited by Robert M. Maniquis and Victoria Myers
16. *Vital Matters: Eighteenth-Century Views of Conception, Life, and Death*, edited by Helen Deutsch and Mary Terrall
17. *Redrawing the Map of Early Modern English Catholicism*, edited by Lowell Gallagher
18. *Space and Self in Early Modern European Cultures*, edited by David Warren Sabean and Malina Stefanovska
19. *Wilde Discoveries: Traditions, Histories, Archives*, edited by Joseph Bristow

20. *Jesuit Accounts of the Colonial Americas: Intercultural Transfers, Intellectual Disputes, and Textualities,* edited by Marc André Bernier, Clorinda Donato, and Hans-Jürgen Lüsebrink
21. *Skepticism and Political Thought in the Seventeenth and Eighteenth Centuries,* edited by John Christian Laursen and Gianni Paganini
22. *Representing Imperial Rivalry in the Early Modern Mediterranean,* edited by Barbara Fuchs and Emily Weissbourd
23. *Imagining the British Atlantic after the American Revolution,* edited by Michael Meranze and Saree Makdisi
24. *Life Forms in the Thinking of the Long Eighteenth Century,* edited by Keith Michael Baker and Jenna M. Gibbs
25. *Cultures of Communication: Theologies of Media in Early Modern Europe and Beyond,* edited by Helmut Puff, Ulrike Strasser, and Christopher Wild
26. *Curious Encounters: Voyaging, Collecting, and Making Knowledge in the Long Eighteenth Century,* edited by Adriana Craciun and Mary Terrall
27. *Clandestine Philosophy: New Studies on Subversive Manuscripts in Early Modern Europe, 1620–1823,* edited by Gianni Paganini, Margaret C. Jacob, and John Christian Laursen
28. *The Quest for Certainty in Early Modern Europe: From Inquisition to Inquiry, 1550–1700,* edited by Barbara Fuchs and Mercedes García Arenal
29. *Entertaining the Idea: Shakespeare, Philosophy, and Performance,* edited by Lowell Gallagher, James Kearney, and Julia Reinhard Lupton

www.ingramcontent.com/pod-product-compliance
Lightning Source LLC
LaVergne TN
LVHW090156080826
844660LV00013B/835/J
9781487507435